ENGINEERING YOUR RETIREMENT

LIBRARY
THE NORTH HIGHLAND COLLEGE
ORMLIE ROAD
THURSO
CAITHNESS KW14 7EE

D0352167

IEEE Press
445 Hoes Lane
Piscataway, NJ 08854

IEEE Press Editorial Board
Mohamed E. El-Hawary, *Editor in Chief*

J. B. Anderson	S. V. Kartalopoulos	N. Schulz
R. J. Baker	M. Montrose	C. Singh
T. G. Croda	M. S. Newman	G. Zobrist
R.J. Herrick	F. M. B. Pereira	

Kenneth Moore, *Director of IEEE Book and Information Services (BIS)*
Catherine Faduska, *Senior Acquisitions Editor*
Jeanne Audino, *Project Editor*

IEEE Microwave Theory and Technique Society, *Sponsor*
MTT-S Liason to IEEE Press, Robert York

Technical Reviewers
Philip M. Kane, P.E., Esq.
Emerson Pugh, President Emeritus IEEE Foundation and Past President IEEE

ENGINEERING YOUR RETIREMENT

Re
Te

LIBRARY
THE NORTH HIGHLAND COLLEGE
ORMLIE ROAD
THURSO
CAITHNESS KW14 7EE

646.
79
GOL

This book is due for return on or before the last date shown

Mik

IEE

BICEN
1 8
W
2 0
BICEN

WIL
A J

Copyright © 2007 by the Institute of Electrical and Electronics Engineers, Inc. All rights reserved.

Published by John Wiley & Sons, Inc., Hoboken, New Jersey.
Published simultaneously in Canada.

No part of this publication may be reproduced, stored in a retrieval system, or transmitted in any form or by any means, electronic, mechanical, photocopying, recording, scanning, or otherwise, except as permitted under Section 107 or 108 of the 1976 United States Copyright Act, without either the prior written permission of the Publisher, or authorization through payment of the appropriate per-copy fee to the Copyright Clearance Center, Inc., 222 Rosewood Drive, Danvers, MA 01923, (978) 750-8400, fax (978) 750-4470, or on the web at www.copyright.com. Requests to the Publisher for permission should be addressed to the Permissions Department, John Wiley & Sons, Inc., 111 River Street, Hoboken, NJ 07030, (201) 748-6011, fax (201) 748-6008, or online at http://www.wiley.com/go/permission.

Limit of Liability/Disclaimer of Warranty: While the publisher and author have used their best efforts in preparing this book, they make no representations or warranties with respect to the accuracy or completeness of the contents of this book and specifically disclaim any implied warranties of merchantability or fitness for a particular purpose. No warranty may be created or extended by sales representatives or written sales materials. The advice and strategies contained herein may not be suitable for your situation. You should consult with a professional where appropriate. Neither the publisher nor author shall be liable for any loss of profit or any other commercial damages, including but not limited to special, incidental, consequential, or other damages.

For general information on our other products and services or for technical support, please contact our Customer Care Department within the United States at (800) 762-2974, outside the United States at (317) 572-3993 or fax (317) 572-4002.

Wiley also publishes its books in a variety of electronic formats. Some content that appears in print may not be available in electronic format. For information about Wiley products, visit our web site at www.wiley.com.

Library of Congress Cataloging-in-Publication Data is available.

ISBN-13 978-0-471-77616-1
ISBN-10 0-471-77616-5

Printed in the United States of America.

10 9 8 7 6 5 4 3 2 1

LIBRARY
THE NORTH HIGHLAND COLLEGE
ORMLIE ROAD
THURSO
CAITHNESS KW14 7EE

CONTENTS

PREFACE

Retirement means different things to different people and the unique circumstances of each person means that general advice is sometimes difficult to provide. There is one bit of advice, however, that applies to everyone: If you have not yet begun to plan for your retirement, the best time to start is right now.

I first got serious about retirement planning about 10 or 12 years ago. My wife, JJ, and I were fortunate to be electrical engineers earning healthy salaries. We were also conservative spenders so we were saving money. We both had plenty of diverse interests outside of engineering so we were not confused about what to do if we were not required to go into the office. Despite these advantages, we really had no specific plan for how and when to retire.

Prior to this point, financial matters and investing had never interested me. I much preferred a lively discussion about electron transport in semiconductors to one about the real rate of return on government I bonds. Taxes were a nightmare ordeal I had to live through each April. Tax strategies that would need to be applied over three or four decades never crossed my mind. Health insurance was something that came with the job. I had no idea what it would cost to replace it. Wills, powers of attorney and other legal documents were alien to me. When I first began to consider retirement, I had no idea where to go for the kind of quantitative, analytical information my engineering outlook on life demanded. The vast majority of the finance and retirement literature available was not very satisfying. It contained a shortage of data, mathematics, and logical development. Most of the literature seemed to be thinly veiled advertisements. Questions about how much I might need to save, what kind of investments to make, and how long it would take all seemed out of reach.

Eventually I did find good sources of information as well as useful simulation and analysis tools. As with most research projects, discovery of one good source led to another, and another, until I was overwhelmed with substantive material. I discovered literature that was logical, mathematically rigorous, and useful. A combination of sources, including academic financial literature, government reports, independent internet sites, and financial articles from savvy columnists, provided good, quantifiable advice on retirement issues. I poured myself into this literature, and soon realized that all my retirement questions could be bounded and addressed. Retirement could be engineered like a new buffer amplifier or a suspension bridge. In fact, it required that kind of attention.

This book is an outgrowth of my research as well as countless discussions with other technical professional retirees. I have addressed the topics I was concerned about as well as those of highest priority to my friends and colleagues. The text examines primary issues related to each topic and then points to more detailed references. The complementary website, *www.golio.net,* provides supplemental data, tools, spreadsheets, and analysis organized according to the table of contents of the book.

I think you will find this book useful as you engineer your own retirement, and I hope the retirement plan you design is satisfying and enjoyable. Good luck.

ACKNOWLEDGMENTS

My wife, JJ, read and redlined the entire manuscript for this book before any other reviewer saw it. She critiqued grammar, content, and organization. JJ also developed the website *www.golio.net* that complements this book with useful URLs organized according to the book outline. While I was writing, she also took up much of the workload on two other editor projects I am responsible for, including *IEEE Microwave Magazine*. It is not an exaggeration to say that this book would not have been possible without her.

Other people have had impact on this project. My parents taught me to live frugally and living below your means is surely the most critical principle in the development of a viable retirement plan. John Greaney (aka intercst) and Bill Sholar (aka dory36) both developed Internet websites of considerable value to those seeking sound advice about retiring. These sites are free, but you definitely get more than you pay for.

Samir El-Ghazaly backed this project as Publications Chair of the IEEE MTT Society. Wayne Shiroma and Bob York provided further Society support. Cathy Faduska, Jeanne Audino, and the publication professionals at Wiley/IEEE Press have done a great job and been wonderful to work with.

I want to sincerely thank all of these people.

1

RETIRE ON YOUR SCHEDULE

As a technical professional living in an industrialized nation today, choices are available to you that many others do not have. Concerning marriage, children, and jobs, you can choose when, where, and what you want to do. In addition, if you plan appropriately, you can decide when and how to retire.

Although Social Security and Medicare benefits have made most Americans think about retirement as something that occurs in their mid-sixties, no natural law dictates this practice. Many people choose to work much longer. Only 58% of Americans over the age of 65, for example, consider themselves completely retired.[1] Others choose to retire much earlier.

Throughout much of history, retirement occurred only when someone became too frail or sick to work. This is still true today in less-developed countries. Improvements in productivity and work environment during the 20th century, however, have led to a mid-sixties retirement norm. Although available data for people retiring in their fifties or younger is difficult to obtain, Figure 1.1 illustrates the trend toward lower mean retirement age in the United States from 1950 to 2000. By 2000, the average age at retirement was less than 62, with many Americans retiring in their fifties or earlier.

Although countless surveys indicate that most Americans are looking forward to retirement, the same studies reveal ignorance about the requirements for successful retirement. This may be due in part to different motivations for retiring. Some people want to pursue other interests but are limited by job constraints. Some people want to escape a work environment they do not enjoy. Others feel like "wage slaves" and long for freedom to do whatever they want. Another part of the problem may have to do with the broad range of lifestyles that people imagine for their ideal retirement. Retirement can involve traveling the globe, simply sitting on the porch

Engineering Your Retirement. By Mike Golio
© 2007 Institute of Electrical and Electronics Engineers, Inc.

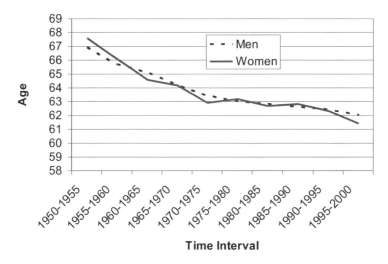

Figure 1.1. Decreasing mean age at retirement in the United States from 1950 to 2000. (Source: Murray Gendell, "Retirement Age Declines again in 1990s," *Monthly Labor Review,* October 2001, pp. 12–21.)

in a rocking chair, finding seclusion, volunteering, or working because you want to, not because you have to.

Regardless of your personal definition and views on retirement, it is a fact that close to 80 million Americans will be either close to retirement or in retirement within the next 20 years. At a time when an unprecedented number of people will reach traditional retirement age, we are also facing funding issues for Social Security and Medicare, witnessing the default of numerous corporate pension plans, and experiencing a personal saving rate of near zero. If aging engineers are to have any chance of enjoying a successful retirement, both financial and social preparation must be completed.

Retirement planning is helpful at any age, but saving early is especially valuable. An early start to saving is the best path to accumulating the resources you will need for a successful retirement. Young technical professionals who begin saving a fraction of their salary at the beginning of their career will be able to retire on their own schedule. Figure 1.2 illustrates the value of starting early.

This figure considers a technical professional with a starting salary of $50,000 per year. An average salary increase of 5.5% per year (3.5% inflation, 2% experience bonus) is assumed. This data is consistent with the IEEE salary survey data for a BSEE graduate with no experience. The salary increase assumptions underestimate the experience of most electrical engineers since they ignore salary increases for promotions into positions of higher responsibility. Similarly, salary increases for obtaining advanced degrees are not considered in the salary increase rates. For example, an individual who obtains an advanced degree after starting work and

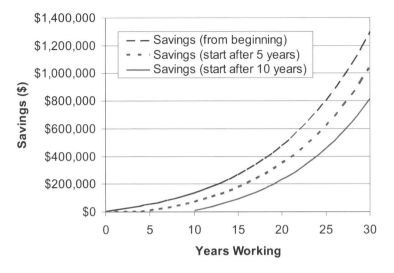

Figure 1.2. An illustration of the value of saving early. The figure represents the savings of an individual with a starting salary of $50,000 per year, an average annual increase in salary of 5.5%, a saving rate of 10% of annual salary, a company match of 3% on 401(k) investments, and assumed earnings on investments of 7%. Three cases are plotted: (a) a person who begins saving as soon as he or she starts working, (b) a person who waits 5 years to begin saving, and (c) a person who waits 10 years to begin saving.

moves into technical management after several years might expect an average salary increase of 8% or higher over the 30-year period illustrated in Figure 1.2.

The hypothetical engineer of Figure 1.2 invests 10% of pretax salary each year and takes advantage of a 3% company 401(k) match. The assumed average return on all investments is 7% over the 30-year period. Three cases are illustrated: (a) a person who begins saving as soon as he or she starts working, (b) a person who waits 5 years to begin saving, and (c) a person who waits 10 years to begin saving.

Even though Figure 1.2 is a simplified case that considers only fixed annual raises, and returns (without variations from year to year) it clearly illustrates the value of starting early. After 30 years, the engineer who starts saving from the first day on the job will have $480,000 more than the colleague who put off saving for 10 years. As in the case of engineering projects, early planning is invaluable.

It is not too late for the slow starter who begins to save in year 10 of his or her career. The time advantage of the early investor can be made up, for example, by increasing the saving rate from 10% to 17.7% once saving starts in year 10. Such a plan reduces disposable income by 7.7% for 20 years, but will result in identical portfolio value in year 30. Achieving a higher rate of return (at least 11.3%) can also compensate for the late start. In the investment world, however, higher returns are always associated with higher risk. Finally, the slow starter could choose to work for 6 years longer to make up the difference in savings.

For the engineer who wants to work beyond normal retirement age, starting to save early may seem of little value. It is worth noting, however, that although 68% of currently working Americans expect to work for pay in some capacity after they retire; only 32% of current retirees actually have worked for pay after retirement.[1] This statistic might indicate that working seems less attractive to the 65+ year old than it did to the 25 year old. It may also be that there are not enough jobs available for 65+ year olds.

1.1. RETIREMENT OPTIONS

Work Until You Drop

Some people feel that work gives them purpose. In a February 1997 article of *The Free Market* titled "I'll Never Retire," William Diehl asserts that "There is a sense of self-worth that comes from working to a purpose that is essential to well-being, whether the task involves major responsibility or physical exertion, as both require diligence and daily attendance." He further sums up his feelings about retirement stating, "As we observe able-bodied citizens hiking the malls or sampling the midnight buffets on the cruise ships, we are struck by their purposelessness, and the overwhelming boredom they manifest. There is no need to arise in the morning, or any necessity to go to bed on time. Their reason for existence has ceased. They have lost the respect of those who support them, and lost their self-respect in the process."

This attitude seems extreme to many, sad and pathetic to others. One might ask if Mr. Diehl believes that working to produce a profit for a company is really a higher calling. If you were granted unlimited possibilities, do you believe the most important thing you could do is work? Is this really more important than focusing on the development of your social and family relationships? On volunteering in your community? On being a better parent? A better spouse? A better person? Nevertheless, if this is how you feel, retirement is not for you. Even if you do not wish to retire, it may be in your best interest to achieve financial independence and to develop some interests beyond the office. Events outside of your control may lead to a time in your life when you are not able to work. A comfortable nest egg (or seed money) might be important. Even if you feel that retirement represents a meaningless existence today, you may change your mind in the future. Preparation today provides opportunity tomorrow.

Normal-Age Retirement (~ Age 65)

On average, men in the United States retire at age 62, whereas women retire at age 61. The Social Security Act of 1935 and the Medicare bill of 1965 have made mid-sixties retirement the norm. In a study by the National Council on Aging, 72% of those surveyed said qualifying for Social Security was their most important reason for retiring. Nearly half of all workers choose to begin taking Social Security benefits at 62, the earliest age they are available.

In the face of continuing economic uncertainty, dwindling company retirement benefits, and escalating medical costs, growing numbers of Americans are pushing back their planned retirement dates. Many aging workers who had expected to ease comfortably out of the labor force in their fifties and early sixties are discovering they do not have the financial resources to support themselves in retirement. Since the mid-1990s, older people have become the fastest-growing portion of the work force. The Labor Department projects that workers over 55 will make up 19.1% of the labor force by 2012, up from 14.3% in 2002.[2]

Get FIREd (Financial Independence, Retire Early)

They had a word for work in ancient Greece: *ponos.* It meant labor, but it also meant suffering. Work was what slaves did. Free men were thinkers—philosophers and appreciators of art.

Many people have to work to live. Not working is not an option so they have become slaves to their jobs and salaries—wage slaves. They may have set high goals for themselves and toiled long and diligently through their careers only to find themselves working for an impersonal company and reporting to someone they do not respect.

To some, the idea of early retirement is appealing—the earlier the better. Early planning and appropriate lifestyle choices can provide financial independence long before a worker reaches his or her sixties. The mantra of early retirees is, "Get FIREd (Financial Independence/Retire Early)."

Job Satisfaction, Retirement, and Financial Independence

Many engineers find their jobs enjoyable and rewarding. Professionals, who find themselves absorbed in their work, may feel it is unnecessary to plan for retirement or develop interests outside of science and technology. Unfortunately, factors outside of their control within the industry, workplace, home, or their own body can quickly change satisfaction to boredom or even dread. Obtaining financial independence can greatly improve job satisfaction and provide insurance against the stress and anxiety associated with many factors outside of your control.

Acceptance of the Workplace. Many people who have worked and saved long enough to retire have found the urgency to do so diminish once they achieve financial independence. That achievement has a way of making office politics or poor management less infuriating. Tolerating an incompetent manager or clueless Human Resources (HR) representative is easy once you have the resources to walk away whenever you want to. Your colleagues' annoying habits may be transformed into minor amusements once you realize that you do not have to face them. Money cannot buy love, but financial security can make life tolerable, even working life.

Workplace Volatility, Industry Downturns, and Management Upheavals. Technical professionals can be performing well in their jobs and still become victims of industrial forces outside of their control. Corporate management can make the decision to refocus resources and eliminate an existing development effort. A large
customer can decide to use a different supplier that is closer, easier to monitor,
cheaper, and so on, leaving the current supplier with too much capacity. Experienced engineers who have lived through periods of volatility do not forget the
lessons of previous upheavals. Figure 1.3 presents a prioritized list of job issues that
U.S. electrical engineers were concerned about in 2004. Although salary tops the
list, the next most important concern was "job market, security, unemployment."

According to a survey of 2185 U.S. electrical engineers, over 45% had been
working in a company that downsized in 2004. Another 19% were part of a company that sold off one of its divisions. Ten percent experienced their company being
sold or merged. Even though most engineers kept their jobs during these volatile
times, 30% were subjected to salary freezes or reductions.[5] Although this data is not
typical for every year in the electrical engineering profession, an engineer can expect to experience periods of job volatility more than once during his or her career.

In start-up ventures, job volatility can be a significant threat. Survey estimates of
the failure rate of technology start-up companies run as high as 85%. Although job
satisfaction is often measured to be higher at smaller companies, job security may
not be as good.

Job loss across an entire industry or across the nation can result from global economic developments. Figure 1.4 shows unemployment data for several groups of
U.S. technical professionals between 1982 and 2002. Unemployment for these occupations tends to run much lower than for the average worker in all fields. The
volatility over time, however, is significant. Over this two-decade period, electrical

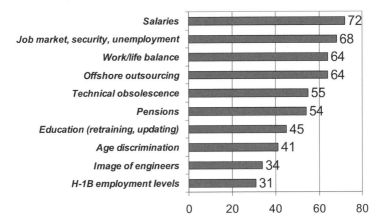

Figure 1.3. Prioritized list of career concerns from a recent survey of 2185 electrical
engineers in the United States. Data represents the percent of engineers who listed each item
as one of their top concerns. (Source: David Roman, "High Pay, High Anxiety," *EE Times,*
Aug 22, 2005, pp. 1–34.)

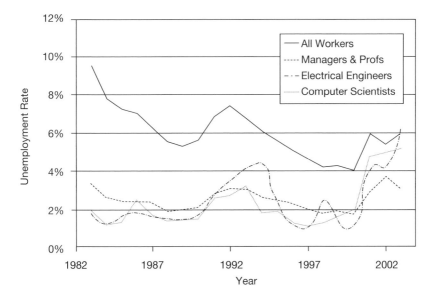

Figure 1.4. Unemployment rate for a number of technical occupations between 1982 and 2002. (Source: US Department of Labor, Bureau of Labor Statistics—Population Survey.)

engineering unemployment rose from nearly 1% to over 4% on two separate occasions. Although a 4% unemployment rate is not considered high for the nation as a whole, it is important to realize that the 3% increase in unemployment rate over a short period (~ 2 years) represents job loss to approximately 150,000 electrical engineers. The worker is not always in control of his/her employment situation.

Workplace volatility and industrywide trends are not the only threat to personal job security. Engineers sometimes find the enemy to be their own management. Power struggles and office politics can lead to stress and job volatility. Workers who are better at technology than playing office politics find themselves easy prey to political careerists in the office. Engineers also become casualties when executives they report to lose high-level power struggles. Unfortunately, there is far too much reality in the newspaper's Dilbert cartoons.

Obtaining financial independence offers significant relief from all kinds of job volatility stress. There is no better insurance against workplace volatility than to possess enough financial resources to be able to live without working. Plant shutdown rumors might cause anxiety in a wage slave with a mortgage and a family, but the financially independent worker is able to view the same rumors as reasons to explore other interesting opportunities.

Possessing the means to retire does not mean you actually have to quit. The ability to retire provides independence for the early retiree or security for the person who chooses to continue working. Financial independence can ease anxieties caused by volatile job markets, corporate politics, management upheavals, outsourced technology, industry downturns, and reorganizations.

Personal Evolution of Attitudes about Work and Family. It should be reiterated that there is a great deal of satisfaction and enthusiasm in the engineering field. It is also true that most engineers will become disillusioned and frustrated with their work or management at some time in their career. These periods of dissatisfaction may be short-lived or they may last for years. Only a small minority of office workers manage to navigate through their entire career without encountering such a period. Career dissatisfaction may be solved by the next reorganization, an industry upturn, the departure of a boss or coworker, or a change in jobs. Sometimes, however, a shift in personal priorities or values leaves technical professionals in jobs that no longer interest them. These people are "retired in place." They arrive at the office and stumble uninspired through each workday. Only the true retirement option may bring inspiration back into their lives.

Even if the job does not become disagreeable or unattractive, it may become less important to an individual. New interests can replace old ones. Becoming a parent or a grandparent, for example, often changes people's priorities. Notice that the third most important job concern of engineers in the survey shown in Figure 1.3 is "work/life balance." It is unlikely that this concern is brought on by too much life and not enough work.

Job Stress. Even when job loss is not an issue, job stress may be. Stress causes a biochemical onslaught that chips away at the immune system, opening the way to cancer, infection, and disease. Hormones unleashed by stress eat at the digestive tract and lungs, promoting ulcers and asthma. They may also weaken the heart, leading to strokes and heart disease. Chronic job stress is like slow poison. Even people who are not sensitized to stress are adversely affected by everything that can go wrong on the job during the day. The self-assurance that comes from financial independence goes a long way toward the reduction of job stress.

Personal Attitude Changes. Regardless of how much financial independence may improve your work attitude or provide a feeling of security, it will not guarantee a successful retirement or enjoyable leave of absence. Someone who has spent a significant portion of his or her life in an office may not have the motivation and interests to fill the days in retirement. For some, achieving financial independence is easier than achieving social and emotional independence.

1.2. IS THERE A RETIREMENT CRISIS?

Future of Social Security

The future of Social Security is clouded by political rhetoric. Financial projections about solvency are based on demographic and economic assumptions of a highly uncertain nature. It is beyond the scope of this book to predict the future of Social

Security, but the following information about the current situation and proposals can be listed. According to the Social Security Administration:

- Presently, Social Security collects more in taxes than it pays in benefits. The excess is borrowed by the U.S. Treasury, which in turn issues special-issue Treasury bonds to Social Security. These bonds totaled $1.7 trillion at the beginning of 2005. Social Security received $89 billion in interest from bonds in 2004.
- There are no plans to cut benefits for current retirees. All current proposals recommend that benefits increase each year with inflation.
- Unless changes are made, a young worker today could be faced with up to a 26% reduction in benefits in the year 2041. Payments could continue at this reduced level or decrease every year thereafter. Some analysis results in estimates of overall benefit reduction from the current formula by as much as 32% by 2079.
- There are no credible plans to replace Social Security as the foundation for the retirement of American workers.
- If Social Security is not changed, payroll taxes will have to be increased, the benefits of today's younger workers will have to be cut, or massive transfers from general revenues will be required. The longer the nation continues without action, the more dramatic the required action will be.

Even though the future of Social Security benefits is uncertain, the information offered by the Social Security Administration does provide a path to retirement planning. For those born before 1950, current benefit levels will probably apply. For those born between 1951 and 1970, reduction of benefits as high as 26% could occur if no action is taken. Reductions as high as 32% should be planned by those born after 1970.

Are You Saving Enough?

Although it should be clear to everyone that retirement requires financial independence, which requires saving, only 58% of working Americans say they (or their spouse) are saving for retirement. It is estimated that less than half are saving enough to retire comfortably by age 65.

Most Americans are not saving enough. Prior to the mid-1980s, the most common retirement plan for American workers was the defined benefit plan (conventional pension). In the past 20 years, however, the number of companies offering a defined benefit plan has dropped by more than 75% and many of these plans are in financial trouble. Defined contribution plans (primarily 401(k)s and IRAs) are the touted replacement for conventional pensions. Americans, however, are not using their 401(k) and IRA opportunities to the extent they should. Poor choices are also being made on which specific investments to hold. When changing jobs, Americans are failing to roll over their 401(k) plans, even when such failure results in large penalties.

A massive amount of data describes our poor saving habits. Traditional IRAs are held by only 33% of U.S. households. Other retirement plans are even less popular. Only 13% of households hold Roth IRAs. All other IRA types cover a combined 9% of households. Since some households hold multiple types of IRAs, only 40% of Americans hold any type of IRA account.

Fewer than half of all Americans are eligible to participate in company 401(k) plans, and almost a third of eligible employees choose not to participate. Twenty-two percent of employees active in their company's 401(k) have a total balance of less than $5000. Low participation among younger workers is persistent, in strong markets and weak ones. To this group of employees, retirement is a distant event and investment decisions are easy to postpone. With rising retiree healthcare costs and declining support for traditional pension programs, however, the younger workers may ultimately need to rely more heavily on their 401(k) savings.

Diversification does not appear to be a top priority for many employees enrolled in 401(k) programs. About one-third of employees' portfolios are concentrated in just one or two asset classes. Company stock is the majority or only investment represented in the 401(k) portfolios of more than one in ten employees, and of over one in three employees over age 60.

Direct measurement of personal savings rates of U.S. households show that Americans are saving too little. The U.S. Commerce Department indicates that the savings rates for average households in the U.S. are below 2% annually. This means that Americans are spending over 98% of their annual income and investing less than 2% for future needs. On a monthly basis, the savings figure has actually dropped to zero on two occasions in recent years. Trying to build up retirement savings while spending more than you earn can be compared to trying to establish voltage across a short circuit.

Figure 1.5 plots the U.S. monthly savings data since 1959. Savings rates have not been as low as they are today since 1934, during the Great Depression. Even though salaries are not keeping up with inflation, consumer spending continues to grow. Where is this growth coming from? Home prices have risen by just over two-thirds since 1999, and the increased value has enabled consumers to spend more money than they earn at their jobs. Homes are being treated like a giant debit card. Home equity loans and refinancing allow consumers to pull out cash and support a higher level of spending. This puts off the short-term need to reduce spending, but it is not preparing American households for economic downturns or for a comfortable retirement.

Record low personal savings rates come at the same time as discouraging news is being released regarding both corporate pension programs and Social Security solvency. U.S. retirement plans for public employees, corporate pensions, and endowments lost $1 trillion between 2000 and 2003. A poorly performing stock market, pensions paying out more than they are taking in, and healthier Americans living longer to collect more benefits have crippled a number of pension programs. The Pension Benefit Guaranty Corporation (PBGC) provides some protection against pension bankruptcy, but insurance guarantees are capped at benefit levels well below most corporate pension promises. For example, United Airlines' recent bankruptcy will cause pilots' pensions to revert to the PBGC. News reports indicate that these pilots may receive as little as 20% of their promised pension benefits.

The data makes it clear that many Americans are not saving enough. How do you know if you are saving enough? The question can only be answered after appropriate personal information has been collected and analyzed.

1.3. HOW MUCH DO I NEED TO RETIRE?

Asking this question is like asking the question, "How much gain does an amplifier need?" Without a great deal of information, the question is not answerable in a meaningful way. In the case of the amplifier, we would want to know more about the specific system into which the amplifier would be incorporated. We need to know specific information about the circuits that preceded and followed the amplifier. The range of signal conditions the amplifier might experience is also important. If we ask enough questions, eventually we are able to answer the original question, "How much gain does an amplifier need?" Electrical engineers go through this exercise every time they develop a spec for an amplifier.

Determining how much is needed to retire is similar to the development of an amplifier spec. It depends on how much you intend to spend, how long you will be

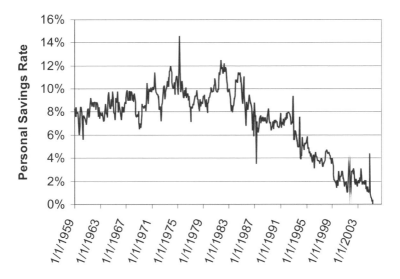

Figure 1.5. A plot of the U.S. personal savings rate (on monthly basis) from January 1959 through June 2005. (Source: U.S. Department of Commerce: Bureau of Economic Analysis, A Guide to the National Income and Product Accounts of the United States (NIPA)— http://www.bea.doc.gov/bea/an/nipaguid.pdf.)

retired, and the rate of return of your investments. These questions may seem to have no reliable answers, but they can be addressed with surprising accuracy, and the results can offer enough certainty to answer our original question. As in the case of the amplifier spec, we might have to conduct research, run simulations, and/or collect data in order to provide detailed specifications before a useful answer is within reach.

Future sections of this book provide a detailed examination of how much money is required for retirement, but the short, approximate answer is simply, "You will need a net worth (or equivalent income flow) of about 25 times your average annual expenses as of your retirement date." For example, if you spend (on average) $40,000 per year, you will need to accumulate approximately $1 million in investments to insure a successful retirement. As will be illustrated in Chapter 2, this approximation considers typical retirement periods (30 years or more), inflation adjusted spending, and worst-case historical investment returns of reasonably conservative investments.

The question of how much money is required to retire can be altered to address spending in retirement: "If I have a portfolio worth P, how much can I spend each year and still be assured I won't run out of money?" Or "What is my Safe Withdrawal Rate, SWR?" The short, approximate answer is

$$SWR = \frac{1}{25} \times (P) = 0.04 \times (P) \tag{1.1}$$

where P is your total portfolio value. Equation 1.1 is referred to as the "4% rule." It is a useful guideline for retirement planning that can be refined as more personally specific information is collected and analyzed. Other information of importance includes:

- Your age at retirement
- Spouse's age at retirement
- You and your spouse's life expectancy
- Your investment allocations
- Your expenses in retirement
- Pension and/or Social Security assumptions
- Heirs and inheritance plans
- Other special circumstances

Although equation (1.1) appears simple, it is based on detailed simulations, has broad application, and is a powerful evaluation tool that has been proven adequate for retirement plans for over the past 130 years. (This is discussed in more detail in Chapter 2.)

Estimating financial needs in retirement is one of the most fundamental of planning steps for later life. According to the Employee Benefit Research Institute, however, almost six out of 10 workers have not made the attempt.[1]

How Long Will I Need to Fund Retirement?

One answer to this question is the obvious—you will need to fund retirement until you die. In reality, you may want to ensure that you can fund retirement throughout not only your lifetime, but that of your spouse or other family members.

Although estimating our exact lifetime is not possible, the Social Security Administration and countless life insurance companies have collected significant statistics on mortality by age. Figure 1.6 presents mortality data from the Social Security Administration. The figure shows the additional years an American can expect to live (y axis) once they have reached a given age (x axis). In addition to the average expectations, data is illustrated for 50th percentile, 75th percentile, 90th percentile, 95th percentile and 99th percentile lifetimes. The data used to produce Figure 1.6 is also tabulated in Appendix C.

For the purposes of safe retirement planning, a conservative approach applied to the general longevity statistics of Appendix C provides a good first estimate to the amount of time you will have to fund your retirement.

Appendix C shows that an American who reaches the age of 65 has an average additional life expectancy of 20.5 years. It is important to note that 20.5 years is the average life expectancy; half of those who reach age 65 can expect to live longer than that. Five percent of 65-year-old Americans can expect to live at least 35.5 more years. To avoid the risk of outliving your retirement portfolio, it is critical that retirement planning consider long lifetime possibilities.

Longevity estimates can be refined to consider gender and race differences, current health habits, family health history, and so on. Appendix A includes links to some online longevity calculators that can be used to compute personal

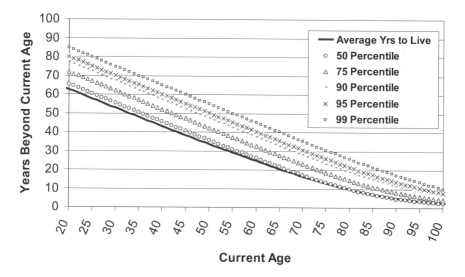

Figure 1.6. Longevity table. (Source: Mortality table in IRS Revenue Ruling 2002-62, Appendix B. See link: http://www.irs.gov/pub/irs-drop/rr-02-62.pdf.)

longevity calculations. Tables of joint survivor longevity are available from actuarial sources.

What Will It Cost?

Although Equation (1.1) provides an estimate of how big an initial nest egg should be for a specified spending level, it is important that retirement planners develop an accurate approximation of their own retirement spending requirements. The closer you get to your retirement date, the more important it is to have a refined and accurate understanding of your spending. The first step in developing an accurate retirement budget is to gain an understanding of your current spending habits. Tabulation of how your money is allocated by major categories of spending can be an important tool for developing a retirement budget. Your current budget can be modified to provide your retirement budget estimate by examining each spending category and estimating how your retirement lifestyle will affect that category. Consider the spending category *clothes,* for example. If you wear nice, relatively expensive clothes to the office but you plan on always wearing shorts and T-shirts in your retirement house on the beach, you may be able to reduce your clothes budget. If you are putting a significant amount of your preretirement budget into investments, this category can be eliminated. The category for income tax is also likely to be reduced. Conversely, if you plan to golf every day in retirement you will probably have to increase your leisure activity budget. Do you want to travel the world when you retire? Vacation and travel budgets need to reflect this.

Retirement literature makes occasional references to rule-of-thumb estimates for retirement spending requirements. Numbers like 70% of preretirement income are often mentioned. These estimates may represent the experience of the average American, but they can be dramatically inaccurate for a specific individual. Many people plan retirements that have greater spending requirements than their work lives. If you live a thrifty lifestyle, however, such a number can be too high by an order of magnitude. In a recent EBRI study, it was found that 13% of surveyed retirees used more than 105% of their preretirement income in retirement. Another 40% required approximately the same income level pre- and postretirement. In contrast, many surveyed retirees required retirement income of less than half their preretirement income. In general, rule-of-thumb estimates for retirement budgets should be avoided. A detailed discussion of the budget estimate process is included in Section 3.4.

What Do I Want to Leave to My Heirs?

A joke among many retirees is that they plan to spend all their money on themselves, and bounce the last check to the undertaker. Such a plan would be possible if we knew the time of our demise, the future return on our investments, and the future rate of inflation. In the real world, however, a retirement plan must survive times of uncertain investment return and inflation. Because of these uncertainties, most well-planned retirements will result in an ending portfolio of significant value. Appropriate estate planning documents, wills, trusts, powers of attorney, and so on should be established early in the retirement planning cycle. This is essential if you wish to leave your heirs a specific gift other than the unknown remainder of your retirement portfolio.

Estate planning is a highly personal issue and will be unique for each situation. The size of the estate, form of the funds, number of heirs and the nature of their relationship with you and each other, as well as other specific issues all contribute to the optimum estate planning strategy for you. Whereas the possibilities are too detailed and personal to cover in this book, a discussion of some of the items that should be considered and guidance on where to seek further direction is presented in Chapters 4 and 8.

1.4. HOW LONG WILL IT TAKE ME TO SAVE ENOUGH MONEY?

Using the rules outlined in this chapter along with some assumptions about return, an equation can be developed to estimate how many years of investing are required to achieve sufficient savings. The required time depends on a number of factors:

1. How much you have today, p
2. How much you save, a
3. How much your investments will earn, r
4. How much you will need to live on in retirement, b_{retire}
5. How large the initial portfolio will need to be to support retirement, P_{ret}

Using Equation (1.1), the quantity P_{ret} can be approximated to be

$$P_{ret} \approx 25 \times b_{retire} \tag{1.2}$$

This simplifying assumption works well for most retirement plans that will last for approximately 30 years or more. The retirement portfolio amount will have to be obtained through a combination of earnings on what you have today, p, the future value of your savings, a, and the earnings on those savings. The formulas for future value of an invested amount as well as for the future value of a recurring investment are given in Appendix B, Equations (B3) and (B4). Subtracting the final requirement, Equation (1.2), from the future value equations of (B3) and (B4) must equal zero when you have earned enough. Solving for number of years, n, gives

$$n = \frac{\log\left(\dfrac{a + rP_{ret}}{a + rp}\right)}{\log(1 + r)} \tag{1.3}$$

The calculation is a crude estimate, since it assumes a fixed rate of return on investments, ignores inflation effects, increases in savings rates, and other nonrecurring expenses or bonuses. Pension and Social Security benefits are also ignored in the equation. Refinements to account for most of these effects will be discussed in later chapters. Despite these limitations, this simple analysis of your retirement saving schedule can be quite useful. It will identify significant shortcomings in your current plan and provide some guidance on the number of years you might expect to work at your current saving rate.

1.5. LEARNING YOUR OWN LIFE VALUES.

Most engineers and technical professionals earn sufficient money to live their lives without ever needing to define a budget or analyze their spending. This is your reward for all that homework and studying you had to do in school. There is a price for this level of affluence, however, and if left unaddressed, it may significantly affect your time to retirement or your lifestyle in retirement. The challenge for prosperous professionals is to use the power of their affluence to gain personal freedom and satisfaction consistent with their life goals and values.

In order to meet the challenge, you first must understand your own life values. What do you want? What do you value? There can be no plan without goals, and without a plan, there is no way to measure progress.

It is easy to use money, salary, or possessions as a metric of success. We can easily quantify those things. When that happens, however, money and things become the end rather than the means to something more valuable. Unbridled consumerism is the result. Money will not increase our self-esteem or buy happiness. It may make the road to happiness easier, but it will not be the source of this kind of satisfaction.

Engineers are notoriously inept at this kind of "touchy-feely" personal value discussion. Many operate under the assumption that if they gather enough information and take action, they will become successful, build wealth, and be happy. But there are several leaps of faith along that chain of events that are neither straightforward nor apparent. A credible plan for success and happiness must first define what those terms mean to you.

The formula expressing personal values should probably include a number of factors other than money. Time is valuable to most working professionals. Do you want to spend more time golfing, fishing, camping, and visiting with family and friends than you do today? If so, it makes sense to set some goals to achieve a better balance than you currently enjoy. This may require reorganizing some things in your life. It may involve saving for a future lifestyle change.

Freedom is valuable to most people, and is tied closely to time. Would you be happier with less regimentation in your life? Would you prefer not to have to go to another Team Building class or hold another Dignity Entitlement discussion with your supervisor? Would you like to sleep in more often? Again, it makes sense to set some goals related to these issues. Even a vaguely defined goal can lead to a plan that could change your life for the better.

Friendship is valuable and good friends are priceless. Life is easier to manage with friends you can count on—for everything from watering your plants while you are on vacation to listening to your problems. Almost everyone would be well served by a simple goal to cultivate more friendships.

Many people find value in charity and volunteer work. There is no shortage of need for help in our schools, hospitals, and nursing homes. Similarly, some find value in environmental or political efforts.

People must find their own values. Only after you have some understanding of what you really value and what you want in the long run, can you begin to analyze whether your spending and investing habits are consistent with your own life values.

In industry, choices have to be made about how to balance spending between current manufacturing operations and future development efforts. There is always pressure to rob development budgets in order to improve manufacturing. This pressure exists because dollars spent to increase manufacturing or manufacturing efficiency result in increased profit almost immediately. But the long-term effect of this practice is to lose business and profits when a competitor develops the next-generation product with far greater value than your own. Technologists and managers often disagree on how the budgets should be split, but only a charlatan does not recognize that some money and resources need to be spent on the future goals. Arguments are about the details, not about the basic principles.

Developing spending habits that support your own life goals is very similar to the manufacturing/development budget issue. The exact nature of your retirement may not yet be completely clear to you. Although the optimum spending balance between current use items and future savings is debatable, it is foolish to ignore your long-term goals and fail to fund your investments.

Effects of Debt

In general, personal debt should be avoided. One of the only things more devastating to a retirement plan than failing to save enough is living with too much debt.

Home mortgage can be a noticeable exception to the general rule against personal debt. This kind of debt can provide powerful leverage to your investment dollars. A buyer can use a home mortgage to purchase a home, then sell the home several years later and make more money from the home appreciation than was spent on the mortgage debt. Money not spent on the initial home purchase can also be invested with the potential to earn higher returns than the mortgage rate. Such debt contributes to personal long-term worth. It is worth noting that such debt is not without risk. In the long term, real estate usually appreciates over time, but it does not always rise monotonically over shorter intervals. Even when it is rising, it does not always rise faster than your mortgage rate. Investment earnings have usually outpaced home mortgage rates over the life of the mortgage, but they are not guaranteed. Although home mortgage is generally considered to be "good debt," it does involve some level of risk.

Low-interest debt is the second type of exception debt. When the interest rate on the debt is lower than the rate you are earning on your investments, debt can be profitable. It is sometimes possible to use initial sign-on offers for credit cards with exceptionally low (even 0%) initial interest rates. You can purchase items at these low rates and put the purchase money in guaranteed savings instruments that pay more than the interest on the purchased items. Providing you remember to pay off the credit card prior to the low rate expiration date, this strategy is a low-risk way to increase your investment returns. CAUTION: read the fine print and do not fail to pay off the purchases entirely prior to the end of the initial rate period.

Americans love credit cards and they have amassed a huge amount of credit card debt. According to figures from the Federal Reserve, revolving credit card balances have increased by nearly 108% over the last 10 years. This debt is devastating to the realization of long-term savings goals and is largely responsible for the near-zero-percent savings rate of American workers. Interest rates of 12%, 18%, and even 22% are common today. These rates are as much as two or three times the available investment returns on most investments. Every dollar in credit card debt erases multiple dollars in investments. The first step on the road to retirement is to eliminate credit card debt permanently.

Lifestyle Choices

If you want to live a happy and successful lifestyle, never measure your financial achievements against anything but your own life goals. Those goals will include the obvious current health, safety, security, and pleasure requirements as well as long-term retirement goals. The tendency toward immediate gratification will compromise your ability to achieve long-term happiness. Evaluate your goals and align your spending habits to support them.

The availability of credit has made it all too easy for affluent professionals to commit future earnings toward consumer goods that contribute little to their real life goals. Armed with healthy salaries and bombarded with advertisements for more and more goods, the professional without a plan can miss the opportunity to achieve a balance between immediate desires and long-term goals.

Quantifying Lifestyle Choices

You pay a price for every item you purchase. A cup of designer coffee, your cell phone bill, a new pair of shoes—every price you pay today directly affects the amount of time required to build a sufficient nest egg. Delays to the achievement of your nest egg goals means additional time until your retirement. There is more than just the investment value of frugal behavior, since the behavior also reduces the size of the nest egg required to support your desired lifestyle.

Evaluation of spending from the perspective of future value as well as current price can be a powerful tool in learning and implementing your own life values. As an example, consider the cup of coffee mentioned in the previous paragraph. At $3.50 per cup, and an average of one cup a day, the coffee purchases amount to $24.50 per week or $1277.50 per year. While that number may seem high to some, it pales in comparison to the time value of that cup of coffee over a 30-year career. If invested in a balanced account earning an average of 7% per year, the coffee allowance becomes worth over $130,000 at the end of a 30-year career. The savings have not stopped here, however. Since the cup-of-designer-coffee habit does have to be supported in retirement, your required nest egg is reduced. Using the 4% rule, the reduction of retirement budget by $1277.50 per year translates into a reduced nest egg requirement of nearly $32,000 dollars. Cutting out the designer coffee turns out to be worth over $160,000—an amount that could shorten time to retirement significantly. Alternatively, the $130,000 additional nest egg amount represents almost $100 dollars per week in additional discretionary spending during retirement.

The analysis described above is not meant to discourage anyone from visiting their local coffee shop, or to convince them that such expenditure is wrong or misguided. If you love the taste of the coffee, relish the experience you get at the coffee shop, understand it's full future value, and feel it is worth it for you, then that is exactly what you should do. If you are not aware of the future value of your regular expenditures, you might want to perform the analysis described above. Whether it is a candy bar each afternoon, a steak dinner every weekend at an expensive restaurant, your cell-phone calling habits, or a regular game of golf, it makes sense to understand the future value of regular expenses and to question whether those expenses are consistent with your life values. Implementation of a handful of frugal habits today could accelerate the achievement of your long-term goals significantly.

Similar analysis can also be applied to less frequent or irregular expenses. Over a person's lifetime, choosing to trade your car every three years instead of every two can be worth hundreds of thousands of dollars (depending on the assumed cost of the car). This savings results since the incremental cost of owning a car for a third year is typically about a third as much as the cost of purchasing a new car. Over a 30 year career, the savings from buying 10 new cars instead of 15 and investing the difference is significant. A choice to drive the same car for a decade can be worth as much as $1 million over the course of an engineering career. Again, the goal of the analysis is not to intimidate people into a life without indulgences, but to provide a simple but effective tool to analyze your spending against your true-life values and your long-term goals. Striking the appropriate balance between immediate gratification and long-term planning is your personal challenge.

REFERENCES AND FURTHER READING

1. Ruffenach, G., The Great American Retirement Quiz, *Wall Street Journal Online,* December 28, 2004, http://pf.channel.aol.com/moneytoday/wsj/investment/retirequiz.adp.
2. Porter, E., and M. W. Walsh, Retirement Turns Into a Rest Stop as Benefits Dwindle, *New York Times,* February 9, 2005, http://www.nytimes.com/2005/02/09/business/09retire.html?ex=1108616400&en=2a85fc81b164930a&ei=5070.
3. Paladino, V., J. Jaffe, and R. Helman, *2004 Retirement Confidence Survey,* Employee Benefit Research Institute, EBRI/ASEC, Washington, DC, April 5, 2004.
4. Stein, B., Brother Don't Spare a Dime, *Legion,* August 2005.
5. Roman, D., High Pay, High Anxiety, *EE Times,* Aug 22, 2005, pp. 1–34.

6. Gleckman, H., The Debate Over Nest Egg Math, *Business Week Online,* April 25, 2005, http://www.businessweek.com/magazine/content/05_17/b3930132_mz021.htm.

7. Sanders, C., U.S. Pensions Lost $1 Trillion in Last 3 Years, *Reuters,* February 28, 2003.

8. Updegrave, W., How Soon Can I Retire? Will My Portfolio of Mutual Funds Give Me Enough to Retire? *CNN/Money Online,* May 24, 2005, http://money.cnn.com/2005/05/24/pf/expert/ask_expert/index.htm.

9. Fore, D., Do We Have a Retirement Crisis in America? *Research Dialogue, TIAA-CREF Institute,* Issue 77, September 2003.

10. Lykken, D., and A. Tellegen, Happiness is a Stochastic Phenomenon, *Psychological Science,* vol. 7, No. 3, May 1996.

11. Whelehan, B., For Happiness, Money's a Tool, Not a Yardstick, *Bankrate.com,* May 25, 2005, http://aol1.bankrate.com/aol/news/BoomerBucks/20050525a1.asp.

12. Vince, G., Intelligence is Irrelevant to a Happy Old Age, NewScientist.com News Service, 15 July, 2005. http://www.newscientist.com/article.ns?id=dn7678.

13. Sahadi, J., Money and Happiness: How Tight the Bond? *CNN/Money,* July 5, 2005, http://money.cnn.com/2005/07/01/commentary/everyday/sahadi/index.htm.

14. EBRI 2004 Retirement Confidence Survey, Can America Afford Tomorrow's Retirees, *EBRI Issue in Brief,* Nov. 2003, p. 24.

15. Isidore, C., The Zero-savings Problem, *CNN/Money,* August 3, 2005, http://money.cnn.com/2005/08/02/news/economy/savings/.

16. Dominguez, J., and V. Robin, *Your Money or Your Life,* Penguin Books, 1992.

17. Gallo, W. T., E. Bardley, M. Siegel, and S. Kasl, Health Effects of Involuntary Job Loss among Older Workers, *Journal of Gerontology Series B: Psychological Sciences and Social Sciences,* vol. 55, pp. 131–140, 2000.

A BRIEF HISTORY OF SOCIAL SECURITY

On August 14, 1935 the Social Security Act became law with the President's signature at approximately 3:30 p.m. on a Wednesday, in the Cabinet Room of the White House.

In the early 1930s prior to passing the Social Security Act, more than 58% of 65+-year-old men were a part of the labor force. Today, less than 18% of men over 65 are still participating in the labor force. While reduced cost of leisure may have influenced this rise in a retirement class, the passage of the Social Security Act of 1935 certainly had a significant impact.

Social Security was designed to extend pension benefits to those not covered by a private pension plan. The Social Security Act consisted of two programs: Old Age Assistance (OAA) and Old Age Insurance (OAI). The OAA program provided federal matching funds to subsidize state old age pension programs. The availability of federal funds quickly motivated many states to develop a pension program or to increase benefits. The U.S. Social Security system was very different from industrial pension systems at the time. In particular, the soon-to-retire worker did not get full credit for past years of work. To receive benefit credit, the retiree must have paid into the system for a number of periods. The U.S. plan was also different from plans in many other countries since it did not means-test benefits.

In 1950, coverage of the OAI program was extended to include farm and domestic workers, and average benefits were increased by 77%. Financed by payroll taxes, the newly liberalized OAI program began to dominate Social Security. Retirees (and later, survivors, dependents of retirees, and the disabled) who had paid into the system were eligible to receive benefits.

In 1965, Medicare was added to the Social Security Act to provide health insurance to the elderly. The Social Security program continued to expand in the late 1960s and early 1970s—benefits increased 13% in 1968, another 15% in 1969, and 20% in 1972.

The formula for determining benefits was adjusted downward in 1977. In 1983, further reforms included the delay of a cost-of-living adjustment, taxation of up to half of benefits, and payroll tax increases.

By 2000, 90% of Americans over the age of 65 received at least some of their income from Social Security. In fact, Social Security benefits are by far the most important source of income for seniors, constituting 40% of all income received by those over the age of 65. Further evidence of the critical role that Social Security has taken for seniors is the statistic that 48.1% of all Americans over the age of 65 would fall below the poverty level without Social Security benefits. That figure rises to 62.1% of all those over the age of 85.

Further Reading:

Short J., Economic History of Retirement in the United States, *EH.Net Encyclopedia,* http://www.eh.net/encyclopedia/?article=short.retirement.history.us.

Williamson, S. H., *The Development of Industrial Pensions in the United States in the Twentieth Century,* Policy Research Working Paper 1542, The World Bank Policy Research Department, Finance and Private Sector Development Division, Nov. 1995.

Fore, D., Do We Have a Retirement Crisis in America? *Research Dialogue, TIAA-CREF Institute,* Issue 77, September 2003, http://www.ssa.gov/history/history.html.

2

ANALYSIS TOOLS AND CALCULATIONS

The ideal tool for retirement planning would provide you with an exact portfolio description required to retire successfully. It would allow you to calculate how much could be spent each year in retirement and not run out of money. An optimization feature would allow you to optimize personal satisfaction obtained from your savings, pension, and Social Security. Unfortunately, that tool does not exist.

Though less than ideal, several approaches for calculating your required retirement nest egg and maximum safe withdrawal rate are available. Since these calculations require estimates of the future (returns, inflation, spending, lifespan), none of the approaches is perfect. Nevertheless, careful use of these methods can provide guidance for planning your retirement.

In order to approach the required-nest-egg problem, you must account for your future return on investments, future rate of inflation, your spending rate for the rest of your life, and your total time in retirement. If you are planning for both you and your spouse, or wish to leave a sizeable inheritance for someone, those factors must also be taken into account. To perform the calculations, you need a model for each of the listed quantities (returns, inflation, spending, and lifespan). The problem is further complicated by the fact that many of these quantities are correlated to each other and to their own immediate past history.

Although this is a difficult problem, there are aspects of it that make it more approachable. First, it is not necessary to maximize your final nest egg in retirement, only to insure that you outlive the nest egg you start with. You are trying to identify a plan that survives worst-case scenarios. Your plan does not need to identify investments that would achieve maximum gain during periods that are not a threat to your portfolio's survival. This is analogous to the problem of choosing your wardrobe for a weeklong vacation in St. Louis next June. Although it would be impossible to predict the exact temperature and conditions during your vacation, it is not as difficult to identify and bring suitable clothing for the likely range of weather possibilities.

A second simplifying aspect of the problem is that it is a long-term problem. Day-to-day or even year-to-year fluctuations in returns, inflation, and spending are not of concern. Your retirement is likely to last 30 years or more. It is important that you focus only on the long-term variations that are much less turbulent than the short-term variations. Stock returns are notoriously volatile, especially on a year-to-year basis, but when examined over 30-year periods, much of the volatility is muted. In Figure 2.1, average 1-year and 30-year returns for the S&P500 stock index are plotted for the years 1900 to 2002. The 1-year returns vary significantly and are actually negative for some years, but the 30-year average returns are much more predictable. There has never been a 30-year period in U.S. history when the S&P500 provided a negative average return. Bond returns and inflation (already less volatile than stocks) also exhibit reduced fluctuations when looking at longer periods.

A final simplification to the retirement survival problem is that you have significant control over one important variable—spending. Investment returns and inflation vary outside of your control, but you decide how much to spend and when. Reductions in discretionary spending during years of poor economic performance can contribute significantly to portfolio survival.

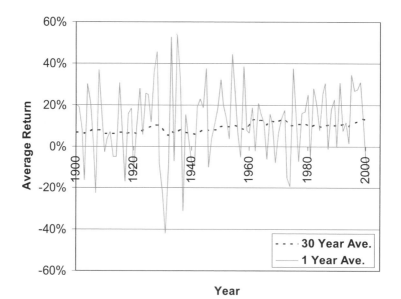

Figure 2.1. One-year and 30-year average returns for the S&P500 from 1900 to 2002. (Source: http://www.econ.yale.edu/~shiller/data.htm, Shiller Data Online.)

2.1. PREDICTIONS BASED ON AVERAGE RETURNS AND INFLATION

Planning for your retirement would be easy if you could depend on earnings and inflation rates remaining the same every year. You would know exactly how much you could afford to withdraw and would never have to deal with uncertainties. The simplest approach for estimating retirement nest egg requirements assumes that every year is the same. This technique makes use of average returns, average inflation, and average spending; then applies those averages to each year. Assuming that a balanced investment portfolio returns an average of 7.6%, and that inflation averages 3.3%, a safe withdrawal rate is computed to be the difference, 4.3%. The difference between investment return and inflation is referred to as the *real rate of return*. If every year were average, retirees could take an amount equal to the real rate of return out of their portfolio each year and never run out of money. Their spending and the size of their nest egg would always keep up with inflation.

The values chosen for the example of the preceding paragraph were arrived at using average return and inflation data over the 100 year period from 1903 to 2002. One hundred-year averages for equity and bond returns are 9.8% and 5.3%, respectively. These numbers also assume a 0.2% expense ratio for your investment accounts. (Expenses will be discussed in Chapter 6.) Using these numbers, a 50/50 diversified equity/bond balanced portfolio would provide a 7.6% average annual return. The average inflation rate over this period is 3.3%.

One problem with this approach is that it is not obvious what data to consider when computing an average value. Figure 2.2 illustrates this problem as it relates to equity and bond returns as well as inflation. Although the 1990s produced a real rate of return for a balanced, diversified portfolio of 10.5%, the real rate of return in the 1970s was *negative* 1.1%. For retirement planning purposes, ten year average values are clearly not adequate.

Although a 100-year database may seem compelling, it is easy to argue that the economy of the United States in the early 1900s may not resemble the economy of the early 2000s. Since the Great Depression, there have been significant changes in laws and regulations that govern stocks, bonds, and investing. Will data from years prior to the establishment of these rules reflect retirement reality today? If 100-year averages are not appropriate for these calculations, what is? 20-year? 30-year?

Even if we could compute correct forward-looking average results for our returns and inflation during our retirement, the average-rate approach to retirement calculations is inadequate. Short-term variations in investment returns and inflation can result in a portfolio running out of money before the retirement period is over, even if the average rates predict success. Figure 2.3 illustrates this using actual historical returns and inflation data for a retiree who retired in 1972 and planned on funding retirement for 30 years. The calculations also assume that the retiree's spending was adjusted each year to keep up with inflation. A combination of low returns and high inflation during the first several years of this period conspire to annihilate the portfolio in just 25 years. The average returns for the period are high largely because of unusually high returns during the mid-to-late 1990s, but the portfolio of the 1972 retiree was too diminished to benefit from these returns. Inflation

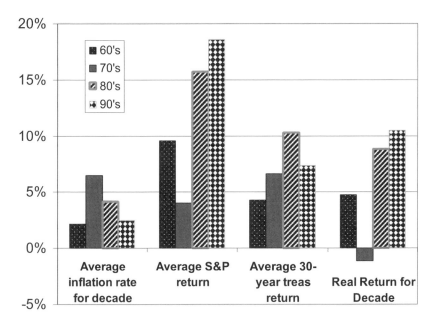

Figure 2.2. Average inflation, S&P500, and 30-year treasury returns by decade. Real return assumes a 50/50 equity/bond rebalanced portfolio.

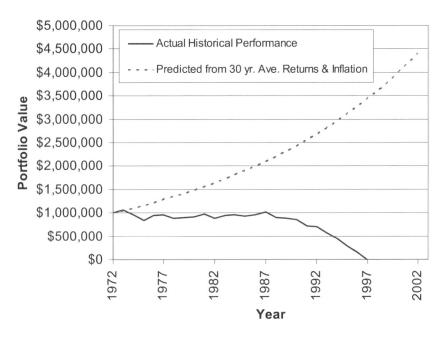

Figure 2.3. A 1972 retiree using average return and average inflation data to predict portfolio performance over the next 30 years would have run out of money in only 25 years. This is true even though the average rates used in this calculation are the exact 30-year averages experienced between 1972 and 2003.

was also high during the early part of the period. Although average inflation over the period was modest, the 1972 retiree had depleted funds too early to benefit from the low inflation of the late 1990s.

Although average-return retirement analysis has many deficiencies, it can still be a useful tool to the retirement planner. One big advantage of the technique is that it can be quickly programmed into a spreadsheet to examine the relative impact of unusual financial events. A more sophisticated simulator using Monte Carlo analysis or historical data is likely to provide more robust predictions, but it may be cumbersome or impossible to examine unusual events using these tools. For example, if a retiree were planning on a retirement lifestyle that involved an unusual spending pattern, this could be easily accommodated in a custom spreadsheet using average-return assumptions. Although the results of such analysis may not be as reliable as you would like, the qualitative effects can be comprehended and applied to more sophisticated tool results.

2.2. SPENDING MODELS

The examples above use an *inflation-driven* spending model. This model assumes a withdrawal rate in year 1 that is adjusted for inflation each year in retirement. The adjustment in annual spending is made regardless of how the portfolio grows or shrinks. For example, a retiree with a $1 million nest egg using a 4% initial withdrawal rate would take $40,000 for living expenses the first year in retirement. If the inflation rate were 5% during the first year, then the retiree would withdraw $42,000 (= $40,000 × 1.05) the second year. An advantage of the inflation-driven spending model is that the retiree maintains his or her standard of living throughout retirement. A disadvantage, however, is that it is possible to run out of money before you die.

An alternative spending model is the *fixed-percentage-of-portfolio* model. Using this model, a retiree would examine his or her portfolio each year and withdraw a fixed percentage of that portfolio for living expenses. For example, a $1 million initial portfolio and a 5% withdrawal rate would result in a $50,000 withdrawal in the first year. In the second year, portfolio performance and the first year's withdrawal would result in a portfolio that may be greater or less than $1 million. The second year's withdrawal would be 5% of the portfolio value regardless of whether the portfolio increased or decreased and independent of inflation. This spending model has the advantage that it will never run out of money. A disadvantage of this model is that if the portfolio shrinks due to bad performance years, the retiree's lifestyle could be reduced dramatically.

A third spending model is a combination of the inflation-driven and fixed-percent-of-portfolio model. This model assumes that certain expenses are required and will increase at the rate of inflation, while others are discretionary and can be delayed, reduced, or eliminated if portfolio performance does not support it.

Figure 2.4 illustrates how each of these models affects the survival of the retirement portfolio for the 1972 retiree. The three models are:

- Inflation-driven model
- Fixed-percentage-of-portfolio model
- Combination model

In this example, the inflation-driven model uses a 5% initial withdrawal rate and is adjusted upward to match inflation each year. This spending behavior would have resulted in the retiree running out of money in 25 years.

The fixed-percentage-of-portfolio model always survives, but in this example requires significant sacrifice of the retiree during the first several years of the period. After the first year, the 1972 retiree would have needed to cut real spending. During several years of the early 1980s, spending reductions would have reached a level more than 20% below inflation-driven withdrawal values and would not have caught up with inflation until the late 1980s.

The combination model offers a compromise that allows the portfolio to survive while reducing the lifestyle deterioration caused by inflation and poor investment

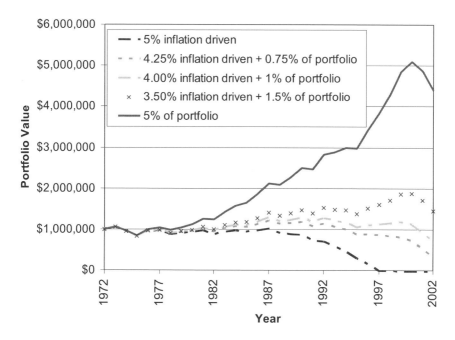

Figure 2.4. Comparison of five different spending models applied to the same portfolio for a 1972 retiree. The inflation-driven spending model uses a 5% initial withdrawal rate and allows the retiree to maintain his or her standard of living, but runs out of money after 25 years. The 5%-of-portfolio model always survives but forces the retiree to reduce spending significantly during the first several years of retirement. Three different combination models are shown in the graph. A required portion of the budget is inflation driven (4.25%, 4.00%, and 3.5% initial withdrawal rate) and a discretionary portion (0.75%, 1%, and 1.5% of portfolio value) fluctuates based on portfolio performance.

performance. Three combination model examples are shown. In the first example, 85% of the initial withdrawal is adjusted for inflation every year and an additional 15% of the initial withdrawal (0.75% of the starting portfolio amount) is adjusted each year according to the portfolio balance. The other two examples use inflation-adjusted initial withdrawal rates of 80% and 70%, and use 20% and 30% of the initial withdrawal (1% and 1.5% of portfolio amount) based on the size of the portfolio. In the first year, the withdrawal of all five cases in Figure 2.4 would have been identical—5% of the initial portfolio. Required reductions in spending for the combination model are small (approximately 2% to 4%) relative to the pure inflation-driven model, but the portfolio life is extended beyond 30 years for all three combination models. This example illustrates the power of extremely modest spending modification on portfolio survival.

Recent research[5] suggests that many retirees reduce spending as their retirement progresses. Based on data from the U.S. Bureau of Labor Statistics' Consumer Expenditure Survey, researchers conclude that retirees generally spend less as they age. The survey data showed that spending in practically every category, from housing to clothing to entertainment, declines with age. The only category in which spending rises with age is healthcare.

According to the data, people over 75 spent 26% less, on average, than those in the 65–74 age group. The greater the age difference, the greater the difference in spending: people over 75 spent 46% less than those aged 55–64, and 51% less than those aged 45–54. Reduced spending during late retirement results in improved portfolio survivability.

2.3. HISTORICAL DATA

Although past performance is no guarantee of future results, historical data plays an important role in retirement planning. Historical performance of the economy is the basis of comparison for all future projections. Investment strategies are back-tested against historical data. Historical retirement simulators use this data directly to perform calculations. Even Monte Carlo simulations and average return models must rely on historical results to calibrate their input variables.

The data illustrated in Figures 2.5–2.7 is the basis for historical results presented throughout this book. This data is also used to compute average returns or inflation values used in average return simulations.

Stock Return Data

In his book, *Irrational Exuberance,*[2] Robert Shiller presents data including monthly stock price, dividends and earnings data, and the consumer price index, all starting in January 1871. The sources for all of this data are described in his book. The data is available as both an HTML and Excel file[1] that can be downloaded without charge. A number of simulators and the historical simulation results presented in this book utilize the Shiller data. Figure 2.5 presents the stock price data from those

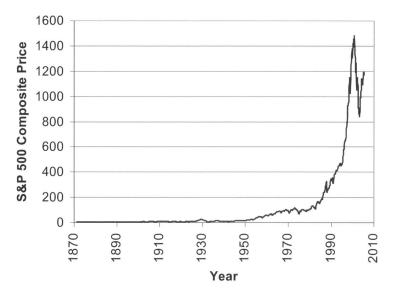

Figure 2.5. S&P500 composite index price by month from January 1871.

tables. The Shiller tables also include dividend and earnings rates as well as the long-term interest rates.

Bond Return Data

A number of historical simulation programs are available over the Internet without charge. These programs[6,7] have tabulated returns for several classes of bonds starting in January 1871 to make the data compatible with the Shiller stock data. The bond data includes rates for 5-year treasuries and 30-year treasuries as well as commercial paper. Figure 2.6 presents bond rate data for the 1871 to 2002 time period.

Inflation Data (CPI-U)

The U.S. Bureau of Labor Statistics calculates and publishes the consumer price index (CPI-U) each month (Figure 2.7). The Bureau samples the purchases of households representing 87% of the population. The index measures prices in a market basket of goods and services that is intended to be representative of a typical consumer's purchases. Goods and services sampled include food; clothing; housing; gasoline; other transportation items; medical, dental, and legal services; and hundreds of other retail goods and services. Taxes associated with the purchases are included. Each item is weighted in the average according to its share of the spending of the households included in the sample. Almost 100 urban areas are sampled.

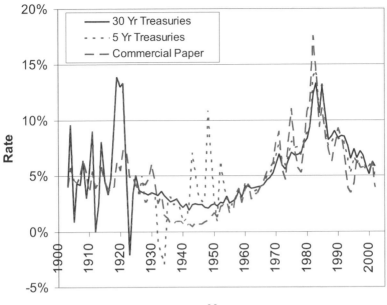

Figure 2.6. Bond rates by month from January 1902.

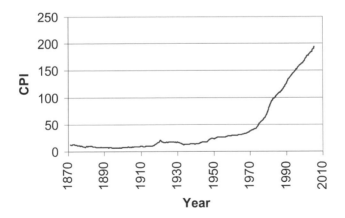

Figure 2.7. Monthly CPI-U data calculated by the U.S. Bureau of Labor Statistics and compiled by Shiller.[1]

The CPI-U is calculated by normalizing the current price of the entire basket of goods and services to the cost of the same basket in the base year. The inflation rate is the increase in CPI-U expressed as a percentage.

2.4. MONTE CARLO SIMULATION

Many engineers are familiar with Monte Carlo techniques as they are applied to design centering and yield analysis. Monte Carlo techniques are also used to model electron transport in semiconductors and in a number of other physics problems. The techniques utilize a random-number generator to produce random sequences of numbers that describe observed variations. In the case of circuit yield analysis, the random sequences imitate the deviations observed in circuit element values (i.e., component tolerances). In the case of retirement planning, the variations imitate the fluctuations observed in investment returns and inflation.

The user of a Monte Carlo safe-withdrawal calculator specifies a retirement plan using the following input parameters:

Original Portfolio Amount—The total amount of money invested at the beginning of retirement.

Stock/Bond Allocation—The ratio of the portfolio dollars invested in equity positions (stocks and stock mutual funds) to the dollars invested in fixed-income investments (bonds and bond funds). Monte Carlo simulators may further subdivide the asset allocation to include real estate, international investments, small cap funds, and so on.

Initial Annual Withdrawal Rate—The percentage of the total portfolio required for living expenses in the first year of retirement. Using the inflation-driven spending model, this annual withdrawal will be increased or decreased to account for inflation/deflation each year.

Expense Ratio of Investments—The expenses required by brokers, mutual fund companies, 401(k) caretakers, and so on expressed as a percentage of total portfolio value. This topic is the subject of detailed discussion in Chapter 6.

Time in Retirement—The total number of years spent in retirement (i.e., age at death minus age at retirement)

In addition to the variables listed above, Monte Carlo simulations require that you describe the assumed distribution of expected returns and inflation over the retirement period. As in the case of circuit element variation, a common way to describe the return probability is to use a normal distribution:

$$G(x, \sigma) = \frac{1}{\sigma\sqrt{2\pi}} \exp^{-(x-X)^2/(2\sigma^2)} \tag{2.1}$$

where X is the mean value and σ is the standard deviation. In Equation (2.1), G can be an approximation for the distribution of S&P500 returns, bond returns, inflation, or expected returns of any other asset class. One advantage of the Monte Carlo method is that it allows you to measure survivability for portfolios containing assets with limited historical data. Few asset classes have documented return data over the 130 years that are contained in the Shiller database. Investigations of the impact of real estate or of international value indexes, for example, are difficult to perform using only historical data. Figure 2.8 presents the S&P500 historical annual-return data as a histogram. The data includes annual returns for the composite index since 1900. Data analysis indicates the statistics are approximated using a normal distribution with a mean of 11.45% and a standard deviation of 18.04%. The normal distribution description is also illustrated in this figure. Similar distributions can be computed for other asset classes and for inflation.

When a Monte Carlo simulation is started, random rates of return are generated by sampling from the assumed probability distribution. The return for each asset class and inflation rate is generated for every year in a hypothetical retirement period. For the first year, the simulator adds or subtracts equity gains or losses and bond gains or losses to the original portfolio amount. It then subtracts living expenses (adjusted for inflation) and investment expenses computed using the expense ratio. The resulting value is the starting point for calculating the portfolio value beginning in year 2. This process is repeated sequentially for each year in the hypothetical sequence until the full time in retirement has been simulated or until the portfolio value is reduced to less than zero. This part of the algorithm results in a computed portfolio value over time for the retirement plan as well as a determination of whether the specified portfolio would have survived the hypothetical retirement period. If the portfolio would have survived the sequence, then a *terminal value* is defined as

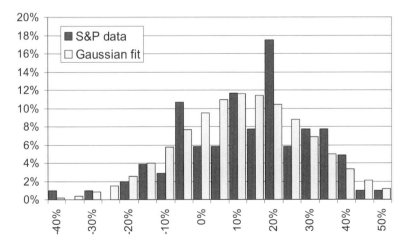

Figure 2.8. Histogram of S&P500 composite index annual returns since 1900. Data analysis indicates the data is approximately described as a distribution with a mean of 11.45% and a standard deviation of 18.04%. The Gaussian distribution curve defined by these terms is also illustrated.

the value of the portfolio after the final annual withdrawal. Each retirement sequence considered by the simulator results in either a determination of failure (i.e., the portfolio falls to zero before retirement is finished) or a terminal value.

The simulator typically runs hundreds or thousands of hypothetical sequences and counts the number of scenarios that provide success. Each simulation includes up and down markets of various lengths, intensities, and combinations. The result is a probabilistic evaluation of your likelihood of success. *Survivability* is defined as the probability that there will be funds remaining in the portfolio at the end of the retirement period. An 80% survivability means that your portfolio still contained money at the end of the retirement period in 8 out of 10 of the hypothetical sequences. A 50% survivability indicates that the portfolio value fell to below zero in half of the simulated sequences.

Table 2.1 presents results from Monte Carlo simulations examining the survivability of a portfolio comprised of 60% S&P500 and 40% short-term, fixed-income securities.[9] Inflation is consistent with CPI-U and a 0% expense ratio was assumed.

Although the probabilistic predictions from a Monte Carlo simulator offer more valuable information about retirement than a fixed-average-rate calculation, it can be difficult to interpret the results. What does an 89.1% survival probability mean? Is that enough?

When deciding what survival probability we feel comfortable with, it is important to understand that the simulator is, overestimating the probability of failure in at least two important ways. First, the Monte Carlo technique does not account for all of the correlations between asset classes and inflation. On the surface, fluctuations in market returns may appear to be random; but in reality, forces in the economy produce correlations between market returns of various asset classes and inflation. Correlations between performance in the present and the recent past are also important. Financial markets obey the principle of causality even if the causes are a mystery to us. Although these correlations are far too complex to quantify using a mathematical formula, they are very important to actual portfolio performance. Uncorrelated or under correlated statistics cause Monte Carlo retirement simulations to produce survival predictions that are slightly pessimistic.

Second, the simulator assumes that the retiree does nothing to modify his or her rate of spending throughout the retirement period. As illustrated in Figure 2.4, a retiree who notices that his her portfolio is being depleted can dramatically improve survival success with only modest modifications in spending. Based on comparisons between Monte Carlo simulations and past history, Monte Carlo predictions could be on the order of 10% to 20% more pessimistic than the worst-case scenarios of the past.

Table 2.1. Results from the Monte Carlo retirement withdrawal calculator[9,10]

Inflation-adjusted initial withdrawal rate	2%	3%	4%	5%
Monte Carlo predicted probability of portfolio survival for 30 years	99.6%	96.3%	89.1%	72.5%

Appendix A provides Internet addresses and information about Monte Carlo programs that are available at no cost. These programs can be used to customize the simulations to describe your own portfolio and analyze it for survivability.

2.5. HISTORICAL SIMULATION AND THE 4% RULE

The historical simulator is a powerful analysis tool that, like Monte Carlo modeling, avoids many of the pitfalls caused by calculations based on average returns and average inflation. Using the financial data presented in Section 2.3, a historical simulator computes performance and evaluates the survivability of a retirement plan. Historical simulation of financial performance is the engineering equivalent of a lookup table model. By its nature, this kind of model captures all important relationships that contributed to past financial performance. This is accomplished without deriving explicit expressions for these relationships or for the correlations between them. Although laws, regulations, and corporations change over time, the fundamental forces that drive corporate competition and profit motive remain relatively unchanged. This is what makes the historical simulation results compelling. It is especially powerful when used to examine worst-case retirement scenarios and to establish portfolio survivability estimates. As with any method used to anticipate future performance, there are limitations to the historical simulation approach. Both strengths and limitations of this methodology are discussed later in this chapter.

The user of a historical simulation program specifies a retirement plan using many of the same input parameters as those required by Monte Carlo simulators:

Original Portfolio Amount

Stock/Bond Allocation—Historical simulators can consider other types of investments such as real estate. Most do not, however, because of the difficulty of obtaining reliable data on the return rates of such investments over a significant period of time.

Initial Annual Withdrawal Rate

Expense Ratio of Investments

Time in Retirement

The historical simulator works in a manner similar to the Monte Carlo simulator. The primary difference is that the historical simulator uses sequences of returns and inflation directly from the historical record, whereas the Monte Carlo simulator uses hypothetical sequences produced by a random-number generator. The historical simulator tests the retirement plan repeatedly, with each year in the historical database serving as the starting year for one retirement sequence. As in the case of Monte Carlo simulation, each retirement sequence considered by the simulator results in either a determination of failure (i.e., the portfolio falls to zero before retirement is finished) or a terminal value. Historical survivability and terminal value are defined in the same way as with Monte Carlo simulations, but the meaning of the values is slightly different. Historical survivability is the actual percentage of years when your retirement plan would have survived throughout history. Our hope in running these simulations is that the future is no worse than the past. In contrast, Monte Carlo simulations represent the percentage of years when your retirement plan survives a hypothetical sequence of returns. The assumption is that the future is well represented by our hypothetical sequence generator.

As an example of what the historical simulator can reveal, consider the following situation. The historical simulator uses the Shiller[2] data (1871 to 2002). The retirement plan is described by the following:

Initial portfolio of $P_i = \$1$ million.
Equity/bond allocation is $S_a/B_a = 50/50$.
Initial annual withdrawal rate is $W_i = \$40,000$.
Expense ratio of investments is $E_r = 0.2\%$.
Time in retirement is $T_{Re} = 30$ years.

The simulator begins with the specified retirement plan and performs computations on a year-by-year basis to determine if the plan would have successfully survived a retirement period starting at the beginning of 1871 and ending at the end of 1900 ($T_{Re} = 30$ years). The plot of Figure 2.9 illustrates the portfolio value as a function of year in retirement for the first sequence. This retirement plan provides for $40,000 to be spent in the first year and an additional $2000 for investment fees. Spending is increased to accommodate inflation each year, yet the overall portfolio grows over the initial 30 year retirement interval to over $2.2 million.

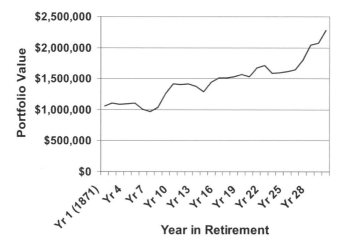

Figure 2.9. Results of historical simulation for first sequence of years (1871–1901). Simulation assumes initial portfolio value of $1 million, equity/bond allocation of 50/50, initial withdrawal rate of $40,000 per year, an expense ratio of 0.2%, and a 30-year period in retirement.

The simulator next repeats the computations for a 30-year retirement beginning in 1872 and ending in 1901, then for the period from 1873 to 1902, and so on. Assuming that the final date of available data is 2004, the last full 30-year simulation includes the dates 1975 to 2004. Further simulations (starting in years beyond 1975) can be performed to see if portfolio failure occurs in less than 30 years. For this example, the historical simulator considers 104 full 30-year retirement scenarios along with 29 shortened-period simulations. A plot of the portfolio value simulations for all sequences is presented in Figure 2.10. All but seven of the sequences resulted in success. The terminal value of the sequences ranges from a high value of over $3 million to a worst-case portfolio performance resulting in failure in just 24 years. Figure 2.11 presents the portfolio performance over time for only the seven starting years that resulted in failure of the specified retirement plan. It is interesting to consider the years that were historically worst for beginning a retirement. Although the Great Depression was a devastating financial era for the United States, 1929 is not the worst time to have retired for many stock/bond allocation plans, as indicated in the example above.

Although historical simulation can be a very valuable tool for the retirement planner, there are limitations of this technique that should be understood. First, a historical simulator can only simulate performance for which reliable historical data exists. Published data exists for total stock market performance and total bond market performance since 1871.[2] This allows us to simulate a portfolio invested in broad total market funds. But if an investor invests some of his or her portfolio in real estate, international investments, microcap funds, and so on, historical simulations cannot analyze the performance. Recently developed indexes track some of these kinds of investments, but without a database of at least 100 years of perfor-

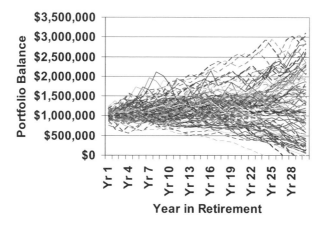

Figure 2.10. Results of historical simulation for 102 30-year sequences with beginning years 1871–1973. Simulations assume an initial portfolio value of $1 million, equity/bond allocation of 50/50, initial withdrawal rate of $40,000 per year, an expense ratio of 0.2%, and a 30-year period in retirement. Survivability for this portfolio is 93.1% and the average terminal value is $1.2 million.

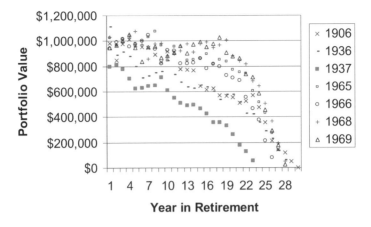

Figure 2.11. Results of historical simulation for seven failed retirement sequences. Simulations assume an initial portfolio value of $1 million, equity/bond allocation of 50/50, initial withdrawal rate of $40,000 per year, an expense ratio of 0.2%, and a 30-year period in retirement.

mance information, the validity of a 30+ year historical retirement simulation is questionable.

The need for several decades of data creates another limitation for this approach. Laws, regulations, corporate structures, international agreements, and many other influences on corporate profits are changed every year. It is appropriate to question how relevant the financial performance of a portfolio invested in 1871 is to the experience today's retiree is likely to encounter over the next 30 or 40 years.

Additionally, *past performance is no guarantee of future results.* This disclaimer should be heeded not only when considering the purchase of stocks, bonds and mutual funds, but also whenever any attempt to predict our financial future is made.

Before abandoning the historical simulator, it is important to realize that we are looking only for worst-case results when using this kind of simulation. The simulator cannot be used to accurately predict the return on our investments next year or the year after. We are not trying to predict the magnitude or timing of the next stock market boom but are trying to find a worst-case estimate for our long-term retirement portfolio performance. All simulations include data from the Great Depression and the poor performance and hyperinflation periods of the 1960s and 1970s (see The Worst Time to Retire at the end of this chapter). The fundamental market pressures of a capitalist economy that produce stock returns, bond returns, and inflation are still similar to those of the past. There are complex relationships between financial returns and inflation, and between financial returns of the recent past and those of today. All of these complex correlations are implicitly included in the historical simulator. No other simulation approach offers this advantage.

Appendix A provides Internet addresses and information about historical simulation programs that are available at no cost. These programs can be used to customize the historical simulations to describe your own portfolio and analyze it for historical survivability.

Safe Withdrawal Rate

The maximum 100% survivable initial withdrawal rate is the highest initial annual withdrawal rate that produces positive terminal values for all retirement periods. This rate of withdrawal is referred to as the *safe withdrawal rate.* Studies completed using historical simulators have examined the safe withdrawal rate for a wide range of portfolios.

Figure 2.12 presents one study of the affects of stock/bond allocation of the portfolio on the historical safe withdrawal rate. The simulation parameters for the study are:

Initial portfolio of $P_i = \$1$ million.

Equity/bond allocation, S_a/B_a, is varied from 0/100 to 100/0.

Initial annual withdrawal rate, W_i is optimized to find the maximum amount that results in 100% survivability.

Expense ratio of investments is $E_r = 0.2\%$.

Time in retirement is $T_{Re} = 30$ years.

Three different bond allocations were considered in the study: commercial paper, five-year treasuries, and I bonds with 1% fixed interest rate. The earnings rate for I bonds is a combination of a fixed rate, which will apply for the life of the bond,

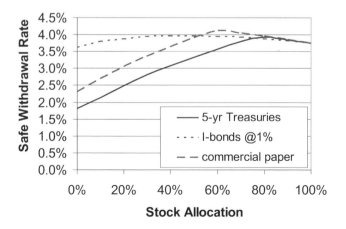

Figure 2.12. Safe withdrawal rate derived from historical simulation for 30-year retirement as a function of stock allocation. For the simulation, three different bond allocations were considered: commercial paper, I bonds with 1% fixed interest rate, and five-year treasuries.

and the inflation rate as measured by the CPI-U. A detailed discussion of each bond type is presented in Chapter 5.

The historical simulation shows that for stock allocations of more than 50% to 60%, the safe withdrawal rate reaches a peak of approximately 4% for all three cases. This means that a carefully chosen, balanced portfolio of $1 million with at least 50% to 60% total stock market index investment and the remainder invested in appropriate bonds, would have survived an approximate $40,000 per year initial withdrawal (adjusted each year for inflation) through any 30 year period in history (1871 to 2002). This observation is the *4% rule* stated in Equation (1.1) of Chapter 1. It provides retirement planners with an initial estimate of how much money is required for a safe retirement.

This rule is not a law of physics or absolute truth. It cannot be confirmed experimentally like Ohm's law or Maxwell's equations, but the 4% rule provides an initial guideline for setting investment targets. Using this rule as a starting point, retirement planners can perform perturbations to the 4% rule to account for pensions, annuities, Social Security benefits, unusual one-time purchases or sales during retirement, and many other details that will affect your ultimate retirement plan.

Longer or shorter retirement periods can also be considered using historical simulation, as illustrated in Figure 2.13. In this figure, a 60/40 stock/bond allocation was used for all three bond types considered in Figure 2.12, but the time in retirement was varied from 10 to 50 years. The figure shows that safe withdrawal rate begins to saturate for retirement periods longer than about 30 years. Longer retirement simulations present another problem for historical simulators. For a 50-year simulation, the earliest possible sequence begins in 1872 and ends in 1921. Similarly, the most recent possible 50-year retirement sequence uses 1955 as its starting year and

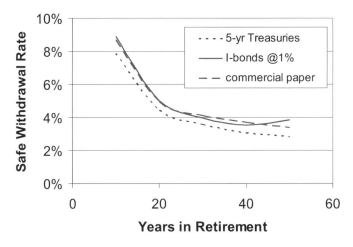

Figure 2.13. Safe withdrawal rate as a function of years in retirement. Three different bond allocations are considered.

ends in 2004. All other 50-year sequences overlap significantly with one or both of these two cases. The 30-year data of Figure 2.11 also illustrates the fact that retirees starting retirement during the mid-1960s faced some of the toughest financial conditions of any retirees in history. We have yet to see the final outcome of their 50 year sequence.

Terminal Value

Another important result from such simulations is the *average terminal value* of the retirement plan. Since most people are not aware in advance of their actual age at death, one risk retirement planners must consider is the potential of outliving their portfolio. The actuarial table of Appendix C might suggest that a 58-year-old man living today will live on average for 26.5 more years to age 84.5. This number is very useful to an insurance company since they will pay benefits to a large number of insured; some will live longer and some will live shorter than the actuarial tables imply. You must plan your retirement, however, for *your* whole life, not for the life of the average person. You may actually live much longer than the actuarial tables imply. For a couple, the odds that one of you will live longer than actuarial table average is higher than for a single individual. A high terminal value of your portfolio at year 30 is good insurance against outliving your portfolio.

Investing Profile

One objection to all of the retirement calculation techniques is that S&P500 index funds are the only equity position considered by many simulators. Real estate, individual stock, and international investments are not considered. The goal of retirement simulation is not to achieve maximum gain from your investments, but to find investments that survive worst-case scenarios. The simple portfolio of S&P500 index funds mixed with bonds or bond index funds is a proof-of-existence of historically safe retirement investments. If the individual investor is able to beat this investment strategy investing in real estate, sector funds, or individual stocks, then their strategy only becomes safer than the simulations have indicated.

Investment options other than simple indexes will be discussed in Chapters 5 and 6. Although some modifications to the allocations used in the retirement simulators may provide better or less risky returns, many investment choices are far more risky. Mutual fund and trading fees can also deteriorate the value of a more aggressive investment strategy. It is not the goal of this book to recommend any particular investment choices. Before committing your retirement funds, however, it would be wise to understand the risk–reward profile of all investments.

Reevaluation and Adjustment of Your Plan

Achieving comfort with a retirement portfolio is an iterative and imperfect process. An initial examination of this problem is likely to include only crude estimates of retirement expenses. Early in your career, your retirement date can only be a guess. Your pension and Social Security expectations are likely to be changed and refined throughout your career. With respect to your retirement plan, the most important action you can take early in your career is to save and invest as much as possible. Simulations using crude estimates as inputs produce crude estimates of ultimate portfolio value and safe withdrawal rate. Application of the simple 4% rule may be an adequate tool for retirement planning for the first several years of your career.

As your retirement date gets closer (six to 10 years out), you should be able to refine your estimates. Social Security and pension benefit estimates should be accounted for in your calculations. Other aspects of your retirement plan are also more defined and understood. You may have chosen a retirement location and made specific decisions regarding some of your assets. Modifications to your investments and your spending can be made that will have a positive impact on your overall plan. You may be able to develop a clear target retirement date.

In the last three to five years before retirement, you should be able to examine your plan with fairly accurate estimates of portfolio, pension, Social Security, and spending expectations. Whether or not to pay off your mortgage may be an important decision at this time. It is time to decide if the portfolio allocation you used during the accumulation phase is the same allocation to take into the distribution phase of your life. It is also advisable to begin thinking about where income flow will come from during retirement. All of these issues can be examined using available retirement simulators.

REFERENCES

1. Shiller, R. J., *Historical Data,* http://www.econ.yale.edu/~shiller/data/ie_data.htm.

2. Shiller, R. J., *Irrational Exuberance,* Princeton University Press, Princeton, NJ, 2000.

3. Bernstein, W., *The Intelligent Asset Allocator,* McGraw-Hill, New York, 2001.

4. Polyak, I., New Advice to Retirees: Spend More at First, Cut Back Later, *New York Times Online,* Sept. 25, 2005, http://www.nytimes.com/2005/09/25/business/your-money/25save.html?adxnnl=1&pagewanted=all&adxnnlx=1127736349-1/oqot7Yt-NieLQglFQrLMw.

5. Bernicke, T., Reality Retirement Planning: A New Paradigm for an Old Science, *Journal of Financial Planning,* June 2005, http://www.fpanet.org/journal/articles/2005_Issues/jfp0605-art7.cfm?&.

6. Greaney, J., *Safe Withdrawal Calculator,* 2002 Edition, December 9, 2002, http://www.retireearlyhomepage.com/re60.html.

7. Sholar, B., FIRECalc: How Long Will the Money Last?, 2002, http://fireseeker.com/.

8. Berstein, W., The Retirement Calculator from Hell, Part III: Eat, Drink, and Be Merry, *Efficient Frontier,* 2001, http://www.efficientfrontier.com/ef/901/hell3.htm.

9. Greaney, J., Where Do These Guys Get a 2% Safe Withdrawal Rate? *Retire Early Home Page,* January 1, 2005, http://www.retireearlyhomepage.com/twoperc.html.

10. Ponzo, P., *Gummy's Stuff, Monte Carlo Simulation,* http://www.gummy-stuff.org/Monte-Carlo.htm.

THE WORST TIME TO RETIRE

The Great Depression began with the stock market crash of 1929. This was one of the worst periods of financial turmoil in American history. Unfortunately, it was not the only period of time that placed retiree's portfolios at risk. Using historical simulation, the plight of retirees throughout history can be analyzed and worst-case retirement dates identified.

In Figure 2.14, the first data points on the left represent the portfolio survival of a retiree who began retirement on January 1, 1920. The three curves represent retirees who made initial withdrawals of 3.5%, 4.0%, or 4.5% of the portfolio in the first year, followed by inflation-adjusted withdrawals each succeeding year. The next data points on the graph represent the portfolio survival of a retiree who began retirement on January 1, 1921, and so on. All simulated retirements start with an initial retirement portfolio of $1 million (invested 50% in S&P 500, 50% in commercial bonds). Simulation intervals are 40 years or until the portfolio runs out of money.

The figure illustrates that a 3.5% withdrawal rate would have survived 40 years regardless of the year retirement was started. The portfolio of retirees using a 4% withdrawal rate would have survived every starting year except 1936, 1937, and 1966. The portfolio of retirees using a 4.5% withdrawal rate reveal significant periods that would not support a 40-year retirement.

It is interesting to note that the beginning of the Great Depression (1929) would not have been a problem for retirees with initial withdrawal rates of 4.0% or less. The late 1930s, the 1960s, and early 1970s were actually more likely to

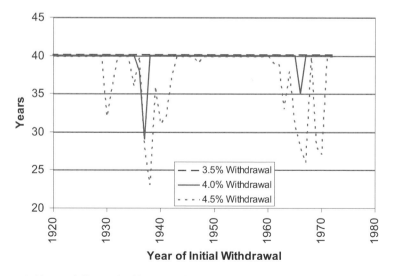

Figure 2.14. Portfolio survival by year of initial retirement withdrawal. Initial withdrawal rates of 3.5%, 4.0%, and 4.5% are illustrated.

devastate a retiree's portfolio. Although stock values were devastated in the market crash of 1929, the period of time immediately following the crash was associated with deflation, which helped portfolio survival for the retiree. In contrast, the 1960s and early 1970s represent a period of devastating inflation and a nearly stagnant stock market. Figure 2.14 illustrates that retirees can be adversely affected by a variety of economic environments.

Further Reading:

Bengen, W., Determining Withdrawal Rates Using Historical Data, *Journal of Financial Planning,* March 2004.

3

LIVE BELOW YOUR MEANS (LBYM)

In the absence of generous, reliable pension benefits, all successful retirement plans depend on one's ability to develop a portfolio of investments that will fund a desired retirement lifestyle. For most technical professionals, this means that successful retirement planning begins with learning to live below your means (LBYM). The critical impact of LBYM principles on retirement planning is easy to understand. You will never have any money to invest if you spend it as fast as or faster than you earn it. Adherence to LBYM principles is required before any investing can take place. If you get this component of retirement planning right, the rest will fall into place; if not, no advice will help you. Exceptions to this rule are lottery winners and recipients of large inheritances. Unfortunately, I know of no way to advise people on how to win the lottery or receive a large inheritance. It is also worth noting that even lottery winners and heirs to fortunes must learn how to LBYM or their windfall will quickly be depleted.

If you live below your means, then you are either investing regularly or collecting money in an idle stash. Practice regular investment and your retirement plan will stay on track. Concerns related to specific investment choices are discussed in Chapter 6, but these issues are neither as complex nor as critical to the ultimate goal as many inexperienced investors believe. The optimum investment portfolio is achieved more by choosing investments that you are personally comfortable with than it is a by choosing investments that produce maximum return. The investment options available will change over time as new investment vehicles emerge. Each investor will learn unique lessons and will settle ultimately on different ideal allocations. Once the LBYM principle is learned and practiced, you are likely to find efficient investment vehicles that will ensure a safe and successful retirement.

There are two major components of LBYM: (1) maximizing means and (2) living frugally relative to those means. The first component is related to career path and job choices and the second is related to spending and living habits. Both are important. More important, however, is the realization that the LBYM principle is only a means to an end. If the achievement of an LBYM lifestyle and early retirement requires that you become a miserly curmudgeon, you have missed the point. It is possible to put too much emphasis on either of the above components. Ruthlessly driving your career to ever higher salaries may not be satisfying or comfortable for you. Similarly, an obsession with the cost of every luxury or comfort item may keep you from enjoying life. Balance is the key to an LBYM lifestyle and a happy and successful retirement.

Although the LBYM principle is simple and obvious, violation of it appears to be the major cause of failed retirement plans. It is not always as easy to apply as it appears. For many, it seems impossible. A young professional forced to take a job in an area with an astronomical cost of living or with a long, gas-guzzling commute faces difficult LBYM challenges. Children, aging parents, or other family issues can produce additional challenges (some of these will be discussed in Chapter 4, Section 4.3). In a consumer-oriented world with advertisers continuously encouraging us to buy things, it is not surprising that many people become materially focused. This chapter will examine LBYM and the components that comprise an LBYM lifestyle. Specific practices that can help in the pursuit of an LBYM lifestyle are explored and some methods of quantifying the effect of financial and purchasing decisions are presented.

3.1. SPENDING

For many people, the words thrifty and frugal carry a negative connotation. They confuse these words with cheap or miserly. The words people use are not important, but seeking strong value propositions in everything you do is key to ensuring a comfortable retirement. Balance the desire for instant gratification with that of achieving longer and more fulfilling goals. Thrifty and frugal people employ strategies to reduce waste, modify costly habits, and seek efficiency.

The control you exercise on spending is the most powerful weapon in your retirement planning arsenal. Spend wisely and you will suffer less stress, your finances will not be so easily derailed by rough financial times, unexpected expenses will be less unpleasant, and you will reach financial independence sooner. You can try to increase your salary and improve your investment returns, but your control over these financial parameters is insignificant compared to the power you exercise to control your spending.

Being frugal is not about sacrifice. It is about getting as much as you can with as little money as possible. Frugality is about understanding the value proposition in every purchase and making the right deals to guarantee your satisfaction, both now and in the future. It is about maintaining your quality of life while maximizing the value gained from money you spend.

Section 1.5 (Chapter 1) presented the example of a daily cup of coffee that is worth over $160,000 at retirement. This example illustrates the fact that no cost is too small to consider cutting. You are not limited to considering purchases of luxury cars or home additions to find ways to live below your means. That daily cup of designer coffee may or may not bring you $160,000 worth of pleasure. The first steps in embracing frugality are to learn how to analyze the cost and to understand the value proposition of your purchases.

The daily cup of coffee may represent value to an individual in ways beyond the simple consumption of a warm drink. Perhaps you meet a valued friend or relative at your favorite coffee shop each morning and chat. The coffee may only be the excuse for maintaining a valuable relationship, a relationship easily worth the money to you. Maybe to you the ability to enjoy a fine cup of coffee in the morning is an important symbol of your success. Regardless of the reason, if value is perceived, then frugality dictates that you make the purchase. You will never be able to maintain an LBYM lifestyle if you cut out the things you value. In controlling your spending, you not only need to cut spending on things that offer insufficient value, but also to save for those things that are important to you.

The value proposition the frugal consumer considers is not as simple as asking, "What do I get if I spend this money right now?" Instead, the frugal consumer also asks, "What do I give up in the future if I spend this money right now?" If you have any long-term goals or large-ticket-item dreams, then foregoing the immediate gratification will sometimes bring you the greatest value.

Luxury items that come with a recurring cost can be especially damaging to achieving long-term satisfaction. While purchase of another telephone feature or hiring a weekly cleaning service may initially bring pleasure, you may find yourself dissatisfied again soon after the initial purchase. You may find yourself looking for another luxury purchase to regain the feeling of gratification. Becoming rapidly accustomed to purchased luxuries is quite common. Although our pleasure from such purchases may be short-lived, the resulting financial drain continues for many years. Becoming accustomed to a higher standard of living also means that a larger nest egg is required to achieve a comfortable retirement.

3.2. BREAKING THE RELATIONSHIP BETWEEN EARNING AND SPENDING

The old cliché is: "It doesn't matter how much we make; we spend it as soon as we get it." A more modern version is, "We spent it before we even saw it." Statistics on U.S. households indicate that these statements are true for many Americans. There are more items of instant gratification available for purchase than any paycheck can cover. In the absence of an LBYM strategy, earning and spending move forward with perfect correlation. Those who do not gain control of this cycle are doomed to be wage slaves for many years.

For many engineers, frugal living comes naturally. Spending much of their working day finding ways to cut costs and achieve optimum efficiency, they find that these habits do not stay in the office. Much of the discussions that follow will seem obvious and unnecessary to them.

There are no calculation tools that can make you save money for the future rather than spend it today. The desire to balance short-term and long-term spending is a matter of self-motivation. For people who have never developed saving habits, changing their relationship with money and learning to live a frugal lifestyle is an empowering transformation. Some people find that frugality becomes their new extravagance. The pleasure from finding new opportunities to save far exceeds the pleasure of purchasing another luxury item.

Evaluation of the financial rewards of a long-term saving decision can also help to motivate frugality. Before committing to a recurring cost, consider the implication of that commitment on your retirement nest egg. Take the example of a fixed monthly expense that is likely to increase with inflation. Using the 4% rule, an annualized expense is multiplied by 25 in order to estimate the additional nest egg required to support that expense in retirement. If you eliminate a few add-on phone services and reduce your monthly phone bill by $25 per month, you not only save $300 per year, but you have also reduced your required retirement nest egg by $7,500. Deciding to mow your lawn, eliminating a $100-per-month landscaping fee, is equivalent to adding $30,000 to your retirement fund. For those who are still several years away from retirement, the savings potential is even greater since the money saved through the elimination of services can be invested to earn money for many years.

One-time and less-frequent purchases can also be analyzed in terms of the impact on long-term savings. If you have a choice between buying two cars with a price difference of $10,000, the additional $10,000 can be considered a direct drain on the achievement of your retirement goal. Alternatively, the $10,000 represents a loss of $33 per month ($400/year) inflation adjusted throughout your retirement. Add the investment value of the money over the time between auto purchase and retirement, and the value can double or more.

When trying to gain control over spending, it may help to consider several issues related to each purchase before you buy. Is the purchase for something you need or something you want? Is there an alternative to making the purchase? Are there other ways to accomplish what the purchase will allow you to do? If purchase of the item or service seems to be the right thing to do, have you shopped to find the best deal? Is there a better time and/or place to make the purchase? You should also consider the consequences of not making the purchase. Is it important that you buy right now?

Opportunities to save exist in virtually every part of our lives. The categorized list below includes a range of ideas covering housing, utilities, transportation, food, health, entertainment, finance, and other areas. The list is a compilation of many ideas from many sources that may help you to find your own ways to LBYM. This list is not a set of recommendations. No single person is likely to find more than a few of these ideas appealing. Some ideas on the list will seem extreme or desperate to almost everyone, especially to affluent technical professionals. Ignore the items on the list that seem extreme to you. Focus only on items consistent with your own value proposition.

Housing and Utilities

1. Refinance your mortgage to get a lower rate and/or switch to a different loan duration.
2. Challenge your property tax assessment.
3. Eliminate premium channels from your cable or satellite TV service or drop the pay TV services altogether. A roof- or attic-mounted antenna may get most major stations for free.
4. If you purchase TV services, compare rates for cable and satellite. Investigate bundled services and purchase only what you need at the lowest cost.
5. Reduce phone extras such as call forwarding or call waiting.
6. Cancel your land line phone in favor of your cell phone service.
7. Cancel your cell phone service in favor of your land line.
8. Seek a cheaper long-distance carrier or switch to Internet calling if you have high-speed service.
9. In nice weather, use a clothesline to dry clothes.
10. Use shades, blinds, and drapes to regulate your home temperature. Keep them open in the winter to let in light and drawn in the summer to block the sun's rays.
11. Install a programmable thermostat so your home is heated or cooled only when you are actually there. Heat and cool only to the level needed to remain comfortable.
12. Wear a sweater in the winter and shorts in the summer so you are not overheating or overcooling your house.
13. Turn off unneeded lights and other electronics when not in use.
14. Use fluorescent bulbs.
15. Turn down the hot water heater or install a timer.
16. Use ceiling fans or portable fans rather than turn on the air conditioner.
17. Take shorter showers.
18. Get multiple quotes on homeowner's or renter's insurance. Consider raising the deductible.
19. Only wash full loads of laundry and dishes.
20. Buy energy-efficient appliances if they will be cheaper in the long run.

Transportation

1. Raise the deductibles on your auto insurance policy.
2. Get all the discounts you deserve, such as good driver, good student, low mileage, and multiple-car discounts.
3. Cancel collision and comprehensive insurance on cars older than five to seven years.

4. Bike, walk, carpool, or use public transportation as often as possible. See if your employer offers any subsidies.

5. Avoid repair bills by maintaining your vehicles properly with regular oil and filter changes.

6. Check air pressure on tires.

7. Group your errands and, if you have more than one car, use the vehicle with better gas mileage.

8. Use regular gas instead of premium.

9. Wash your car at home and skip the car wash.

10. Consider buying a preowned car instead of a new one.

11. Leave early and drive slower to save gas.

12. Keep checking airfare prices even after purchasing. With major airlines, you can get a voucher for the difference if the price goes down after you purchase.

13. Keep checking prices on rental cars even after you make a reservation, as there is no penalty for canceling.

Food

1. Bring your lunch to work or find inexpensive places to buy lunch.

2. Dine out less.

3. When you do dine out, eat dessert at home.

4. When traveling, eat outside of the hotel.

5. Cook in bulk and freeze; multiply whatever you are making and freeze the excess for a later meal.

6. Avoid overpackaged, overprocessed, and highly advertised foods. The closer a food is to its natural state, the less it tends to cost.

7. Buy fruits and vegetables in season.

8. Examine what is in your refridgerator daily to use items before they go bad.

9. Give up high-priced eating habits (alcohol, soda, snack foods).

10. Be a smart grocery shopper: cut coupons, shop at discount stores, and stock up on sale items.

11. Make a list before shopping. Resist buying outside your list unless the item is something you use and reduced in price.

12. Use newspaper ads and weekly grocery store circulars to plan meals around sale items.

13. Cut back on designer coffee. Bring your own coffee to work.

14. Make meal preparation as well as meal clean-up an enjoyable family/social event.

15. Bring snacks and water with you when you will be away from home for more than a few hours.

Health

1. Take advantage of free health screenings at work or through other organizations.
2. If you are self-employed, consider switching health insurance plans to a high-deductible plan to take advantage of HSAs (see Chapter 6).
3. Take advantage of medical prescription drug cards.
4. Give up expensive health club memberships. Learn to do exercises outdoors or at home. Form a walking, jogging, or riding club.
5. If your doctor approves, fill prescriptions with generic drugs.
6. Buy non-name-brand equivalents of over-the-counter drugs.
7. Get annual physicals. They can prevent costly future problems.
8. Look for free and low-cost clinics.
9. Ask for discounts when you pay cash for medical services.
10. Carefully review hospital bills for errors.
11. Monitor insurance claims to make sure they get paid.
12. Exercise.
13. Stop Smoking—save on cigarettes, life insurance, and medical costs.
14. Eat Less. Eat better. Save on food and life insurance.
15. Get enough sleep.
16. Volunteer at your local YMCA in exchange for membership.

Entertainment

1. Take advantage of free days at local museums, Zoos, and so on. Look for free days when you travel to other cities on vacation.
2. Use the public library to borrow movies or books for free. Library books on tape can also provide entertainment during long car trips.
3. Read.
4. If you fish, find your own bait.
5. Prerecord any TV you watch. When you watch, fast-forward through commercials and be less tempted to spend.
6. Look for free summer opportunities: free movies, free tennis/swim lessons, free parks programs, and so on.
7. Go to matinees and discount movie theatres.
8. Plan parties at which everyone brings something.
9. Do not subscribe to magazines and newspapers you do not have the time to read.
10. Use your senior discounts. Do not be afraid to ask if a discount is available.
11. Surf the Internet. Find sites that interest you and visit them often.
12. Play, talk, and cook with your children.

13. Visit friends.
14. Listen to music.

Clothing

1. Stop buying clothes that are "dry clean only."
2. Learn to iron.
3. Shop resale stores and estate sales.
4. Shop the clearance racks.
5. Inventory your wardrobe and buy pieces that work with what you already own.
6. Hold a clothing swap with friends.
7. Ask friends and relatives for hand-me-downs.
8. Give kids a clothing allowance or offer "matching funds" for what they want to buy.
9. Avoid the mall.
10. Sew and repair your own clothes.

Finance

1. Pay off your credit cards monthly. Do not charge if you cannot pay off the balance.
2. If you must keep a balance, switch to a no-fee or low-fee credit card.
3. Pay off auto loans with a home equity loan. The interest is tax-deductible.
4. If your house down payment was for less than 20% of your home value, cancel your private mortgage insurance (PMI) once your mortgage balance is 80% or less of the value of your home.
5. Only use ATMs that do not charge service fees.
6. Check your credit history. Ensure accuracy. If mistakes have been made, you might be paying more in interest charges than necessary.
7. Take advantage of employer matching contributions on any 401(k) or other tax-deferred retirement plans.
8. Consider using company-sponsored reimbursement plans for medical, education, or child care.
9. Defer taking retirement distributions until you are over age 59 years and six months to avoid paying penalties. Start required minimum distributions (RMDs) from traditional IRAs by the time you reach age 70 years and six months.
10. Make IRA contributions early in the year to take advantage of additional months of tax deferral.
11. Place investments that generate ordinary income in tax-deferred accounts.

12. Place tax-exempt bonds in taxable accounts.

13. Place investments that generate capital gains or dividends (both taxed at lower rates than ordinary income) in taxable accounts.

14. Pay attention to the expense ratios and fees on mutual funds you buy.

15. Pay attention to the brokerage fees you pay when buying stocks.

16. Do not buy mutual funds just before capital gains are distributed. You will save on taxes.

Miscellaneous

1. Do not buy brand-name products when low-cost equivalents are available.

2. Make hair appointments at beauty schools, rather than full-priced salons.

3. Cut your family's hair.

4. Look up phone numbers in the phone book or from the Internet instead of paying for directory assistance.

5. Get a roommate and share expenses.

6. Make your own greeting cards on the computer.

7. Send free e-cards and save on postage.

8. Track your spending.

9. Watch out for shipping and handling costs when buying via the Internet or from catalogues.

10. Postpone buying decisions. Wait a week to see if you still really want it.

11. Review your bills and insurance policies regularly. Buy only what makes sense today.

12. Pay bills by phone or Internet to avoid paying for stamps.

13. Use rags or washcloths instead of paper towels.

14. Avoid disposable plastic bags if a reusable container works.

15. Declutter your house, sell items in a garage sale, and do not buy replacements.

16. Sell or donate stuff you do not need or use any more.

17. Shop garage sales, reuse stores, and auctions.

18. Repaint or refinish older furniture.

19. Associate with other people who avoid conspicuous consumption.

3.3. ESTABLISHING BUDGET PROJECTIONS

Establishing a budget is a practical way to get a grip on your spending and to ensure that your money is used the way you want it to be used. The first step is to identify how much you spend and what you spend it on. There are a number of software programs available to help with this task, or you can use a spreadsheet to track spending by category. Although the categories you choose for your personal expenditure survey are not critical, there is no reason to invent them. Table 3.1 presents the categories used by the U.S. Bureau of Labor Statistics to perform their consumer expenditure studies and also to compute the CPI inflation rate. One advantage to tabulating your spending using the categories of this table is that you can compare your spending to other U.S. households and examine your personal inflation rate based on the Bureau's studies.

Table 3.1 may include more subcategories than you care to consider as you tackle your cost accounting exercise. For example, you may choose not to subdivide the food category into multiple grocery items. Perhaps a single category of "groceries" provides all the detail you wish to consider. If after several months of accounting, the single "grocery" category appears much larger than you are comfortable with, subdivide it to learn why your expenses are greater than you hoped. Since the goal of this exercise is to develop an estimate of your retirement spending prior to retirement, make sure you include all categories you expect will change once you have retired. Do not forget to include income taxes. For some reason, the federal government neglects this expenditure in their calculations. Unfortunately, you will not be allowed to neglect it.

An important consideration in developing your expenditure accounting is how to capture large capital items that may not occur on an annual basis. A car purchase may only happen every 6 years; a water heater might have to be replaced in 15 years; the house needs reroofing after 20 years; and so on. It is possible to keep track of everything you spend for one full year without witnessing any of these events. Table 3.2 lists a number of typical household capital items along with an associated purchase cost, lifespan, and an annualized cost. The list is not intended to represent typical or average values for these items. It merely serves as a starting point for your estimates. Your own capital list, item lifespan, and costs will vary. When calculating your average annual expenditures, the average annualized value from Table 3.2 should be added to your normal recurring expenses that are captured in Table 3.1.

Before you reach retirement, the information from Tables 3.1 and 3.2 can be combined with information about your total income to analyze your cash flow and to determine the amount available for investment each year. An example of a cash-flow worksheet is presented in Table 3.3. A final planning worksheet to help capture your present net worth is illustrated in Table 3.4. Unlike the first three tables, Table 3.4 contains no example or average data. The net worth of individuals will change dramatically as they progress through their careers. Technical professionals just starting out may have a negative net worth due to education, housing, and auto loans. After several years, the value of their investments should surpass their debt and continue to grow dramatically until retirement.

Completion of the four tables of this chapter will require you to assemble a great deal of financial information. It may be useful to locate the following items before you begin:

- Checkbooks
- Credit card statements for a full year

Table 3.1. Consumer spending by category. The data presented represents the average annual expenditures and characteristics from a survey of over 115,000 U.S. households in the United States in 2003 (the latest date with statistics available). The average household consisted of 2.5 persons (0.6 under the age of 18, 0.3 over the age of 65) with 1.3 earners and 1.9 vehicles. Sixty-seven percent of the households were homeowners.

Item	Annual expenditure
Food	$5,594
Food at home	$3,236
Cereals and bakery products	$456
Meats, poultry, fish, and eggs	$837
Dairy products	$343
Fruits and vegetables	$556
Other food at home	$1,044
Food away from home	$2,358
Alcoholic beverages	$442
Housing	$13,654
Shelter	$7,922
Owned dwellings	$5,247
Rented dwellings	$2,220
Other lodging	$455
Utilities, fuels, and public services	$2,820
Household operations	$730
Housekeeping supplies	$582
Household furnishings and equipment	$1,600
Apparel and services	$1,744
Transportation	$8,040
Vehicle purchase (net outlay)	$3,871
Gasoline and motor oil	$1,353
Other vehicle expenses	$2,416
Public transportation	$400
Healthcare	$2,495
Entertainment	$2,155
Personal care products and services	$559
Reading	$133
Education	$792
Tobacco products and smoking supplies	$307
Miscellaneous	$658
Cash contributions	$1,458
Personal insurance and pensions	$4,710
Life and other personal insurance	$414
Pensions and Social Security	$4,296
Total annual expenditures	$40,586

Data from U.S. Department of Labor, *Consumber Spending in 2003,* U.S. Bureau of Labor Statistics, Report 986, 2005.

Table 3.2. Household expenses that do not occur on an annual basis

Captial item	Cost	Lifespan (years)	Annualized cost
Car	$24,000	5	$4,800
Water heater	$250	13	$19
Furnace	$2,000	20	$100
Air conditioner	$4,000	15	$267
Housepaint	$200	20	$10
Refrigerator	$600	17	$35
Freezer	$240	20	$12
Dishwasher	$350	10	$35
Range	$400	12	$33
Microwave	$175	6	$29
Washer and dryer	$750	15	$50
Car tires	$600	2.5	$240
Computers	$600	5	$120
Printer	$130	10	$13
Television	$300	8	$38
Stereo	$500	15	$33
Living room set	$4,000	15	$267
Bedroom set	$1,700	15	$113
Dining room set	$1,000	10	$100
Patio furniture	$400	7	$57
Gas grill	$500	7	$71
Exercise machines	$425	10	$43
Vacuum cleaner	$115	17	$7
Steam cleaner	$650	10	$65
Major house maintenance	$7,500	14	$536
Total			$7,093

- Bank statements for a full year
- Recent pay stub
- Income tax returns from previous year
- Investment statements from all investment accounts

In order to gain an estimate of your expenses in retirement, examine each item in Tables 3.1 and 3.2. Consider whether the item will increase, decrease, or remain the same in retirement. Job-related items such as clothing, commuting, and lunches will probably decrease or disappear. If you plan to move to a smaller home, housing costs might also decrease. Social Security and medicare taxes disappear and income taxes typically decline. You may find more time to shop better values and prepare meals, thus reducing grocery costs. In contrast, you may plan on spending more money on travel. If your healthcare is not covered by your ex-employer, you might spend more in this category. After completing Tables 3.1 and 3.2 for your present situation and estimating any anticipated changes, a reasonable projection of your required retirement budget is obtained.

Your estimated retirement budget figure is an important number. The 4% rule, can be used to obtain a first estimate of your retirement nest egg requirement. Simply multiply your projected budget by 25. Compare the nest egg requirement to your net worth (from Table 3.4) and see how close you are. Finally, examine your cash flow from Table 3.3 and use Equation (1.3) to estimate how much longer you will need to save.

The estimates described in the paragraph above are crude first-order approximations. More refined estimates can be obtained when the data from the tables of this chapter are used with the tools described in Chapter 2.

If the projections from these exercises leave you dissatisfied, revisit the tables. Does your budget really describe your values? Can you apply some LBYM techniques to help achieve your goals more quickly? Consider how a reduced expense propagates through the spreadsheets. A reduction in spending from either Table 3.1 or 3.2 leads to an increased amount available to invest in Table 3.3. It also reduces the amount of nest egg required to support your retirement. A reduced nest egg target and increased investment both reduce your time to retirement.

Table 3.3. Cash flow statement

Income:	
Salary/wages	$61,128.00
Commissions/bonus	$4,500.00
Interest/dividends	$4,000.00
Business/partnership income	$0.00
Pensions	$0.00
Social Security	$0.00
Trust distributions	$0.00
Alimony/child support	$0.00
Sale of assets	$0.00
Gifts	$0.00
Tax refunds	$0.00
Other income	$800.00
Total Income	$70,428.00
Expenses:	
Normal recurring expenses from Table 3.1	$40,586.00
Average nonannual expenses from Table 3.2	$7,093.00
Income taxes (state and federal)	$15,494.16
Total expenses	$63,173.16
Cash surplus (available for investment)	$7,254.84
Company 401(k) matching funds	$3,056.40
Total invested	$10,311.24

Table 3.4. Net worth statement

Assets:	
Cash/cash equivalents:	
Cash	$0.00
Checking accounts	$0.00
Savings accounts	$0.00
Money market accounts	$0.00
Savings bonds	$0.00
Life insurance cash value	$0.00
Other	$0.00
Total cash/cash equivalents	$0.00
Fixed-income investments:	
Certificates of deposit	$0.00
Government securities and funds	$0.00
Nongovernment bonds and bond funds	$0.00
Other fixed-income investments	$0.00
Total fixed-income investments	$0.00
Stock investments:	
Stock	$0.00
Stock funds	$0.00
Other	$0.00
Total stock investments	$0.00
Real estate investments:	
Undeveloped land	$0.00
Rental/income-producing property	$0.00
REITs/real estate partnerships	$0.00
Other	$0.00
Total real estate investments	$0.00
Business ownership/interests	$0.00
Retirement assets:	
Individual retirement accounts	$0.00
401(k)/403(b) plans	$0.00
Keogh/SEP plans	$0.00
Stock purchase/employee thrift plans	$0.00
Pension/profit sharing plan vested interests	$0.00
Tax-deferred annuities	$0.00
Other retirement assets	$0.00
Total retirement assets	$0.00

Table 3.4. Continued

Assets (*cont.*):	
Personal assets:	
Personal residence(s)	$0.00
Automobiles	$0.00
Furnishings	$0.00
Jewelry	$0.00
Antiques/collections	$0.00
Computers and related equipment	$0.00
Personal property	$0.00
Total personal property	$0.00
Other assets	$0.00
Total assets	$0.00
Liabilities:	
Outstanding bills:	
Credit cards	$0.00
Taxes payable	$0.00
Utilities payable	$0.00
Miscellaneous/other payable	$0.00
Total outstanding bills	$0.00
Installment loans:	$0.00
Mortgages on personal residence(s)	$0.00
Mortgages on investment real estate	$0.00
Automobile loans	$0.00
Student loans	$0.00
Personal bank loans	$0.00
Other loans	$0.00
Total installment loans	$0.00
Other liabilities	$0.00
Total liabilities	$0.00
Net worth (assets less liabilities)	$0.00

The completed tables of this chapter provide a snapshot of your current situation and a first-order extrapolation of where you are headed financially. You can download Excel versions of these spreadsheets by directing your browser to www. golio.net, selecting "Table of Contents and URLs," and then navigating to the section on "Personal Budget Spreadsheets" at the end of Section 3.3. As you approach retirement, the picture offered by this analysis becomes increasingly clear. It is advised that you revisit these tables regularly and monitor your progress toward retirement.

3.4. CREDIT CARDS

Borrowing money with a credit card can provide flexibility in what you buy and when you buy it. More than three-quarters of American households have at least one credit card. These cards offer many benefits. They make Internet purchases possible, generate cash rewards or reward points, provide grace periods from payments, free you from the need to carry cash, and offer a ready source of emergency financing. Most people manage their credit cards well. Statistics indicate that more than 95% of credit card accounts are paid as agreed. In the hands of a frugal shopper, credit cards can save time and money.

If living below your means is difficult for you, however, there is a good chance that credit card expenditures are a major contributor to your problem. Credit card loans come with a price. A balance on your credit card could result in high interest payments that make your loan very expensive. A recent Federal Reserve survey showed that the median credit card balance for Americans is about $1,900 and the average balance is nearly $9,000 dollars. Approximately 4% to 5% of credit card holders have lost control of their spending and are paying large amounts of interest and fees. Fees and interest make any credit card purchase expensive when the balance is not paid off on time each month. Credit cards make it easy to overspend and often lead to serious credit problems. When overextended by credit card purchases, your lifestyle can be affected well into the future.

Even if you are not thinking of borrowing money in the near future, you should try to remain a good candidate for credit in case you ever need it. Credit card records are an important component of credit history. To establish a good credit history, pay your bills on time and check your credit report annually. Avoid charging more than you can afford to pay. Avoid predatory lending practices by making sure you understand all the terms of your credit card agreement.

If you have not read the fine print on your credit card agreement lately, you might be surprised at the arrangement you have entered into. Pay off your balance on time every month or you are subject to a wide range of penalties and fees. Here are a few typical credit card terms you need to be aware of:

- Banks may increase cardholder interest rates based on financial events completely independent of the cardholder's relationship with the bank (universal default penalty). They can double or triple rates with little or no warning.
- The card you get is not necessarily the card you apply for. The card issuer can advertise their premium card with extremely low interest rate, but decide to issue you one of their less attractive cards with a higher annual percentage rate.
- Some banks want to collect their interest more than once. Rather than calculate interest based on the previous months' balance, banks can base it on the

two previous months. If you carry a balance on the card (never a good idea) you will pay more interest using the two-month method.

- Some banks will charge you if you do not offer them a chance to charge you. Inactivity charges can be applied for not using your card for a specified interval (typically 6 months).
- Make a late payment and the banks will make you pay—typically around $30. But that is not the end of the financial pain. The late payment may trigger higher interest rates, not only on the card you paid off late, but on any other card you hold.
- Watch your credit limit. If you go over, you can be charged extra. Interestingly, bank charges (such as a late fee) can cause you to go over limit and result in an additional over-limit fee.
- Accept an offer to transfer your balance from one high-interest card to a low-interest card and you may be hit with a transaction fee of 3%–5%. Make sure you have read the fine print.
- Do not count on the courts to help you out if you have a dispute on any charges. There is a good chance that you have given up your right to anything but mandatory arbitration.

Credit cards are a great convenience and a potential aid in your effort to LBYM, but they can also contribute to spending problems that lead to spiraling costs. This can undermine your attempts to LBYM and impede your progress toward retirement. Establish a good credit history by understanding your card agreements and using credit wisely.

3.5. INCREASING EARNINGS

Living below your means is a general principle that can be applied by any person or family at any income level, but the principle becomes easier to apply with increased means. For that reason, an aspiring retiree should focus some attention on maximizing earnings. Although this book is not intended to be a career planning guide, career decisions will have significant impact on retirement timing and lifestyle. Choices we make each day on the job as well as major career decisions affect not only our job satisfaction, but also our total earning power.

Some people do not get paid what they are worth because they settle for less. They lack confidence to negotiate for more or they fail to recognize their own self-worth. These people may possess significant talent, ability, and knowledge; but they are reluctant to establish aggressive earning goals and seek more money.

There are, of course, some aspects of earning power that we have little control over. A study released recently by two professors at the University of Florida and the University of North Carolina shows that tall people earn considerably more money throughout their careers than their shorter coworkers. Each additional inch of height increases their pay about $789 a year. Similar results were reported in a survey of male graduates of the University of Pittsburgh, where it was found that the tallest students' average starting salary was 12% higher than their shorter colleagues.

An even uglier finding is the affect that appearance has on earnings. According to research from the University of Texas and Michigan State University, plain people earn 5 to 10% less than people of average appearance, who in turn earn 3 to 8% less than those deemed good-looking.

Regardless of our superficial physical attributes, there are a number of things technical professionals can do to improve their compensation. Ross Perot at 5'7'', Jack Welch at 5'8'', and Bill Gates at 5'9'' prove that there is hope for height-challenged engineers with less than movie star good looks. It is important to focus attention on the compensation factors we can control.

Technical professionals tend to be paid well relative to the population as a whole. A healthy starting salary plus initial job satisfaction, however, do not automatically lead to sustainable career vitality or competitive compensation. Your job must continue to satisfy your needs as well as those of your employer or the long-term relationship can be undermined. If you feel cheated, you will contribute less. Conversely, if your employer perceives a decline in your contributions, opportunities and rewards will be withheld.

Figure 3.1 illustrates the impact of only a 0.5% additional annual salary increase over the course of a career. The figure assumes a starting salary of $50,000 per year and considers two cases: a person who receives a 4.5% annual raise and a person who receives a 5% annual raise. At the end of 30 years, the salary differential is over $26,000 per year. The cumulative difference in these two cases is over $271,000. And if the salary difference were invested with 6% annual return, the additional 0.5% of raise would produce an excess of over $280,000. Using the 4% rule, this addition-

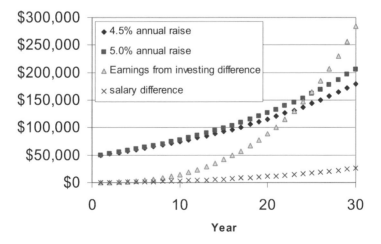

Figure 3.1. Illustration of the impact of negotiating a 0.5% additional increase in salary over a 30-year career. Starting salary is assumed to be $50,000 per year. Investments of the salary difference are assumed to earn 6% per year.

al nest egg could provide over $11,000 per year (inflation adjusted) of additional spending money in retirement. Alternatively, the additional earnings could be used to speed you to retirement years earlier than you could otherwise manage.

How do you avoid settling for less? The following steps can help you determine, and receive, what you are really worth.

1. Assess Your Values

In the pursuit of greater compensation, balance is still important. Except for the shallowest careerist in the office, blind pursuit of maximum compensation is not likely to result in long-term job satisfaction. It may even result in burnout and periods of underemployment. Technical professionals are best advised to look at career choices that excite them. If you choose what you enjoy, you are more likely to excel and advance your career. Do not let your job choices be determined by someone else's advice. Do not select jobs based on expectations of making lots of money instead of doing what you enjoy. It will be difficult to spend an entire career in a field that you eventually acknowledge as being a bad choice. If you enjoy doing something, you are more likely to be good at it.

Developing a description of your ideal job may help you to understand your own values as they apply to your current position. The nature of your work and the work environment are critical to your job satisfaction. Some work environments stimulate and satisfy, whereas others may leave you bitter and unhappy. Consider the list of job attributes below and determine which ones are important to your ideal job. The prioritized list will tell you a lot about your own job values.

salary/rewards	strict routine	convenient schedule
benefits	influence	time for life outside of
stock options	prestige	work
upward mobility	formal recognition	climate
working with people	visibility	near family
teamwork	autonomy/independence	security/structure
collaboration	being in charge	predictability
working with ideas	leadership	exploration/adventure
innovation	management support	ambiguity
creativity	competitive environ-	limited structure
publication	ment	flexibility
working with things	supervisor's style	research
challenge	impact	development
variety	travel	manufacturing
clear direction	daycare	support

After you have included the most important characteristics from the list above, include additional characteristics that you feel are important. The resulting list describes your job-related values and should be a significant consideration in any attempt to advance your career.

2. Understand What Your Company Values

In addition to understanding and satisfying your own values, it is equally important to understand your company's values and that you contribute to satisfying the goals of corporate leaders. Read memos and listen to presentations from senior leadership in your company. Understand what they value and try to learn more than the "buzz-words" they promote. When possible, discuss these issues with your management. Learn to describe your strengths and accomplishments in terms of the issues senior leaders value. Find ways to apply your strengths to these issues in your job. Consider changing jobs if your own values and those of the senior leadership of your company are incompatible.

3. Establish Personal Goals

Establishing personal goals is an important step to advancing your career. These goals should describe, in general terms, how you will add value to the company and provide satisfaction for yourself. Goals should be associated with a schedule or time-line. One- or two-year goals will be different from longer-term goals. In developing goals, you may want to identify your target job, the type of company you want to work for, the industry you want to be part of, the salary range, the level of responsibility, and even the location of the job. Do not neglect goals for your personal satisfaction outside of work, such as free time and time with family and friends.

Your long-term personal goals may not be compatible with your present experience, qualifications, education, and/or training. If not, additional short-term goals focused on gaining the necessary job qualifications may be helpful. Seeking additional training, experience, certification, or advanced degrees can be extremely valuable if these exercises advance your progress toward reaching your job goals. According to the U.S. Bureau of Labor Statistics, a Master's Degree in Engineering is worth an 18% increase in earnings over a Bachelor's Degree in Engineering, on average. Bureau statistics also indicate that a Doctoral degree is worth 9% more than a Masters in engineering. Education and training should be considered long-term investments in your career. The younger you are, the more potential you have to make these investments pay off. Many companies make this investment decision easier by helping technical professionals with both the financial and time investment required to gain additional knowledge. It is important that any additional training you pursue be related to your job goals. Obtaining an advanced degree that does not contribute directly to achieving your ideal job is not likely to be time well spent. Do not stack qualification lines on your resume if they do not advance your career toward your ideal job.

Another important source of advanced learning is involvement in professional activities. Professional societies or organizations exist to represent most engineering fields as well as scientific disciplines. The Institute of Electrical and Electronics Engineers (IEEE), for example, consists of over 365,000 electrical engineers from approximately 150 countries. Professional groups offer opportunities to advance your career in several ways. Attendance at group meetings, conferences, or symposia allows you to network with world-class experts in your field. Knowledge you gain from this interaction may be invaluable to you in your work. These contacts may also come to you seeking employment, or they may direct other engineers to your organization in the future. Similarly, they may become a source of employment leads for yourself. Participation in the organization and management of professional group activities can provide you with valuable planning, budget management, and organization experience. This is experience that you can leverage in your career planning. Serving as an author and/or reviewer for such organizations provides you with valuable presentation experience and offers access to state-of-the-art developments several months ahead of published literature.

Involvement in formal training and/or professional activities is a clear indication of your effort to learn. In a rapidly changing world, learners have a clear advantage over the learned. As your career progresses, that advantage can be exploited to gain you the job you want at the salary you deserve.

4. Prepare Your Case

If you complete the three steps outlined above, you are likely to achieve greater job satisfaction and work/life balance. In order to leverage that into superior compensation, however, you will probably need to present the case to your management and explicitly state what you want. As you prepare your case, it is important that you understand what you are worth and document that understanding. Your expectations need to be based on realities in the marketplace. Sources such as the Bureau of Labor Statistics, online salary calculators, and compensation surveys are a great place to gain information about what others in your field with similar education and experience are earning. IEEE members can access their website and use the online salary calculator. This tool benchmarks base salary and income from primary sources (base salary plus bonuses, commissions, and net self-employment income) for individual professionals in specific positions, based on a regression model derived from the current survey year's database. The regression model considers the following factors: size of company, area of specialization, area of technical competence, job function, type of employer, line of business, education level, geographic region, years of professional experience, tenure with current employer, and number and type of personnel supervised. The salary calculator is useful to estimate compensation for a present position or to project your expected compensation in different circumstances. The results are presented as estimated median salary with decile rankings for compensation range.

In most companies, being a hard worker or nice person is not enough to gain a superior raise. You will need to document your accomplishments in writing and illustrate how they have contributed to the company's values. Provide concrete examples of how you have met or exceeded individual and team expectations. List major responsibilities and identify new responsibilities you have taken on at work. You should also include accomplishments in your education, training, and professional activities. Be prepared to explain how each of these accomplishments has increased your value to the company.

5. Negotiate

High earners tend to negotiate. It is unlikely that you will achieve your maximum earning potential if you do not engage in negotiation. After completing the first four steps listed above, you should know what you want and why you deserve it. Do not be apprehensive about discussing these findings with your current supervisor. Be prepared to offer creative solutions during the negotiation process if your initial suggestion is rejected. If your salary is capped by your job grade, pursue a promotion instead of a raise. Discuss what the company would have to pay to replace you. Ask your supervisor to describe what he or she feels is fair compensation. Request incentive bonus compensation based on achieving personal goals. Ask for stock options or access to additional benefits.

Most people are surprised by the outcome of their first compensation negotiation. If negotiations do not result in compensation you consider fair, with a viable career plan, then consider changing jobs. A job search may cause you to reevaluate your worth in the marketplace, or it may lead to a new opportunity a step closer to your ideal job.

REFERENCES AND FURTHER READING

1. Lorenz, K., Do Pretty People Earn More? careerbuilder.com, 2005, http://jobs.aol.com/article?id=20050808184809990111.
2. Kilbane, D., To Live Well, Follow Your Passion, *Electronic Design,* p. 68, June 16, 2004.
3. *Career Planning Guide for IEEE Members, version 3.0,* IEEE—USA, 2005, http://www.ieeeusa.org/careers/cpg/default.asp.
4. U.S. Department of Labor, *Consumer Spending in 2003,* U.S. Bureau of Labor Statistics, Report 986, 2005.
5. Federal Reserve Bank of Dallas, *Time Well Spent: The Declining Real Cost of Living in America,* 1997 Annual Report.
6. Pulliam, L., 50 Ways to Trim Your Budget, *MSN.money,* 2005, http://moneycentral.msn.com/content/Savinganddebt/Learntobudget/P120498.asp?GT1=6708.
7. Dominquez, J., and V. Robin, *Your Money or Your Life: Transforming Your Relationship with Money and Achieving Financial Independence,* Penguin Books, 2000.
8. Stanley, T., and W. Danko, *The Millionaire Next Door,* Pocket Books, New York, 1996.
9. Wiles, R., Climbing Out of Credit Trap, *The Arizona Republic,* September 4, 2005.

ESTIMATING YOUR MARKET VALUE

For more than 30 years, the Institute of Electrical and Electronics Engineers—United States of America (IEEE-USA) has conducted one of the most thorough salary and fringe benefit surveys in the United States. The project provides information on current and long-term trends related to the income, salary, and benefits of electrical engineers in the United States. Analysis of the survey data and the resultant regression models help to form an accurate understanding of compensation practices in these occupations. Although the results may not apply directly to other technical professionals, many of the factors that affect electrical engineering compensation will affect salary levels in other technical fields. Important compensation factors include:

Company Size—Employees of large companies (>10,000 employees) may make over 10% more on average than equivalent employees in a small firm.

General Area of Technical Specialization and Area of Technical Competence—These two factors can also impact compensation level by more than 10%.

Primary Job Function—General management pays an average of almost 13% more than computer programming, engineering support, or design and development engineering. Basic research is worth about 5% more than these jobs.

Type of Employer—In general, electrical engineers working for the federal government will earn approximately 6% to 7% less than utility workers, whereas private sector employees earn almost 5% more.

Line of Business—Computers and communications businesses tend to pay 6% to 7% more than other businesses. Education tends to pay that much less.

Highest Degree—An MSEE is worth about 5.4% over a BSEE degree. An MBA is worth slightly less. A PhD is worth about 15% more. A two-year degree is worth approximately 9.3% less than an BSEE.

Region and Metro Area of Workplace—Regional differences in pay can cause median salaries to vary by as much as 20%.

Figure 3.2 illustrates the impact that experience and responsibility level have on median compensation for electrical engineers. The curves can change absolute value depending on the factors listed above. An important observation that can be drawn from the figure is that experience is worth far less than promotion. A single year of experience is worth 2% in the first few years of employment, then is gradually reduced, and levels off to no compensation advantage by the 30th year of experience. In contrast, a promotion from one level to the next is worth 7% to 12% regardless of experience.

Figure 3.3 presents the range of salaries expected based on performance ranking. As in the case of grade-level promotion, performance ranking can be far more important to compensation levels than years of experience. A top performer can make more than 50% in additional compensation over the median salary for an engineer in the same situation. Poor performers can see a reduction of nearly 40% in compensation from the median.

Further analysis can be obtained at http://salaryapp.ieeeusa.org/rt/salary_database/Compensation (requires IEEE membership).

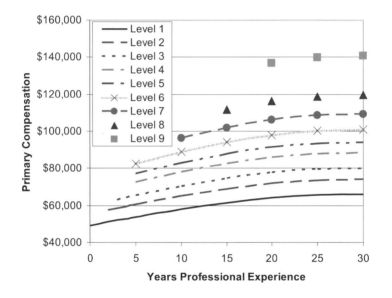

Figure 3.2. Median compensation levels for electrical engineers in the United States as a function of years experience and level of responsibility. Level 1 is the entry level of professional work, requiring a bachelor's degree in engineering and no experience. Level 1 is equivalent to a GS-5 government employee. Levels 2 through 7 are increasing experience levels for technical engineers and technical management. Levels 8 and 9 correspond to government ratings of GS-15 or higher. These levels represent general management positions.

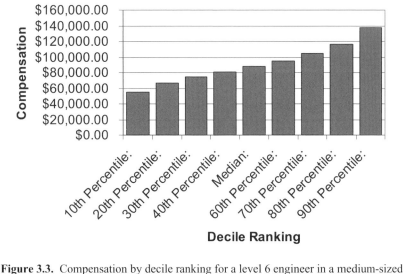

Figure 3.3. Compensation by decile ranking for a level 6 engineer in a medium-sized communications company with a BSEE degree and 10 years experience. The engineer is also assumed to be a design and development engineer in non-defense-related private industry living in the Rocky Mountain region of the country. The 90th percentile engineer (stellar performer) can earn as much as 56% more than the median salary for this position, whereas the 10th percentile engineer earns 37% less.

4

EMERGENCY FUNDS AND INSURANCE (FIRST TAKE CARE OF STABILITY)

Put first things first. Before doing anything else on the road to financial independence, prepare for unexpected emergencies that may occur along the way. This chapter can help to guide you through the process of establishing your catastrophe safety net, but the details of your preparations will be unique to your personal situation. If you are not sure what steps should be taken or how best to take them, seek competent legal and medical advice.

Essential preparations typically include purchasing appropriate insurance, building an emergency cash fund, and development of a few important documents. A small life crisis can turn into a major setback in your progress toward financial independence if you have not put appropriate plans in place. Your emergency strategy should include plans for the welfare of your family as well as yourself. Put emergency and catastrophe plans in place first, and then focus your energy on the rest of your financial and retirement strategy.

The purpose of insurance is to protect your income and assets. Part of planning for retirement is making sure that you have the right insurance coverage for you. First examine all of your current insurance policies. Do you need them? Are the premiums competitive? Do you get good service from your agent? If the answer to any of these is, "no," you should shop for better coverage. Next consider insurance you do not carry that you may need. Consider these types of coverage:

- Automobile
- Homeowner's or renter's
- Disability (if you are still working)
- Health

- Life
- Long-term care

Not all of these types of insurance make sense for every family or situation. A single engineer with no family or heirs has very different insurance needs than a head of a household of five with aging parents. People all have different fears and levels of comfort with risk. Since insurance is partly about providing a sense of security, the amount and kind of insurance you need depends on what you personally feel comfortable with. Although a particular policy may make sense at one time in your life, it may be the wrong policy a few years later. It is important to think about what you want to insure against and who you are trying to protect. Review your insurance policies regularly and add, delete, or modify them as your insurance needs change.

It is also important to have an emergency fund to pay for unexpected expenses as well as appropriate documents to protect your family in case you become incapacitated or die. Additional discussion of these topics is included later in this chapter.

4.1. MEDICAL INSURANCE AND HEALTHCARE BUDGETS

The leading cause of personal bankruptcy in the United States is unpaid medical bills. Half of those without medical insurance owe money to hospitals and a third are being pursued by collection agencies. Another important reason for having health insurance is that uninsured patients are billed at full price, whereas a 40–60% discount is typical for those with insurance. Insurance companies negotiate for lower prices from healthcare providers. Without medical insurance, not only can an illness destroy you financially, it can adversely affect your health. Studies, for example, show that people without health coverage are less likely than the insured to receive treatment for lung cancer, heart attacks, or pneumonia. The uninsured are 25% more likely to die in any given year than those with insurance. Having a health insurance policy is not enough to buy immunity from financial catastrophe due to illness. In 2005, 76% of people who had a medical-related bankruptcy had health insurance when they became ill. These facts illustrate the importance of creating a family healthcare budget to complement a health insurance policy. Establishing that budget could mean the difference between being able to pay future bills and having to seek relief from creditors.

The complexities of the various insurance offerings make health insurance far more difficult to understand and plan for than most other types of insurance. Health insurance can be tricky to obtain, expensive to own, and exhibit rate increases that far outstrip average inflation. Figure 4.1 presents the per-capita health insurance costs in the United States between 1990 and 2002. During the latter half of this period, the inflation rate on health insurance ranged from 6.4% to 10.9%. These numbers are far higher than increases in either inflation or workers' earnings during that period. Since 2000, premiums for health insurance in the United States have been rising five times faster, on average, than workers' earnings.

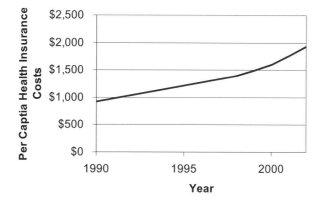

Figure 4.1. Per-capita health insurance costs in the United States by year. (Source: Centers for Medicare and Medicaid Services, Office of the Actuary, National Health Statistics Group; U.S. Dept. of Commerce, Bureau of Economic Analysis and Bureau of the Census, 2003. http://www.cms.hhs.gov/statistics/nhe/projections-2003/t2.asp.)

According to the U.S. Dept. of Commerce, future health insurance rate increases will remain well above the average national inflation rate for at least the next decade. Figure 4.2 presents the projected average annual percent change in health insurance costs from 2006 through 2013. Although the rate of increase in medical expenses is projected to decline beginning in 2008, this rate still exceeds projected inflation and wage increases. These rates of increase need to be accounted for in your healthcare budgeting process.

Planning for health emergencies begins by building a health budget. In order to address the high medical inflation rate, you will need to put aside money both for

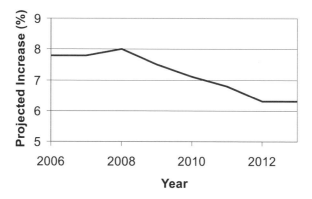

Figure 4.2. Projected average annual percent change in health insurance costs. (Source: Centers for Medicare and Medicaid Services, Office of the Actuary, National Health Statistics Group; U.S. Dept. of Commerce, Bureau of Economic Analysis and Bureau of the Census, 2003. http://www.cms.hhs.gov/statistics/nhe/projections-2003/t2.asp.)

current expenses and to build a nest egg for future healthcare costs. Fidelity Investments has estimated that a couple retiring in January 2004 without an employer-sponsored healthcare plan would have needed to set aside $175,000 to pay future healthcare costs. If you are fortunate enough to have employer-sponsored retiree health insurance, this number will be reduced. Fewer and fewer U.S. technical workers, however, have such insurance; and recent trends in corporation policies have been to eliminate retiree healthcare plans or to increase the out-of-pocket expenses in the plans they currently have. Even retirees with employer-sponsored plans may need to budget for future healthcare needs.

Your health budget should include all your healthcare expenses including:

- Premiums—your regular health insurance bills
- Out-of-pocket expenses—deductibles, copayments, coinsurance percentage —the costs you pay for covered products and services
- Products—over-the-counter medications, etc.
- Noncovered services—dental and vision care
- Miscellaneous—fitness expenses, alternative medicine

When computing your health budget needs, it is important that you consider not only your present costs in each of the categories above, but also the inflation projections of Figure 4.2. A medical inflation rate that outstrips your investment earnings by only 2% requires a nest egg of approximately 40 times your current annual medical expenses to support those payments for 30 years.

One alternative to save money on healthcare expenses is to open a Health Savings Account (HSA). HSAs allow you to use tax-free income to pay for healthcare products and services. Using money that has not been taxed is like getting a discount on your medical expenses equivalent to your tax rate. There are limitations and restrictions to these accounts. You can only contribute to an HSA if you have a high-deductible health insurance policy that meets IRS requirements. You cannot contribute to your account if you are on Medicare or if you are covered by another policy (although you can collect from an account that was established earlier). More details about Health Savings Accounts are provided in Chapter 6, Section 6.3.

Planning for the Transition to Retirement

Health insurance is often the greatest deterrent to retirement, especially for those under the age of 65. Many people underestimate the complexity of finding and obtaining an appropriate policy, while others misjudge the amount of nest egg required to pay for it. These two mistakes keep many technical professionals employed long past the time when they want to retire

If you need to find health insurance to cover you and your family after you retire, do not underestimate the time required to research available companies, decide on a type of policy, complete applications, and be approved by insurance underwriters. This process often takes 3 to 6 months. It can take more than two months from the time you complete an application to when the underwriters approve your policy alone. If you have had any medical problems in the past 10 years, it may take longer.

Comparison shopping for medical coverage is difficult because no two policies offer the same benefits. As a result, your assessments tend to be based on apples-to-cumquats comparisons. Policies will offer different coverage and different copay schedules for doctors visits, emergency care, prescription drugs, and every other health service. Some policies offer certain types of services such as annual check-ups and breast exams for free. Some will have a single deductible amount that applies to all health products and services. Others will apply a different deductible for prescription drugs than for other services. Policies have different payment schedules that apply after deductibles and different caps for maximum out-of-pocket expenses.

Depending on the insurance company, protection may be in the form of traditional coverage, health maintenance organizations (HMO), preferred provider options (PPO), or provider sponsored organizations (PSO). If you are over 65 years old, you may be eligible for Medicare supplemental plans (MEDIGAP). Each of these options needs to be researched and understood before making a decision. The size and stability of the insurance company is also important. The negotiated hospital rates and benefit pay-out practices of insurance companies are not all equal. Factor this information into your decision. Insurance companies will apply different exclusions and preexisting condition clauses to policies if you are considered a medical risk for previous health issues.

The above issues are compounded by the fact that every state is different. State laws governing health insurance vary significantly and will affect your insurance strategy. Some states protect people with high-risk situations much better than others. Some have highrisk pools that guarantee coverage. Some require insurance carriers to cover everyone regardless of health risk situation. Depending on the state where you choose to retire, you might find it reasonable to take out a catastrophic policy before you retire (even though you do not need it because of your employment). You are more likely to qualify for coverage today than sometime in the future after you have been diagnosed with an illness that insurance companies consider a risk. In many states, an insurance company cannot stop coverage or increase your rates (outside of the rates for your insurance age group) once a policy has been issued. So if you qualify today and pay your premiums, you will continue to be covered in the future.

Because every state and the needs of every family are different, it will require some research to choose the best health insurance for your situation. The discussion above lists many of the primary issues for consideration. It is important to complete at least cursory research early enough in your retirement planning to establish a healthcare budget and nest egg requirement. That research should be updated periodically to account for changes in your family's healthcare needs, insurance companies' healthcare rates, and Medicare regulation developments. At least six months before your final retirement date, perform a serious healthcare insurance evaluation and apply for appropriate coverage.

To begin your retirement insurance evaluation, analyze the total annual medical expenses using the insurance you have today. If your health insurance is company sponsored, you will need to determine both the cost to you and to your employer. Your company's Human Resources department or the insurance company should be able to help with this. Include all of the costs listed previously in this section (premiums, out-of-pocket expenses, products, noncovered services, miscellaneous). The resulting annual expense establishes a baseline number for your comparisons.

Low-deductible and/or small-copay coverage is the type typically offered by large employers. This is not likely to be the most cost-effective health insurance you can find. Use your recent medical history along with an insurance quote from a company with a high-deductible policy to estimate your annual expenses for this alternative. Consider your estimated required budget as well as your comfort level with high-deductible insurance. Once you decide on the insurance option you feel most comfortable with, seek additional quotes from other companies for similar products. Consider any organizations you are a member of that may offer group insurance. Many professional organizations offer group insurance to their members. The Institute of Electrical and Electronics Engineers (IEEE), for example, provides a wide range of insurance offerings for their membership (see http://www.personal-plans.com/product/ieeeinsurance/usa/index.html). Once an insurance policy is selected, the portfolio requirement to support your medical expenses is likely to be 30 to 40 times your projected annual health budget.

Options for the Retiree

A working engineer or scientist is likely to be eligible for a company-subsidized group healthcare plan. These plans typically offer a range of options at a very affordable cost. They are easy to enroll in and relatively simple to use. Corporate group health plans can lead to the false assumption that medical insurance is easy to come by. If you are retired or not covered by such a plan, you will find that it is a much more difficult task to find adequate and affordable healthcare.

Health insurance is a particularly harsh problem for people aged 50 to 64. Many in this pre-Medicare age group find themselves in the individual insurance market at the very time they are developing health problems that insurers consider a risk. As a group, technical professionals in this age bracket are more vulnerable to layoffs or forced early retirement. This also represents a point in their careers when it can be difficult to get another job with benefits. These factors are exacerbated by the trend of employers to cut health benefits and transfer more expense to the employee and retiree.

COBRA coverage (acronym for Consolidated Omnibus Budget Reconciliation Act of 1985) is one alternative for the retiree who has not identified another insurance option. COBRA laws guarantee you the right to continue in your former employer's group health plan for up to 18 months, at your own expense, even if you leave your job voluntarily. Although COBRA laws guarantee the right to coverage, the coverage cost can be quite high—up to 102% of the total company-plus-employee cost prior to your separation. Extensions of COBRA coverage beyond 18 months may be available under certain specific conditions, but COBRA should be thought of only as a stopgap measure that buys time required to find alternative insurance. Make sure you obtain individual coverage before running out of COBRA coverage. If you have been on an employer-subsidized group plan and then on CO-BRA, you have certain rights under the Health Insurance Portability and Accountability Act (HIPAA). This includes the right to force the sale of an individual policy to you. It does not make a guarantee on the cost of that insurance.

Medicare is a large federal health insurance program. It is the major health insurer for Americans over 65 years of age. Once you reach age 65 and qualify for Medicare, you can use a traditional fee-for-service plan or a managed care organization that contracts with Medicare. The type of coverage Medicare offers depends on whether you qualify for Medicare Part A, Part B, or both. Medicare Part A covers certain in-patient benefits with no premium charge to you. Medicare Part B (if you qualify) offers additional coverage for which a monthly premium is charged. Everyone with Medicare, regardless of income, health status, or prescription drug usage, has access to prescription drug coverage. The details of Medicare and the associated drug coverage can be very complex, with literally dozens of possible options to consider and select from.

Even with Medicare, there are still some costs you will be responsible for. Medigap is a type of insurance policy designed by private insurers to supplement Medicare coverage. There are ten standardized benefit plans for Medigap insurance, from Plan A with "basic benefits" alone to Plan J, which offers the most coverage.

Although Medicare and Medigap insurance are more standardized than independent insurance policies, there are still significant differences in the coverage from state to state. Be sure to get answers to your questions in order to obtain the best coverage for you and your family. Fortunately, there are free services in each state that will help you understand the details of Medicare eligibility and coverage.

4.2. EMERGENCY FUND

After acquiring appropriate insurance and paying off your credit card debt, the next stop on your road to financial independence is the establishment of an emergency fund. A portion of your financial assets should always be kept liquid and readily accessible for day-to-day calamities or crises. Sooner or later a leak appears in the roof, your car has to be replaced, the refrigerator compressor gives out, or some other required expenditure surprises you. Whatever the disaster, preparing for the unexpected is not only smart, but will likely decrease the stress associated with such an event. An emergency fund can lessen the need to dip into your retirement savings for a financial emergency.

If unforeseen expenses related to your home and automobile were the only things you needed to plan for, your emergency fund would not need to be very large. A much more expensive emergency that you need to consider, however, is how you would pay your expenses if you were suddenly unemployed for several months. Financial planners recommend that your emergency fund contain enough cash to pay your monthly expenses for anywhere from three to eight months. Notice that the value of your emergency fund should be tied to your living expenses rather than your salary. If you have completed the budget process of Chapter 3, you can analyze your expenses and include only those that will continue while you are unemployed. Income tax, Social Security payments, and Medicare payments, for example, are not expenses you face during periods of unemployment. The budget might also point to other places to reduce costs during this time. Although 3 to 8 months of expenses may seem excessive, you should consider that when technical professionals lose their jobs, it is often because of industrywide downturns or nationwide recessions. At these times, finding another job may take several months.

Your emergency fund should be in a liquid, interest-bearing account so it can be accessed without penalty if needed, while allowing growth at the same time. Traditionally, emergency funds are held in local bank accounts or money market funds (cash equivalents). With this kind of account, you simply write a check to tap your emergency fund. You have immediate access to the money. As you build wealth, you can become more flexible in how your emergency fund is invested, but starting out it is best for the money to be invested in some type of cash account. After you have at least two months of living expenses in your emergency account, you can move one month of expenses to a one-month CD or other stable, interest-bearing investment. A collection of I bonds held for at least one year, for example, can serve as part of your emergency fund. Short-term government bond funds can also be used.

Investments that experience significant short-term fluctuations in value or that are not readily converted to cash should not be used as part of your emergency fund. Most individual stocks, stock funds, and other similar investments should only be part of your long-term planning since you do not want to be forced to sell them during a down market. Real estate should not be part of your emergency fund since it is not always possible to turn property into cash in a short period of time.

Your emergency fund is money that should not be touched unless it's absolutely necessary. Think of it as a dedicated fund. Use of the fund to purchase a new luxury item defeats the purpose of the fund and places you at risk. Also, emergency funds should be replaced as you use them, so they are available the next time something unexpected arises.

4.3. PERSONAL FINANCIAL CONCERNS

The size and particular needs of your family have a major impact on all aspects of your retirement planning. Your family income, budget requirements, saving goals, necessary emergency fund, and insurance needs should reflect your family's specific situation.

Family Size

An estimate of how family size and type affects a budget has been developed by the U.S. Bureau of Labor Statistics and is presented in Table 4.1. We can use the table

Table 4.1. Equivalence scale used by U.S. Bureau of Labor Statistics.[12] The equivalence scale is used to adjust financial thresholds for differences in household size and composition.

Family type	BLS normalized family budget
Single adult	0.360
Two adults	0.600
Two adults, one child	0.820
Two adults, two children	1.000
Two adults, three children	1.116
One adult, one child	0.570
One adult, two children	0.760

to consider cost-of-living changes along a typical family life cycle. The normalization basis for this table is a family of four (two adults and two children). All other budget entries represent the normalized funding required for the specified family to maintain an equivalent lifestyle to the base family. For a single young person prior to marriage, the cost of living is 36% that of our normalized family of four. The cost of living for a married couple increases to 60% of the normalization base. When one child is added, the family budget is at 82% of the base. A second child puts the family at base budget level. A third child places the couple at 111.6% the cost of a family of four. For cases not shown in the table, the equivalence family budget can be roughly approximated using the expression

$$E = \frac{(A + pK)^F}{2.751} \tag{4.1}$$

where A is the number of adults in the family, K is the number of children, $p = 0.92$, and $F = 0.75$.

The equivalence scale data indicates how difficult it can be for a family to grow, maintain a lifestyle threshold, and continue to save for future retirement. If they hope to maintain a constant lifestyle, a family of three (two adults and one child) requires a 36.7% higher budget than the married couple with no children. If the wage earner(s) of that family earn a salary increase of 5% over inflation per year, their income does not reach a level to support a first child until they have worked for more than 7 years. To achieve an income that would support a second child at the same standard of living would take an additional 4 years on the job.

A single professional who wants to marry, or a couple that desires children, have other options. If they do not want to wait until their salaries reach the level indicated by the equivalence table, they can choose to lower their lifestyle and carry on with family plans. They could also choose to invest less money toward retirement, maintain their standard of living with family additions, and work more years before retirement. A combination of the two choices is also possible. When going from single to married, a couple consisting of two wage earners might easily exceed the required 66.7% income increase implied by the table simply by combining salaries. While two cannot live as cheaply as one, two wage earners can live a more comfortable lifestyle or can save more toward their long-term goals.

In addition to financial considerations, family additions usually signal the time to review insurance coverage and other important documents. Life insurance, disability insurance, and health insurance should be reviewed. It may also be time to change your will, set up a trust, or start a college fund. Do not forget to take advantage of the positive tax implications of additions to the family. These include claiming an additional dependent and placing up to $10,000 a year into a tax-deductible college fund.

Although the expense of having a family should not be ignored, it is not the primary consideration in most couples' decision. Parents usually reply with an unqualified, "yes," when asked if their children are worth the expense. Despite the costs, the lower savings, the sleepless nights, and so on, parents tend to consider their children a valuable enhancement to their lives. Decisions about family involve more than a financial side. People planning both a family and retirement need to be extremely cautious and brutally honest to themselves about where their money goes. Spending money on children may result in less being placed into the retirement plan, and cause retirement to be pushed out to a later time. Couples who understand the cost implications of a family, and plan appropriately, are more likely to achieve their family and retirement goals.

Children and LBYM

Raising children can be expensive. Teaching them values you believe are important can be difficult. You hope to provide the things they need without spoiling them. It is difficult to balance the wish to give children every advantage they need to succeed while at the same time allowing them to become self-sufficient.

With the rise of single-parent families or families with two working parents, children often get less attention than their parents would like to provide. Many parents feel guilty for their lack of available time and attempt to compensate by spending. Even when a parent is not using money to compensate for their own demanding schedule, their children live in a community where other parents are. Affluent technical professionals choose to live in affluent neighborhoods surrounded by families with expensive toys, clothes, and after-school activities. Children feel peer pressure to have what others have. They are continually inundated with advertisements. Parents are likely to be faced with an extraordinary number of purchase battles with their children. Modern parents are forced to pick their battles. It can be difficult to maintain family unity while constantly explaining to your children why you are unwilling to buy them the latest, overpriced, brand-name jeans or toy when all their friends have them. Yet a good question to ask yourself is what lessons about financial responsibility will your children learn if you buy them every trendy item that comes along?

The lessons of financial responsibility are best taught by experience and example. If children are provided money to buy every item they desire without considering the impact on long-term goals, they will learn to spend without thinking. Giving in to social pressure to ensure that your child has everything the other children have teaches your child to give in to social-pressure spending. Conversely, if your children are taught ground rules for spending their allowance and particular expenses that they must pay with that money, then they will learn to spend wisely and save for what they really value. As they get older, both the allowance as well as the range of expenses they will be responsible for can be increased. One method to test a child's commitment to larger expenditures is to split the saving goal with them. Make a deal: if your child saves some portion of the cost of something they wish to buy, you contribute the remainder of the cost. A part-time job can also provide valuable financial lessons, but the hours must be limited so that school work does not suffer.

Teaching a child the lessons of frugal living can be challenging. But if you succeed, you will have prepared them for a satisfying life with fewer financial crises along the way. Your own retirement plans will also benefit significantly.

Funding College

The cost of college is high. Costs of tuition, room and board, books and supplies, transportation, and other expenses at a four-year college typically amount to over $13,000 per year. For many colleges, the figure can be much higher. Private schools are even more expensive. Trying to save for a child's college fund and for your retirement can be competing goals. If you are unable to fund both completely, focus first on your own retirement accounts. Your tax-deferred retirement accounts reduce your taxes, grow tax-free, and often offer employer matching funds. Then, when college bills come due, you may be able to borrow some portion of your funds for college expenses. This is not an optimum solution in most cases. There are consequences to borrowing against your 401(k) to pay for college expenses. Paying this money back may require that you work additional years before retiring.

If you can afford it, the time to start saving for you child's college fund is now. The sooner you begin to invest, the longer those funds will have to grow, and the better your chances of funding an education bill without damaging your own financial position.

There is good news concerning college funding. The government has established a number of different saving and investment plans designed to help save for your children's future education. The optimum choice depends largely on your income. Some of the most popular college saving plans include:

Roth IRA Account. Although these accounts are normally used for retirement savings, they can also be exploited for college funding. There is a cap on annual investment amounts allowed in a Roth IRA, but the limit is higher than that for Coverdale ESAs and rises each year through 2008. The Roth allows you to withdraw your original contributions (though not your earnings) at any time for any purpose without owing taxes or penalties. A limitation that some highly compensated technical professionals face is that their income exceeds the levels that make them eligible to contribute to Roth IRAs.

Coverdale Education Savings Account (Education IRA). This is a tax-advantaged program that was created specifically to help parents fund a child's education. The Coverdell Accounts place a cap of $2000 per student on your annual contributions. The earnings in the account grow tax-free as long as distributions are used for eligible expenses. Parents who exceed legislated adjusted gross income limits are not eligible to contribute to these accounts.

Section 529 College Savings Plan. These plans are state-run, tax-deferred savings plans specifically designed to fund a child's education. Because they are state managed, they vary significantly from state to state. They potentially offer significant tax savings advantages, but because they are state-run, there is a degree of uncertainty in the Section 529 landscape. New state programs can be launched or changed and both state and federal laws can also generate changes.

Uniform Gifts to Minors Act (UGMA). These accounts were created to make tax-free gifting of money or assets to children easier and more efficient. There can be significant tax savings benefits with this kind of account. The plans come with limitations in terms of ownership and qualifying for financial aid.

Prepaid Tuition Plans. States offer these plans for tuition at state schools. You select the state school, a payment plan to fit your budget, and tuition is taken care of when your child is ready to attend school. The plans offer tax incentives as of 2002. An important limitation to these kinds of plans is that you are choosing the school your child will attend before they have developed their own educational interests. If they decide to attend another school, you may have to forfeit some or all of your prepaid tuition. You should also note that these plans cover only tuition costs. Room and board, books, supplies, and other college expenses must still be funded.

The government also provides two tax credits and a tax deduction to help you finance your children's college education. The Hope Scholarship and Lifetime Learning Credit offer eligible tax filers some relief from tuition and related expenses. The Hope Scholarship provides families with up to $1500 a year for the first 2 years of college. The credit only applies to a student's tuition and fees expenses. A $2000 tax credit is allowed with the Lifetime Learning Credit. This tax credit is offered on a per-family rather than per-student basis. For those beyond the first two years of college, or taking classes part-time to improve or upgrade their job skills, the family will receive a 20% tax credit for first $10,000 of tuition and fees. One eligibility requirement for both of these credits is based on a maximum allowable adjusted gross income. The credit is phased out for joint filers between $80,000 and $100,000 of income, and for single filers between $40,000 and $50,000. These limits are indexed upward each year after 2001. The eligibility cap on adjusted gross income for the education tax deduction is slightly higher than for the tax credits. Those eligible can deduct up to $4000 of higher education expenses from their income each year.

Financial Beliefs & Control Issues

Family financial issues are not typically limited to planning for family additions or for college funding. When couples fight over finances, they may be discussing the most recent credit card bill, but the real issues are about investment beliefs and control.[17,18] There are savers and spenders and a continuum of behaviors in between. Some couples manage budgets best when they pool their finances; some find they need separate accounts. Money might be viewed as the currency of freedom and adventure to one partner whereas it buys safety and security for the other. No couple is likely to agree entirely on financial strategy. To ease financial friction, it is important for a couple to share some long-term priorities. A shared priority might be to save more for retirement, save for a home down payment, put a child through college, or go on a special vacation. The shared goal changes the spending discussion from, "you can't buy that new gadget," to "let's put the money toward our goal." The shared goal helps couples think like a financial unit and fight together to reach their goal rather than battle each other.

It may take time to achieve financial harmony with your partner, but it is important and valuable. Learn to discuss your financial plans during a calm moment rather than during a tense period. Take issues such as who pays bills off the table by automating these items. Make sure your cash flow plans provide enough money for both of you to get some short-term pleasure as well as pursue long-term goals.

Divorce

If the budget and financial control issues of family life seem expensive or difficult, they pale in comparison to the cost and turmoil of divorce. Ask someone who has been through a divorce how much it will cost and you may hear the answer, "It will cost as much as you can afford." The more contentious the divorce, the higher the cost will be. Divorce proceedings for middle class couples can cost $50,000 or more in attorney and legal expenses alone. Uncontested divorce costs as low as several hundred dollars are possible, but rare. An often overlooked, but major cost of divorce is related to the expense of moving into and running two households instead of one. From Table 4.1, we can compare the equivalence budget of a married couple with no children (0.6) to that of two divorced single adults ($0.36 \times 2 = 0.72$). The divorced pair requires a budget increase of at least 20% to maintain two separate but equivalent lifestyles. A similar analysis for a divorced couple with one child shows that a required budget increase of more than 13% is needed to maintain two homes instead of one. These figures do not include the cost of moving or expenditures required to initially set up a new home (first and last months rent, utility deposits, purchase of essential household items that have to be duplicated, etc.). An expensive divorce procedure resulting in the distribution of half of all assets and followed by an effective reduction to future earning power of 13% to 20% can be devastating to any retirement plan.

The amount of time required to get divorced can also be detrimental to your career. You will need to gather countless documents required by your attorney, meet with your attorney to discuss the information, make appearances in court, and commute to and from various offices and court buildings. It is not always feasible to handle these requirements outside of work time. Some of the people you need to contact are only available during regular working hours. A divorce is damaging not only to your current financial situation, but also to your work performance and, therefore, to your career.

Divorce can be a devastating event on the road to retirement. The cost in time, money, and emotional energy is extremely high. Investments of your time and energy to maintain a fulfilling family life for you and your partner is not simply good emotional advice, it makes great sense from a practical perspective. If divorce is not avoidable, then think with your head instead of your heart. Seek appropriate help. Work to minimize the contention and, therefore, the expenses. When it is over, take an accounting of your situation and re-map your financial future.

Aging or Ailing Parents

Your parents are likely to need your help eventually. Don't wait for a crisis. One or both of your parents may become ill or incapacitated. They may lose their ability to take care of their own financial affairs. The sooner and more often you talk to them, the easier it will be to ensure that their wishes are appropriately addressed. While you are developing a plan with your parents, make sure your siblings also understand what your parents want.

Taking care of an aging or ill parent is a significant responsibility. There may be a number of concerns related to housing and healthcare that need to be addressed. Who in your family will take principle responsibility to oversee caregiving or will be the caregiver? How will other members of the family support the caregiver?

Discussions of these issues are almost always awkward and difficult. Let your parents know that it will be easier for you to help them later if they share with you the financial and insurance plans they have made. At a minimum, they should inform you of where they keep critical documents related to their finances. You need to know if they have a will and where they keep it. It is also important to know if they have a medical power of attorney (POA) or medical directives document and where it is kept. Preparation of POA and living trust documents should be done while your parents still have their mental faculties.

Under ideal conditions, it might also be helpful if you know all of the following:

- Social Security numbers
- Location of recent tax records
- Location of important insurance policies
- Medical records
- Saving and investment accounts
- Home safe combinations or safe deposit box keys
- Information for medical, legal, financial, and insurance contacts

Long-term Care

If you reach a point in your life when you can no longer take care of yourself, there are a number of ways to address your needs. Assisted-living facilities, nursing homes, adult daycare centers, and home-health services are available options. If you are forced to use one of these options for more than 30 to 60 days, however, your health insurance policy will almost certainly *not* pay for your care. Long-term healthcare expenses will need to be funded either from your own nest egg, by your family, or through a special long-term-care (LTC) policy.

When purchasing a LTC policy, the annual premium will be based on your age at the time of purchase. The principle behind LTC policies is simple. You pay premiums today to cover potential long-term-care expenses in your future. But the list of issues you should consider before purchasing a policy is complex. One important question to ask is, "Will the insurer you choose be around when you need the policy?" Not all insurers will have stable finances for the two to four decades that might come between your purchase of a policy and your need to use it. Consider how much insurance is sufficient. As with the case of other healthcare, LTC costs are escalating at alarming rates. If you purchase a policy to cover daily nursing-home costs today, it may be insufficient to cover the cost of a nursing home when you actually need to be admitted to one. Make sure you understand what conditions have to be met before you qualify for benefits. The conditions are likely to be linked to a very specific list of activities of daily living. If you are capable of performing too many of these, you may not qualify. It is important to understand the limitations of the policy.

Long-term-care policies are not appropriate for everyone. If you have built a sufficient nest egg, you will be able to afford your own care. If your net worth is small enough, you will qualify for Medicaid, which will pay the expenses once you exhaust your funds. People who are married and/or have children are less likely to need LTC than those who are not.

4.4. DOCUMENTS

In case of your death or incapacitation, someone will have to make decisions about your finances, assets, and family. Depending on personal circumstances, it is probably advisable to complete legal and/or instructional documents to establish what decisions are made and who will make them. You can legally establish who will take care of your finances, who will inherit your assets, who will take care of your children, or who will make medical decisions on your behalf. These issues can usually be addressed with a few legal documents and a well-designed letter of instruction. It is prudent that you obtain advice and assistance of a qualified attorney licensed in your jurisdiction who will be obligated to look after your interests as you have expressed them while drawing up the documents discussed below.

Here are some examples of types of legal documents you might need. Although it will vary depending on the individual circumstances and the state you live in, many people can satisfy their requirements with two or three of these documents:

- Will
- Trust
- Durable power of attorney for finances
- Medical power of attorney for healthcare issues

It is unlikely that you will need all of these documents to ensure that your wishes are addressed. Investigate each of these options relative to your personal situation, consider the state laws where you live, and then choose the right documents for you.

Will

A will is a legal document that specifies how to distribute your money and property after your death. Your wishes regarding funeral, burial, and guardians for children can also be designated in a will. A will can also be used to decide who should receive your assets upon your death, who will take care of your children, and/or who will take care of your financial affairs. Conversations with your spouse or a good friend are not adequate. Your wishes need to be in writing and notarized or witnessed as required by the laws of your state. In the absence of a will, each state has a default set of rules that determine how all of these issues are handled.

Trust

A trust is a written agreement that sets forth who will manage the assets placed in it during your lifetime, in the event of your incapacity, and upon your death. It allows you to transfer the legal title of your assets to a trustee (another person or yourself). There are a number of different kinds of trusts, and it may be advisable to seek professional legal advice regarding the right choice for your situation and state. In many cases, a living trust can be a more cost-effective alternative to a will.

Durable Power of Attorney (POA) for Finances

A POA document authorizes another person to act for you in the event of temporary or permanent incapacitation. The document can specify which events must take place before the POA goes into effect and can also limit the range of actions allowed by your named representative. When you give someone durable POA for your finances, that person is legally able to decide how your funds and assets are dispersed. If there is someone you trust, who understands your wishes, and who will represent your interests, you can name that person in a durable POA document. A spouse is a logical representative for durable POA for many people since that is someone who is likely to be familiar with your wishes and finances regardless of any recent changes in their situation. Many life changes that can lead to required changes in a will or trust may not necessitate changes to a durable POA.

Medical Power of Attorney (POA) for Healthcare

A medical POA document provides authority to someone you specify to make medical decisions for you. Under circumstances in which you are unable to make medical decisions for yourself, physicians may be forced to choose medical options based on legal constraints rather than on reasonable medical judgment or undocumented personal wishes. Someone identified as a healthcare representative in a medical POA document can direct doctors to make decisions consistent with reasonable medical judgment and the patient's personal wishes. You literally trust your POA healthcare representative with your life. It is important that this person be familiar with your wishes and willing and able to see them carried out on your behalf. To make these decisions easier for the representative, it is advisable that you explicitly indicate in the document what you want done in terms of healthcare, tests, and so on in the event that you are unable to make your own choices. Some states have a requirement for a document called an *Advanced Directive,* which you give to your primary care physician. It becomes a part of your permanent medical records. This document details your wishes in the event of inability to communicate those wishes to the medical providers treating you, and is designed to minimize or eliminate the conflicts among family members and medical providers that may arise. Some states have a very specific form that has to be used for that purpose. Check with your attorney, physician, and medical plan administrator to determine what your requirements would be.

Letter of Instruction and Distribution of Documents

The existence of appropriate legal documents may be of little help to your loved ones if they are unaware of the documents, their location, or their contents. Once appropriate legal documents have been created, several witnessed and notarized copies will need to be prepared. Named representatives in any of the documents should get a copy. It is advisable that your family physician be provided with a will or medical POA document. If you work closely with any financial planners or bankers, they should get a copy of your POA for finances document. Finally, you should keep copies of all the documents in your safe and/or safety deposit box.

The final document you should prepare is not a legal document, but a letter to those who might need instructions in case of your death or incapacitation. Discussions held in the past are not sufficient. The letter should be simple, but very specific. It should not repeat instructions included in other legal documents, but simply instruct others of where copies of those documents are located. An example template for a couple's letter of instruction is included in the box beginning on page 88.

Instructions in the Event of Our Deaths or Incapacitation
Updated:_____

Our Social Security numbers are: <u>you</u>:_____ and <u>spouse</u>:_____

We have the following checking accounts and savings accounts:
- *Bank_____ Account type_____ Account #_____*
- *Bank_____ Account type_____ Account #_____*

We have the following insurance policies:
- Health Insurance: *Company, policy #, agent, premium*
- Long-term-care insurance: *Company, policy #, agent, premium*
- Life insurance: *Company, policy #, agent, premium*
- Home insurance: *Company, policy #, agent, premium*
- Auto insurance: *Company, policy #, agent, premium*
- Other insurance: *Company, policy #, agent, premium*

The location of critical documents:
- Our wills *(location and attorney information, who has copies)*
- Other legal documents such as POAs *(location, who has copies)*
- Life insurance policy *(location)*
- Long-term-care policy *(location)*
- Home insurance *(location)*
- Auto insurance *(location)*
- Auto title/deed/registration *(location)*
- Pension information *(location)*
- Financial account information *(software and paper record locations)*
- Abstract/deed for house *(location)*
- Income tax records *(software and paper record locations)*

Make sure that the following bills are paid:
- Medical insurance premium *(payment details, date due, amount due, accounts where automatic payments are taken from, etc.)*
- Property taxes *(dates of tax bills)*
- Home insurance *(dates of policy renewal)*
- Other insurance, or recurring expenses that must be maintained
- Other debts (mortgage, car loans, etc.) *(dates of bills, institution details)*
- Regular expenses

We have a safe deposit box: *key location, number, bank location*
We have a safe in the house: *location, combination*
We have a post office box for some mail delivery: *PO Box #, information*
We have a storage locker: *location, number, key location*
We have additional assets we keep at: *details*

We have the following investment and retirement accounts:
- *Company/Broker_____ Account type_____ Account # _____ Approximate Total_____*
- *Company/Broker_____ Account type_____ Account #_____ Approximate Total_____*

Information about other assets
- House *(owned free and clear or mortgage information)*
  Autos *(owned or car loan)*
- Credit Cards: *number_____ bank or institution_____*

The following people/institutions owe us money
  List with details

We have made the following arrangements or have the following wishes in case of our deaths
- Cemetery plots: *location and details*
- Funeral arrangements: *preferences, spending desires*

If possible, we would like you to use the assets you inherit to pay for the following items as your first priority:
- Pay for children's college *(list children still in college and any directions)*
- Charity contributions *(list desired charity and amount or percentage that should be donated)*
- Other spending desires

You should contact the following friends and family:
  List friends, relatives and contact information

REFERENCES AND FURTHER READING

1. Snyder, J., Hospitals Reducing Rates for Uninsured, *The Arizona Republic,* July 28, 2004.
2. Gladwell, M., The Moral-Hazard Myth, *The New Yorker,* August 29, 2005.
3. Jaffe, C., Better Off in the End, *Market Watch,* July 27, 2005.
4. Rubenstein, S., Health Insurers Often Reject "Near Elderly," *The Wall Street Journal Online,* November 16, 2004.
5. Orman, S., *The Road to Wealth,* Riverhead Books, New York, 2003.
6. The National Coalition on Healthcare, *Health Insurance Cost, 2004,* http://www.nchc.org/facts/cost.shtml.
7. Smith, C., C. Cowan, A. Sensenig, and A. Catlin, Health Spending Growth Slows in 2003, *Health Affairs,* 2005.
8. Pear, R. U.S. Healthcare Spending Reaches All-Time High: 15% of GDP, *The New York Times,* January 9, 2004.
9. Centers for Medicare and Medicaid Services, Office of the Actuary, National Health Statistics Group; U.S. Dept. of Commerce, Bureau of Economic Analysis and Bureau of the Census, 2003, http://www.cms.hhs.gov/statistics/nhe/projections-2003/t2.asp.
10. Powell, R., Of Little Benefit: Study Shows Need to Rethink Healthcare in Retirement, *MarketWatch,* March 23, 2005.
11. Bruce, L., Building an Emergency Fund, *Bankrate.com,* December 7, 2004, http://www.bankrate.com/brm/news/financial-literacy/emergency-savings1.asp.

12. Burns, S., There's a High Cost of Living as A Family, *The Dallas Morning News,* August 21, 2005.

13. Johnson, D., J. Rogers, and L. Tan, A Century of Family Budgets in the United States, *Monthly Labor Review,* May 2001.

14. Futrelle, D., Are Your Kids Normal about Money? *Money,* pp. 55–56, December 2005.

15. Pollitz, K., R. Sorian, and K. Thomas, How Accessible is Individual Health Insurance for Consumers in Less-Than-Perfect Health? Henry J. Kaiser Family Foundation, June 2001.

16. Do You Need Long-Term-Care Insurance? *Consumer Reports,* pp. 20–24, November 2003.

17. Dunleavy, M. P., Uncommon Sense: 3 Big Reasons Couples Fight about Money, *MSN.Money,* November 14, 2005, http://moneycentral.msn.com/content/Collegeand-Family/Loveandmoney/P134920.asp?GT1=7533.

18. Knuckey, D., *Conscious Spending for Couples: Seven Skills for Financial Harmony,* Wiley, Hoboken, N.J., 2002.

OUTSIDE THE BANDWIDTH

The Secret to the Universe

One warm, sunny day in late September a few years ago, George Stotlemeyer accidentally discovered the secret to the universe. At the moment he made the discovery, George thought to himself, "Wow, that's pretty neat."

Now you might think that if George had really made such a discovery, he would have exhibited a more enthusiastic response than simply thinking to himself, "Wow, that's pretty neat." But it turns out that the secret to the universe, when discovered, is most likely to result in exactly this kind of response. Often, the discoverer is not even aware that what they have discovered is indeed the secret to the universe. But they almost always recognize that what they have discovered is "pretty neat."

George was not at his desk at com.Wireless.com at the time of the discovery. He was not sitting in front of his computer at home. Instead, George made this amazing discovery while enjoying a weekend outing with some family and friends.

When George Stotlemeyer came back into the office on the following Monday, he did not advertise his discovery. In fact, he appears to have been intentionally hiding his discovery from the rest of the workforce at com.Wireless.com. He did not write a memo about it, or call a meeting to present it. Actually, George did not discuss his discovery with a single coworker or with any member of Bo's & Leary's management team. Over the course of the next several weeks and months, George did not stand up in a single pointless and misguided meeting to reveal, "I happen to know the Secret to the Universe and I can assure you that this meeting is pointless and misguided." George did not attempt to publish any documents or manuscripts taking credit for the secret he had happened upon. He filed no patent applications. Quite the opposite is the situation. George actually seemed to become less involved in interoffice political battles. He withdrew from pointless and misguided meeting debates. George went so far as to leave the office early if he had other personal and family activities going on. He quit working weekends entirely. His actions seemed to indicate anything but the fact that he was holding knowledge about the secret to the universe.

So it is quite remarkable that George's office mate, Brittany Gateway, began to suspect that George was on to something big. In addition to George's shifting priorities and lack of interest in office politics, she noticed that George began to hum or whistle songs as he moved down the hallways. (He seemed to favor head-banger rock-and-roll, but Brittany wasn't sure whether that had anything to do with the change in George or not.) Once Brittany was sure that George knew something, she began to discuss it with other office coworkers. They too, noticed the changes and began to wonder what George knew.

Finally, Brittany called an informal meeting of several of George's coworkers to discuss how they might uncover and exploit George's apparent secret. The meeting was held one evening at a local establishment that was rumored to have a surplus of beer. The group decided that they could help with the establishment's surplus problem while discussing the problem of the whistling George. Neil Rails wondered if George had perhaps been given a promotion, raise, or bonus. Maybe that's why he seemed more relaxed and happy. This possibility was ruled out since Joe Nors was George's immediate supervisor and he was also at the meeting. He would have to have known about any kind of promotion, raise, or bonus. Gladys Best speculated that perhaps George had developed a solution to the Aphrodite project. This project seemed doomed as long as it continued along its present course. Could he be waiting until management became desperate so that he could step in and be the hero? This possibility was also ruled out since all of the engineers present agreed that there was no solution to this Aphrodite problem short of the demise or departure of the program's current management. Ed Forsythe wondered out loud if George might have dug up some dirt on Bo or Leary and was able to blackmail them. Although it was easy enough to believe that there was dirt in the background of Bo and Leary, this seemed too far-fetched an idea to most of the group. Finally, it was agreed that the group would keep a close eye on George for the next month and if he continued to appear to hold some important secret, they would confront him directly. They also agreed to come back and work on the beer surplus problem some evening in the not-too-distant future.

Unfortunately, George showed up the following Monday morning with his letter of resignation. It seems he just decided to take early retirement. George took his stored-up vacation over the next few weeks and spent little time in the office. He did make it a point to go around and say goodbye to his coworkers. He seemed very relaxed and happy during this time. He wished everyone well. Although Brittany tried to bring up the subject of the secret George was hiding, he played dumb and acted like he didn't know what she was talking about.

So George left com.Wireless.com without ever revealing the secret to the universe to any of his coworkers. Now he is sometimes seen on warm, sunny days in late September enjoying an outing with friends and family. Brittany stays in touch with George hoping he might someday reveal the secret that she could use to bring her recognition and promotion. Of course, Bo and Leary have never suspected a thing.

(From *IEEE Microwave Magazine,* September 2004.)

5

INVESTMENT INSTRUMENTS

5.1. BONDS

Bonds are loans for which the investor is the lender. They are like IOUs. When a bond is purchased, the buyer is lending money to a government, company, or other organization. Bonds are sold in fixed increments, normally $1000. The organization that sells a bond is known as the *issuer.* Like other loans, there is an amount borrowed (*face value* or *par value*), an interest rate (*coupon rate*), and a specified time when the bond must be paid off (*maturity date*). Bond maturities can range from days to decades. Interest is paid to the bond owner on a schedule specified by the bond—typically every 6 months, although quarterly or monthly payments are sometimes specified. Because the cash flow from them is fixed, bonds are also known as fixed-income securities. On the maturity date, the face value of the bond is returned to the bondholder.

Investors include bonds in their portfolio to provide stability, not higher returns. For long-term investment periods, the stock market has always beaten bond performance. For periods of a decade or less, however, stable bond interest can outperform the more volatile stock market. For most investors, it makes sense to have at least part of their portfolio invested in bonds. A detailed discussion of the value of stock/bond diversification is provided in Chapter 6, Section 6.1.

Bonds are debt, whereas stocks are equity. This distinction means that equity holders are owners of a company, whereas bondholders are creditors. Legally, the creditors (bondholders) have a higher claim on assets. In case of bankruptcy, a bondholder will get paid before a stockholder. An organization's bonds carry less risk than their stock certificates. Since the bondholder is taking less risk, he or she almost always receives lower returns.

Engineering Your Retirement. By Mike Golio
© 2007 Institute of Electrical and Electronics Engineers, Inc.

Not all bonds carry the same risk. The more risky the investment, the higher the rate of return offered by a bond. Companies sometimes default and fail to pay back bonds. Time is also a factor in bond risk. A bond that matures in 30 years is much less predictable, and therefore more risky, than a bond that matures in 1 year. For this reason, longer time to maturity is usually associated with higher interest rates. Bond investors should consider underlying risk before investing in a bond.

Bond ratings can be useful in evaluating the default risk of bond issuers. Bond ratings are developed and published by two major rating organizations in the United States: Moody's and Standard & Poor's (S&P). These ratings are similar to a report card on the issuer's stability. The highest grades are awarded to government bonds since they are the closest thing to a risk-free investment available. Large, blue-chip firms tend to receive fairly high ratings because of corporate stability. Financially unstable companies receive low ratings. Table 5.1 presents the issuer ratings of the two rating organizations in order from highest to lowest quality. Bonds with ratings near the bottom of Table 5.1 are referred to as *junk bonds*. These bonds offer high yield, but at greater risk.

A bond can be sold before its maturity date. When bonds are sold on the secondary market, the price can fluctuate from the face value. If a bond is bought at face value, the yield is equivalent to the coupon rate of the bond. If the bond is purchased at a price greater than face value, the payments remain fixed, providing a yield less than the coupon rate. Similarly, a bond purchased at below face value will produce a higher yield than the coupon. The *yield to maturity* (YTM) is the return an investor will receive from a bond purchased on the secondary market at a price different than the face value. YTM can be larger or smaller than the bond coupon. Bond prices and bond yields are inversely related. The discussion above does not apply to government bonds sold at below face value on the primary market.

The entire bond market can be categorized along a dual continuum. The classifications that apply to bonds are maturity and credit rating. Conventional maturity classifications are *long* (greater than 10 years), *intermediate* (4 to 10 years), and *short* (less than 4 years). Credit rating is the Moody's or S&P's credit rating as discussed above and presented in Table 5.1. As an example, a U.S. treasury bond with

Table 5.1. Bond issuer ratings used by Moody's and Standard & Poor's

Moody's	Standard & Poor's	Bond grade
Aaa	AAA	Investment
Aa	AA	Investment
A	A	Investment
Baa	BBB	Investment
Ba, B	BB, B	Junk
Caa/Ca/C	CCC/CC/C	Junk
C	D	Junk (in default)

a 20 year maturity would be classified as a long-term, low-risk bond, whereas a bond from a financially struggling small company with a 3 year maturity would be a short-term, junk bond.

In addition to the maturity and credit rating, bonds can be divided into United States or foreign debt. Foreign bonds can be further classified either as emerging- or as developed-country debt. Bonds can also be classified by the business sector of a company.

The most common types of bonds are treasury bonds, treasury notes, treasury bills, agency bonds, municipal bonds, corporate bonds, and zero-coupon bonds.

Government Bonds, Notes, and Bills

Debt securities from the U.S. government are known collectively as *Treasuries* because they are sold by the Treasury Department. There are a number of different types of debt securities, available maturities, and payment arrangements associated with treasuries. The word *bond* is used by the U.S. Treasury only for their issues with a maturity longer than 10 years. Bonds with maturities as long as 30 years are sold by the U.S. Treasury. Bonds pay interest every 6 months. *Treasury Notes* are government securities that have maturities of 2, 3, 5, and 10 years and also earn interest every 6 months. *Treasury Bills* are short-term government securities with maturities ranging from a few days to 26 weeks.

Treasury Inflation-Protected Securities, or TIPS, provide protection against inflation. The TIPS principal increases with inflation and decreases with deflation, as measured by the Consumer Price Index. When TIPS mature, you are paid the adjusted principal or original principal, whichever is greater. TIPS pay interest twice a year, at a fixed rate. The rate is applied to the adjusted principal; so, like the principal, interest payments rise with inflation and fall with deflation.

I Bonds are low-risk, liquid savings products backed by the U.S. Government. While you own them, they earn interest and help protect your savings from inflation. I bonds are sold at face value in increments of $25. You can invest as little as $50 or as much as $30,000 per year in paper I Bonds. In addition, you can invest as little as $25 or as much as $30,000 per year in electronic I Bonds. They grow with inflation-indexed earnings for up to 30 years but can be cashed anytime after 12 months. If an I Bond is redeemed before 5 years, a 3 month interest penalty is applied. You can defer Federal taxes on earnings for up to 30 years and I bonds are exempt from state and local income taxes.

EE Bonds are a secure savings product that pays interest for up to 30 years. Series EE savings bonds issued on or after May 1, 2005 earn a fixed rate of interest. You can cash Series EE bonds anytime after 12 months, but if a bond is redeemed before five years, a 3 month interest penalty applies. They are sold at face value electronically. Paper EE Bonds are sold at half the face value. Regardless of whether they are electronic or paper, EE Bonds will increase in value every month as interest accrues monthly and compounds semiannually. You are limited to $30,000 maximum electronic purchase plus $30,000 maximum in paper bond purchase each calendar year. Interest earned on your Series EE bonds is exempt from state and local income taxes. You can defer federal income tax until you redeem the bonds, or after 30 years when they stop earning interest. There are also special tax benefits available for education savings. If you qualify, you can exclude all or part of the interest earned on Series EE bonds from income when the bonds are redeemed to pay for postsecondary tuition and fees.

Agency Bonds

Some government agencies and quasigovernment agencies sell bonds. The Government National Mortgage Association (Ginnie Mae), Federal National Mortgage Association (Fannie Mae), and Federal Home Loan Mortgage Corporation (Freddie Mac) are among the better known agencies that issue bonds. These are low-risk bonds backed by the full faith and credit of the United States.

Municipal Bonds

Municipal bonds are also known as "munis." They are issued by state or local governments and are considered almost as safe as U.S. government bonds or agency bonds. The major advantage of munis is that the returns are free from federal tax. Furthermore, local governments will sometimes make their debt nontaxable for residents, making some municipal bonds completely tax-free. Because of the tax savings, the yield on munis is typically lower than that of a taxable bond. An investor in a high tax bracket may achieve higher after-tax returns from a muni than from higher-yielding, taxable bonds.

Corporate Bonds

Corporations can issue bonds just like they can issue stock. Corporate bonds pay higher yields than government bonds because of the higher risk of default associated with companies. The company's credit rating is a very important consideration when assessing corporate bonds. *Junk bonds* are high-yield corporate bonds issued by companies with poor credit ratings.

Zero-Coupon Bonds

This is a type of bond that makes no coupon payment during the life of the bond. Instead, the bond is issued at a price considerably below face value. At maturity, zero-coupon bonds pay the bondholder one lump sum equival to the initial investment plus interest that has accrued. Zero-coupon bonds are usually associated with long maturity dates—10 or more years.

Investors can purchase different kinds of zero-coupon bonds in the secondary markets. The bonds are issued by a variety of sources, including the U.S. Treasury, corporations, and state and local government entities.

The prices of zero-coupon bonds fluctuate more than other types of bonds in the secondary market. Investors may be required to pay federal, state, and local income tax on the imputed or "phantom" interest that accrues each year, even though no actual interest payments are made until maturity.

5.2. STOCKS

Stocks are certificates of ownership in a company. They are sold in units of shares, so the terms *stockholder* and *shareholder* are interchangeable. Typically, when people refer to stock, they are referring to *common stock.* Most stock is issued in this form. Owning common stock or shares is also known as owning *equity* in the company. Although stockholders possess a claim on assets and earnings, they do not have any say in the day-to-day operations of the company. Instead, they have the right to one vote per share in the election of the board of directors at annual meetings. In theory, company management can be voted out at the next annual meeting if they fail to increase the value of the firm for shareholders. In practice, individual investors hold very little influence over company management. Institutional investors (pension fund and mutual fund managers), however, can hasten changes in corporate management and policies.

There are no guarantees that an individual stock will ever produce positive earnings for an investor. Some companies pay regular dividends, but even these are not guaranteed. A company has no obligation to pay out dividends and can choose to stop issuing them at any time. Many companies pay no dividends. The investor only makes money from these companies if the stock price appreciates in the open market and the stock is sold while the price is high.

As a stockholder, you are not personally liable for company debts or mismanagement. You can never be forced to pay creditors from your personal funds. The maximum amount you can lose when investing in stocks is the value of your investment, even if you are a shareholder of a company that goes bankrupt. On the other hand, your participation in earnings has no limit. Although you can lose no more than 100% of your investment, you can earn more than 10,000% on your stock if the company is successful. For the greater risk of owning stocks, the investor demands greater returns. This is the reason that throughout history stocks have outperformed other investments over the long term.

A company's *market cap* is an indicator of the total value of a company. It is determined by the outstanding number of shares times the price of the stock. Price of a stock alone is not an indicator of company value. When companies issue more stock, they dilute the value of existing stock and prices drop. When they buy back stock, they concentrate value and stock prices rise.

Like bonds, the entire stock market can be categorized along a dual continuum. Companies are often classified by their market cap on one continuum, and potential for growth or value along the other. Companies are typically ranked into one of three size categories: issuers of *large-cap stocks* (company value greater than $5 billion), *mid-cap stocks* (company value from $1 to $5 billion), and *small-cap stocks* (less than $1 billion). The growth-value ranking of a company is not always easy to establish. Growth stocks have high average annual growth (greater than ~

25% or more) and tend to be issued by small companies. Dividend income from growth stocks is usually small or nonexistent. High-tech companies with a "hot" product are often in this category. Growth stocks are expected to earn money because the company will grow its profits and that growth will be reflected in the stock price. Associated with higher average growth is greater volatility. The same growth stock that provides a large increase in value one year may exhibit declines of equal or greater value the following year. Value stocks are typically stocks that have limited growth potential, but are capable of producing steady, regular profits. Stocks that have seen recent declines and are selling at a price below the fair value of the company's underlying potential are candidates for value stock classification. Value stocks are expected to earn money as the market comes to recognize the value of steady earnings production. Dividend payments are typically an important component of a value stock's perceived worth. Although large annual growth is not typically expected from a value stock, steady growth and dividends can make value stocks outperform their growth counterparts over some periods of time.

In addition to the market cap and value-growth potential of a company, stocks can be divided into U.S. or foreign assets. Foreign stocks can be further classified either as emerging- or as developed-country assets. Stocks can also be classified by the business sector of the company issuing them.

Stock prices change every day. Capitalism and the laws of supply and demand drive stock prices up or down depending on what people with investment dollars believe about the future of a company. Unfortunately, it is very difficult to understand or anticipate what the entire investment community believes about the future of a company. It is fairly easy to determine past earnings. Earnings are the profit a company has made. Past profits are no guarantee of future performance, however. Investing in last year's most profitable company is not likely to result in an optimum performance record.

When discussing stock value and what investments will be "good," some investment advisors talk about *valuation* of a company. Valuation is a seductive term. How can something called "valuation" not be an important factor in determining the value of a company's stock? Unfortunately, "valuation" is an example of a misleading financial term. In reality, when most advisors are talking about valuation, they are simply referring to the ratio of the current stock price to the past year's earnings, or P/E. In some cases, investment advisors will attempt to smooth out the inherent volatility of the market and use the ratio of the current price to the average earnings over the last 10 years, or P/E10. It should be obvious that the current stock price is not an indicator of future corporate performance. Similarly, past performance is no guarantee of future results. Yet, somehow through the magic of division, P/E is supposed to indicate what companies or markets to invest in.

If all investors used the same models to decide what stocks were worth, we could predict what stock prices would do. As rapidly as we could predict, however, every other investor could also predict and it would be nearly impossible to buy or sell ahead of the market. Making money would come down to who had the fastest internet link to their broker. Understanding what a majority of investors believe is also of little value. It is not the number of investors but the number of investment dollars that determines price. Predicting the rise or fall of stocks is further complicated by the fact that, in general, the investors who panic and bring the price down today are not the same investors who get greedy and bid the price up tomorrow.

Stock prices change, but it is very difficult to determine why or how. Two important things investors need to remember are that (1) stocks have outperformed other investments in the long term, and (2) stock prices are volatile and can change extremely rapidly.

A second type of stock (other than common stock) is *preferred* stock. Preferred stock provides shareholders with some claims on assets, but without voting rights. Preferred shareholders get guaranteed fixed dividends, making the stock similar to a bond, but without a maturity date. Preferred stockholders continue to receive dividends forever, or until the company "calls" the shares. A company usually retains the right to buy back (call) preferred stock shares at any time for any reason. Preferred stock calls usually include a premium, so that the investor is paid more for the repurchased shares than the original share price. In case of bankruptcy and liquidation of a company's assets, investors in preferred stocks are also paid off prior to common-stock shareholders.

Preferred stocks tend to perform more like bonds than like equity investments. Since their primary value is in fixed dividends, preferred stock prices are not as volatile as common stocks. The upside potential is limited regardless of how well the company does because the primary value of preferred stocks is the fixed dividend payments.

5.3. REAL ESTATE

Real estate is land plus any structures permanently fixed to it. Unlike other investments, real estate value is primarily affected by the immediate area around the investment—location, location, location. It is the local, not the national, investment environment that matters. In 2005, Arizona house price appreciation led the nation with a 34.9% increase according to the Office of Federal Housing Enterprise Oversight. Michigan house price appreciation was the lowest in the nation at only 3.76%. When examined at a city level, the variations are even greater. House prices in Phoenix–Mesa–Scottsdale, Arizona appreciated by 39.67% in 2005, whereas house prices in Burlington, North Carolina dropped by 1.16%.

Many investors consider real estate ownership to be similar to fixed-income investments because mortgage payments are fixed for specified periods of time. This view overlooks many important distinctions between real estate and bonds. Real estate is more like a business than a loan. With bonds, an investor is loaning funds at a fixed rate and the entire principal is repaid at bond maturity. With real estate, both principal and income of the investment is subject to change based on market forces. There is no maturity date. Property owners also have to manage, repair, pay taxes, and insure their investment. Bonds are entirely passive investments. These distinctions between bond investment behavior and real estate do not imply that real estate is similar to the stock market. Although local real estate markets can exhibit boom and bust trends, property values are not typically nearly as volatile as the stock market. Real estate also exhibits low correlation with equities. The value of holding a portfolio comprised of assets that exhibit low correlation will be discussed in Chapter 6, Section 6.2.

Some investors prefer real estate investment to stocks, bonds, or mutual funds because real estate seems more tangible to them. Unlike the value of a stock or bond security, a piece of property can never disappear. For some reason, real estate seems to attract large numbers of hucksters selling "get rich quick" schemes through books, tapes, and short courses. Some experts have suggested that more money has been made selling real estate investment schemes than has ever been made from actual property sales.

Since real estate is typically purchased using a low-interest, long-term mortgage, it provides investors with an opportunity to leverage their investments in a way that is less difficult and risky than stock or bond leverage. Leverage is the use of borrowed capital to increase the potential return of an investment.

The rise in the median U.S. home price between 1970 and 2004 was only 6.05%. This increase barely beat inflation during that period. In contrast, during the same period the S&P500 returned 11.41%. On the surface, real estate would appear to have underperformed the market significantly. Using leverage effectively, however, the real estate investor could easily have come out ahead of the stock investor. An example can illustrate this point. A real estate investor who invests $30,000 in a $180,000 home obtains a mortgage to cover the other $150,000 in the price. Each year, the investor will make mortgage payments, pay insurance premiums, pay property taxes, and perform necessary maintenance. These costs might be on the order of 10% of the original purchase price of the house ($18,000 per year in this case), but will be at least partially offset by any rent collected on the property. If able to recoup only 90% of these costs through rent, the real estate investor must contribute another $1,800 per year into the house investment. Table 5.2 presents (1) the total cumulative investment in the house; (2) the value of the house if it appreciates at 6.05% per year; (3) the principal remaining on the mortgage, assuming a 6%, 30 year fixed mortgage; and (4) the net profit a real estate investor would make by selling the house at the end of that year. Data is shown for an investment period of 10 years. Also shown in the table is the data that would apply to the same amount of investment dollars invested in the stock market if it returned 11.4% per year. From the table, it is seen that by the end of year 6, the real estate investor's earnings are greater than the stock market investor's earnings. By the end of year 10, real estate has produced almost 25% more profit than the stock market.

The example above illustrates *how* it is possible for real estate to produce superior returns, but actual results from real estate investment vary significantly by locality. There are several significant points that should be considered in evaluating the results of Table 5.2:

- The assumptions made about mortgage, insurance, tax, and maintenance costs are reasonable for many areas, but may not be applicable for some properties.

- The example assumes that 90% of annual costs could be recovered through rent. This might be unrealistic in many areas of the country.
- Closing costs at the purchase and sale of the home were not considered in the example. The costs required to purchase or sell property can significantly reduce real estate investment profits.
- Although an investment in a stock market index fund is completely passive, the real estate investor is required to keep the property rented and maintained. Property owners also have to keep up to date on insurance, taxes, and so on.
- The stock market index investor is diversified, whereas the real estate investor holds one property. Holding only one investment is an investment risk.

Investment Property

Investment real estate is property that generates income or is otherwise intended for investment purposes rather than as a primary residence. Examples of investment properties include apartment buildings, condominium buildings, duplexes, and rental houses. The example of Table 5.2 illustrates one way that real estate investments can work for an investor. Real estate is expected to generate capital gains as the property value increases over time, but collection of rent is also critical to achieving superior returns on real estate investments. Successfully investing in real estate usually requires an investor to become a landlord and being a landlord is work. Real estate should not be considered a "get rich quick" or "easy money" strategy. In many ways, real estate is not an investment as much as it is a job.

Table 5.2. Evaluation of the performance of a leveraged real estate purchase (real estate value increases at 6.05% per year) versus an investment in the stock market returning 11.4% per year. The real estate purchase price is assumed to be $180,000. One hundred fifty thousand dollars is financed with a 6%, 30 year fixed mortgage.

Year	Cumulative dollars invested in real estate	Home value @ 6.05% per year increase	Principal remaining on mortgage	Net profit if house is sold	Cumulative dollars invested in stock market	Portfolio value @ 11.4% per year return
1	$31,800	$190,890	$147,999	$11,091	$31,800	$35,323
2	$33,600	$202,439	$146,034	$22,805	$33,600	$41,252
3	$35,400	$214,686	$143,947	$35,339	$35,400	$47,857
4	$37,200	$227,675	$141,732	$48,743	$37,200	$55,216
5	$39,000	$241,449	$139,380	$63,069	$39,000	$63,413
6	$40,800	$256,057	$136,883	$78,374	$40,800	$72,544
7	$42,600	$271,548	$134,232	$94,716	$42,600	$82,717
8	$44,400	$287,977	$131,418	$112,159	$44,400	$94,050
9	$46,200	$305,400	$128,429	$130,771	$46,200	$106,674
10	$48,000	$323,876	$125,257	$150,619	$48,000	$120,737

A landlord has to choose appropriate tenants, plan for required legal obligations, arrange financing, and direct or perform maintenance. For a small landlord, there are no economies of scale when addressing these obligations. Volume discounts do not apply. There is no staff of accountants or attorneys. The landlord has to find and pay for appropriate services. There is no maintenance staff; so plumbing, electrical and structural repairs involve paying full price to skilled tradesmen. The more tasks that the landlord can do for himself or herself, the better the investment performs.

A single irresponsible tenant can have a devastating impact on real estate returns. If a tenant does not pay rent or refuses to pay for damages, the required court and lawyer's fees reduce investment returns. It can take months to evict a bad tenant. As landlord, you may have to carry your mortgage without rental income during this process. Not only the cost, but the time and energy required to evict tenants from the premises can be significant. Keeping a contingency fund and understanding reasonable occupancy rates in your area can help address this type of problem, but choosing the right tenants and maintaining good tenant–landlord relations is even more valuable.

Identifying a building with good location, value, general maintenance, and a clean title is important. Understanding local zoning restrictions and who the current tenants are is just as important. In areas with rent control laws, knowing current-tenant rent status is critical.

Many landlord issues are solved by selecting the right tenants and setting the right expectations to begin with. Topics that should be addressed in advance include pets, smoking, parking, garbage removal, yard work, property maintenance, and noise. A videotaped walk-through with new tenants can be useful if issues arise at a later date.

Fix'n'Flip

One way to invest in real estate without embracing the headaches of being a landlord is to use a *fix'n'flip* strategy. This strategy involves buying a house at a low price, improving and repairing it quickly, and then reselling it for a significant profit. As with rental property, this is not a "get rich quick" scheme. The technique works best for people who want to turn their own skills and hard work into equity. It requires a significant commitment for a potentially great return.

The formula for fix'n'flip success is flexible. Some investors look for great bargains requiring few and minor repairs. In a rising real estate market, quick flips can be profitable. Investors with a real estate license often use a rapid buy-and-sell strategy. They benefit from savings on commissions. Other investors use their own contractor skills and look for houses requiring major renovation. They may choose to live in the house while they perform the repairs, and may choose to own the house for over a year to reduce the capital gains tax impact.

For fix'n'flip investments, the key to making a profit is getting a good deal when you buy the property. If you pay too much, you start with a handicap. No matter how nice the repairs and renovations turn out, you may not be able to recover all your costs. Costs include not only the purchase price, but also closing fees, document preparation fees, homeowner's insurance, title policy, repair costs, interest on loans, property taxes, sales commissions, and so on. The final sales price minus all of the costs is the profit you clear on the deal. The longer the period of time between purchase and sale of the property, the more profit is required to make the deal worthwhile.

Practicing fix'n'flip real estate strategies is a job. It can be a rewarding and fulfilling job if you enjoy shopping for real estate bargains, arranging financing, contracting, and repair work. The retiree looking for more recreation time, however, would be well-advised to seek other investments.

REITs

Real Estate Investment Trusts (REITs) are equity investment vehicles that allow investors to own a portion of many real estate properties or real estate mortgages. Investing in REITs is a liquid, dividend-paying method of participating in the real estate market. It provides diversification not possible from individual property purchases. Over the past two decades, REITs have become very popular. Today, there are over 200 publicly traded REITs. They generally pay no federal income tax but are required by the federal government to annually distribute at least 90% of their taxable income in the form of dividends to their shareholders.

REITs are neither stocks nor bonds, but share some characteristics of both. They pay out regular dividends often typical in magnitude to that of bonds. Like stocks, however, they can exhibit significant growth in price as the trust's property appreciates in value. Technically, REITs are not mutual funds, but they work in an almost identical fashion to one for the investor.

Like stocks or bonds, the REIT asset class can be subdivided. There are *equity REITs* that own commercial properties, *mortgage REITs* that lend money to real estate owners, and *hybrid REITs* that both own property and lend money. Most of the revenues of equity REITs come from property rents. Equity REITs invest in all kinds of property, including shopping malls, office buildings, apartments, warehouses, and hotels. Some REITs will invest specifically in only one kind of property, or in one specific region, state or, country. The revenues from mortgage REITs are generated primarily by the interest they earn on mortgage loans.

5.4. ANNUITIES

An annuity is a contract with an insurance company to provide a stream of income for a period of years or for the lifetime of an individual or couple. Annuities are often used as a form of income during retirement. Benefit payments are based on the total account balance and the expected longevity of the investor. In certain states, annuities are sheltered from creditors.

There are two major classes of annuities: *fixed annuities* and *variable annuities.* Fixed annuities offer a guaranteed rate of return over the life of the contract. They operate much like a certificate of deposit. The rate of return offered by a fixed annuity is typically competitive with CDs of similar time frames. Variable annuities are a family of mutual fund investments with an associated insurance company policy. They allow money to be invested in mutual funds in a tax-deferred manner. Their primary use is to provide a tax-deferred investment option for retirement at amounts greater than permitted by individual retirement or 401(k) plans.

Annuities can also be classified as either immediate or deferred. With an *immediate annuity,* investors make a single lump-sum deposit and the insurance company guarantees an immediate monthly payment until their death. *Deferred annuities* place invested dollars in an account that grows tax-deferred until the annuity contract is converted to an immediate annuity or is cashed in. A deferred annuity can be either fixed or variable depending on the underlying accounts investments are placed into.

There are two phases to an annuity. The *accumulation phase* occurs when the investor is making investments into the annuity. This phase can be stretched out over decades or can occur in a single deposit event. Once the insurance company begins paying regular benefits, the annuity has entered into the *distribution phase* or the *annuitization phase.* Distribution is comprised of a series of fixed payments at regular intervals over a period of time specified by the annuity contract.

People with no interest in managing their own finances sometimes see annuities as a simple solution to guaranteed lifetime income. Rather than choosing among a myriad of investment options, an annuity participant simply decides on an insurance company, fixed or variable returns, deferred or immediate income, and lumped or periodic contributions.

When shopping for an annuity investment, an investor should consider the financial strength of the insurance company that underwrites the annuity. Although a fixed annuity eliminates market risk, it replaces it with a risk that the underwriting insurance company may not remain solvent. Annuities are viewed by many savvy investors as a poor investment because these policies are associated with some of the highest commissions and fees in the investment community. They are also associated with high surrender charges. Annuities vary in quality and the variation in fees charged by different companies is significant. Fees typically include commissions, underwriting, and fund management. Other costs include penalties for early withdrawal and unexpected tax consequences.

Once money is invested in an annuity, it is inaccessible to the investor except under very restrictive conditions and with steep penalties. This should be considered before entering into any annuity contract. An investor should also consider the impact of an annuity investment on their heirs. Once annuitized, fixed monthly benefit payments are made until you die. If you do not outlive the longevity tables, the insurance company, not your heirs, receives the surplus investment you made. Even if you die as early as a year after annuitization, the insurance company keeps all of the remaining balance of your investment.

Variable annuities offer versatility in investment choices and an opportunity to participate in market upswings, but at fee rates as much as eight times that of typical mutual funds. The fees come out of your return. These policies also include insurance fees for a benefit that is of questionable value. The insurance benefit is paid only if you die and the market has dropped. If you require insurance, it is much more efficient to simply buy insurance, not tack a dubious policy onto an expensive investment instrument. Surrender charges may apply for as long as 10 years. These steep charges dramatically reduce an investor's flexibility. Even without surrender charges, an investor is restricted by federal law from withdrawing prior to age 59½. Although variable annuity investments are tax-deferred, withdrawals are taxed at ordinary income tax rates. In contrast, much of the money invested in stocks or mutual funds outside a variable annuity get taxed at the lower capital gains rates. This tax liability is transferred to your heirs in the event that you die before spending the accumulated income in the variable annuity.

A new category of deferred annuity called the *equity indexed annuity* emerged In 1995. Insurance companies guarantee a minimum return for this class of annuity. A rate of return higher than the minimum is offered in years when the stock market performs well. In those years, the rate of return is determined by the performance of the target stock market index, excluding dividends. Interest rate caps and administrative fees also apply.

Equity indexed annuities are being heavily pushed by insurance companies. If the sales hype is replaced with analysis, however, most individual investors will avoid them. Giving up dividends plus imposing a cap on market capital gains is far too severe a penalty to pay for protection against periodic market losses. Indexed annuity contracts are sold because the greed-without-fear sales hype resonates with less astute investors.

Careful and thorough evaluation of the numbers leads some financial gurus to avoid annuity products. Despite this, many investors are attracted to the longevity risk insurance and simplicity offered by them. They are willing to pay for the stability offered by an annuity. Immediate annuities purchased at retirement offer the most efficient way to invest in guaranteed lifetime income for most investors. Coupled with a diversified portfolio of other types of assets, an annuity can reduce longevity risk while reducing portfolio returns only modestly.

5.5. DEFINED BENEFIT PLANS (PENSIONS)

The term "pension" can apply to both defined benefit plans (tradtional pensions) and defined contribution plans [401(k)s, 403(b)s, and 457 plans]. In this section, only traditional pensions will be discussed. Defined contribution plans are discussed in detail in Chapter 6, Section 6.3.

Traditional pensions are a form of deferred compensation. An employee is promised a regular income stream after retirement for services performed prior to retirement. The pension benefit is determined by a formula, which typically incorporates the employee's pay, years of employment, age at retirement, and other possible factors. Most corporate pension plans in the United States use the average salary over the last 3 or 5 years of employment as a primary factor in calculating pension benefits. Inflation indexing is not included in most U.S. corporate pensions. This means that during retirement, the buying power of the pension is reduced each year by inflation. Inflation indexing is more common for state and federal government pension plans. Expected Social Security benefits are also included as a factor in some pension calculations.

In addition to the postretirement cash flow benefit, pension plans are usually advantageous to both employee and employer for tax reasons. There is also an insurance component to many pensions, since they often pay benefits to survivors or disabled beneficiaries.

Because of the accrual formula, the present value of traditional benefit plans grows slowly early in an employee's career and accelerates significantly in midcareer. There is usually a vesting period for the first 1 to 5 years of pension plans that further reduces their value early in an employee's career. Pensions are not generally portable, and are payable only after the employee reaches retirement age (as defined by the plan). Even if the employee leaves the company prior to retirement age, he or she is not allowed to receive benefits until retirement age is reached. A recent trend in corporate America has been to offer employees who are vested in a pension plan the option of taking their pension in lump-sum form when their employment is terminated. The employee can roll the lump-sum pension plan into another qualified plan to maintain the tax advantages and can choose to purchase an annuity with the pension lump sum if they wish to maintain the same level of longevity risk offered by the original pension.

Although it is probably not wise to choose a job based on pension benefits, consideration of the value of a pension is important when planning retirement. The present value of a future pension can only be estimated based on economic and financial assumptions. An estimate of the present value of a pension, PV, at retirement can be calculated from the formula

$$PV = C \times \left[\frac{1 - (1 + i)^{-n}}{i} \right] \tag{5.1}$$

where C is the cash flow per benefit period, i is the assumed interest rate, and n is the number of payments the retiree expects to receive during his or her lifetime.

In order to evaluate Equation (5.1), retirement planners have to determine the amount of monthly pension benefit, C, they are presently qualified to receive. This value will be unique to the company plan and the employee. A competent Human Resources representative should be able to provide this number. In the absence of such a person, employees must locate the documents that describe their corporate plan and perform the calculations themselves. The value of n represents the total number of payments the retiree expects to receive. This can be estimated by subtracting life expectancy (see Appendix C) from retirement age and multiplying by the number of payments per year (typically 12). The remaining variable in Equation (5.1) is interest rate, i. This value represents the interest rate expected on money invested during the payout period of the pension. Since a pension performs similarly to a bond during the payout period, the value of i should be representative of expected bond rates. An annual rate of 4% to 5% is a reasonable value. For monthly payments, this rate should be divided by 12 (i.e., $0.04/12 = 0.0033$).

The result calculated from Equation (5.1) provides an estimate of the value of a pension benefit on the day of retirement. The value can be used in retirement simulators as part of the retiree's total portfolio value. Using a calculated present value of pension benefits in portfolio simulations is only an approximation. Unlike other portions of the portfolio, a pension is not susceptible to longevity risk. Pensions also cannot be left to heirs. These distinctions should be considered for various aspects of retirement planning.

Defined benefit plans are becoming an endangered species for engineers and scientists working in corporate America. Two decades ago, 40% of American workers were covered by traditional pensions. Fewer than 20% of today's workers are covered by such plans. In addition, about 75% of the existing corporate plans are currently underfunded. The recent trend is clear. As recently as 2005, the Social Security Administration determined that about two-thirds of households age 65 and older received pension benefits. On average, these pensions were the source of 16% of postretirement income. This represents a significant consideration for retirement planning. If you have a pension, you need to include that income in your planning. If you do not have a pension, you need to ensure that your retirement plans are adequate to produce all of your required income.

5.6. CASH AND CERTIFICATES OF DEPOSIT

Not all of your money should be engaged in long-term investments. Every investor has monthly expenses. As discussed in Chapter 4, Section 4.2, an emergency fund comprised of several months of regular income should be available in liquid investments. In addition, you might be saving for an anticipated near-term, large-item purchase. For all of these reasons, investors need to keep some funds in short-term liquid accounts.

Cash, checking accounts, and savings accounts are some of the options for short-term saving needs. Other options include money market mutual funds (see Section 5.9), Treasury Bills (see Section 5.1), and certificates of deposit (CDs). Banks, Credit Unions, and Savings and Loan associations offer checking and savings accounts that offer convenience and immediate access to funds. Unfortunately, they do not offer competitive interest relative to other types of investments. It is not wise to leave more money in these accounts than is needed to pay regular monthly expenses.

A certificate of deposit, or CD, is a short-term savings instrument issued by a bank or other financial institution. Like individual bonds, CDs pay a specified rate of interest over a specified period of time. Maturity dates on CDs range from 3 months to 5 years. They can be issued in any denomination. At the end of the period, they pay back your principal. CDs are insured up to $100,000 by the federal government. CDs offer slightly higher yield than regular banking accounts or Treasury Bills (see Chapter 6, Section 6.4) and are extremely safe investments. The interest on CDs is determined by the current interest rate environment, how much money you invest, the maturity date, and your specific financial institution. Rates vary and not all banks offer competitive rates, so it pays to shop around.

When comparing CD rates, it is important to understand the difference between annual percentage rate (APR) and annual percentage yield (APY). APR is the interest rate that will be applied at each compounding event. APY is the total amount of interest you will earn as a percentage of your investment. If interest is compounded annually, APR and APY are equivalent. APY will be greater than APR when compounding is more frequent. As an investor, APY is clearly more important to you.

The main disadvantage to CDs is that withdrawal prior to maturity triggers a harsh penalty. CDs should be chosen with maturity dates that match an investor's spending needs in the near future. As a long-term investment, CDs do not offer competitive returns.

5.7. SOCIAL SECURITY

Your Social Security benefits are likely to be the foundation on which you build a secure retirement. Under current law, a person with average earnings will replace about 44% of their preretirement earnings with their Social Security benefits once they retire. People in upper income brackets will replace slightly less of their income with Social Security benefits, whereas the benefits received by lower income workers may replace over half of their preretirement income. Pension benefits, savings and/or other investments are required to supplement Social Security for the remainder of a retiree's postretirement income requirements.

Social Security benefits are inflation indexed and guaranteed for life. This makes these benefits extremely valuable since this portion of your postretirement income is safeguarded against both inflation and longevity risks. Do not overlook or neglect this benefit in your retirement considerations. The Social Security Administration should be mailing you an annual estimate of the monthly amount of Social Security benefits you can expect to receive at retirement. If you are not receiving this information, log onto www.ssa.gov and view your statement online. If there is a problem and your statement is not available or inaccurate, contact the Social Security Administration immediately.

Retirement benefit calculations are based on your average earnings during a lifetime of work under the Social Security system. For most retirees, the 35 highest years of your earnings are averaged. Years in which you have low earnings or no earnings may be counted to bring the total years of earnings up to 35. Your actual earnings are indexed to account for changes in average wages since the year the earnings were received. A formula is then applied to these earnings to arrive at a basic benefit, or *primary insurance amount* (PIA). This is the amount you would receive at your full retirement age. For older retirees, this is age 65. Beginning with people born in 1938 or later, however, that age will gradually increase until it reaches 67 for people born after 1959.

The benefit computations are not trivial. Simple tables or rules-of-thumb are not useful. The Social Security Administration provides a downloadable program as well as an online calculator so that you can perform your own calculations. In order to use these tools, you will need to reference your personal detailed report of your lifetime earnings from the Administration. If you do not have your most recent copy of this report, request one from Social Security. Both the program downloads and the request can be accomplished over the internet at www.ssa.gov.

When a worker dies, certain family members may be eligible for survivor's benefits if the worker had enough Social Security earnings credits. For many survivor cases, the number of required earnings credits is based on the worker's age at the time of death. Younger workers need fewer earnings credits than older workers and no worker needs more than 40 earnings credits (10 years of work) to be fully insured for any Social Security benefit.

Under appropriate circumstances, Social Security survivor's benefits can be paid to a widow/widower, an unmarried child under 18 years of age, or dependent parents over the age of 62. A former spouse can also receive benefits under the same circumstances as a widow/widower if the marriage lasted 10 years or more. Benefits paid to a surviving divorced spouse who is 60 or older will not affect the benefit rates for other survivors receiving benefits.

The amount of the survivor's benefit is based on the earnings of the person who died. The more he or she paid into Social Security, the higher the benefits will be. The amount a survivor receives is a percentage of the deceased's basic Social Security benefit.

5.8. MUTUAL FUNDS

A mutual fund is a security that provides small investors access to a well-diversified portfolio of equities, bonds, or other assets. They have become very popular in the last 20 years, with more than 80 million Americans invested in mutual funds today. Each shareholder participates in the gain or loss of the fund. The mutual fund investor can purchase or redeem shares at the end of any business day. Share prices for the fund rise and fall according to the *net asset value* (NAV) of the fund. The NAV is calculated by summing the entire value of the portfolio of securities, less any expenses and liabilities, divided by the outstanding shares.

An investor makes money from a mutual fund if the underlying securities pay dividends or interest. The fund pays out this income in the form of a distribution. Investors are usually given an option of taking distributions in the form of a check or reinvesting the distribution back into the fund. An investor also profits if the fund manager sells securities that have increased in price. This capital gain income may also be passed to the investor as a distribution. Finally, an investor can make money from a mutual fund if the fund holdings increase in price and the investor sells shares.

It is important to understand how a financial advisor or broker makes money from mutual funds. Mutual funds can be classified as front-end-load funds, no-load funds, and back-end-load funds. This discussion can be kept very simple. No-load funds are funds that do not cost you to buy or sell. No-load funds are the only type of mutual fund an investor should ever buy. Front-end loads and back-end loads are generally restrictive, with obscene commissions that severely erode your earnings. They do not help you in any way.

The primary advantage of a mutual fund is the diversification it offers. A small investor is not able to purchase 5000 different stocks, but purchase of a mutual fund that invests in this many stocks can often be done with as little as $1000 or less. Even when an investor could afford to purchase a large number of individual securities, transaction costs would be extremely high. Mutual funds enjoy the economies of scale, and are able to keep transaction fees low.

Mutual funds are not all well managed. Most *managed mutual funds* fail to outperform the market over time periods of several years or decades. The longer the period of time considered, the fewer funds there are that outperform. Investors can pay significant fees for this underperformance. Fees vary significantly from fund to fund. Mutual funds do not necessarily trade in a tax-efficient manner. Gains realized from a fund that trades often can be diminished by taxes.

Mutual funds have stated objectives, and investments are made by the fund manager to match those objectives. The fund's assets, regions of investments, and investment strategies are all specified by the objectives. This makes mutual fund investment simple. Investors who wish to add to an allocation of a specific asset class, or include a new asset class in their investment plan can almost always find a mutual fund with a stated objective to invest in that class.

There are hundreds of different kinds of mutual funds, each with slightly different objectives. Some of the kinds of stock funds an investor can choose include growth, value, blended, international, emerging market, sector, and balanced funds. The growth-versus-value distinction for stocks discussed in Section 5.2 can be applied to the stocks that comprise a mutual fund. A fund that buys only growth stocks is a growth fund. Similarly, value funds are comprised of value stocks. Blended funds invest in both growth and value stocks. International stocks are the underlying securities in international funds. Some international funds focus only on stocks from a specific region of the world—Japan or Latin America, for example. Emerging-market funds invest in developing regions of the world as opposed to industrialized nations. Sector funds invest in the stocks of a particular industry. Pharmaceuticals, telecommunications, and energy are a few examples of investment sectors that a fund could focus on. A balanced fund is a mutual fund that invests in both stocks and bonds. Mutual fund objectives often specify the size of companies that will be included, so other fund types include large-cap, mid-cap, and small-cap funds. Bond funds can similarly be classified in terms of the maturity and grade of bonds that will constitute the fund. Bond funds also specialize in international bonds or bonds from specific business sectors.

One important type of mutual fund is the *money market fund*. Money market securities are essentially very short-term bonds issued by governments, financial institutions, and large corporations. These instruments are very liquid and very safe. Safe, short-term, conservative securities naturally offer a lower return than most securities. In general, money market securities are offered only in denominations that are far too high to be purchased by individuals. The money market is also without a central trading floor or brokerage houses. An individual investor can gain access to the money market only through *money market mutual funds* or *money market bank accounts*. These instruments pool assets of individual investors in order to buy money market securities on their behalf. Money market funds offer a liquid, low-volatility parking place for money that is needed for short-term investor needs.

Mutual funds can be *actively managed* or *indexed.* An actively managed fund involves a fund manager who chooses which investments to make, when to make them, and when to sell. The fund manager attempts to pick securities and time the market. An index fund tracks the result of a target market index by purchasing securities on that index. Index funds are referred to as passive investments since buy and sell decisions are determined only by the amount of money invested in the index and the index itself. Over many years, index funds have outperformed approximately 90% of all managed mutual funds. In addition, index funds are the lowest-cost funds and among the most tax-efficient funds in the mutual fund industry. Most investors are well advised to seek no-load, low-cost index funds as described in Chapter 6, Section 6.2, Develop an Investment Plan.

5.9. EXCHANGE-TRADED FUNDS (ETFs)

Exchange-traded funds (ETFs) are relatively recent investment vehicles that offer an attractive alternative to indexed mutual funds for some investors. Like an indexed mutual fund, ETFs track either an index of the broad stock market or a bond market, stock industry sector, or international stock. They move up or down in value based on the stocks or bonds of the index they are tracking. Trading ETFs is like trading individual stocks. They are traded in real time throughout the trading day, unlike mutual funds that only settle when the market closes. When you buy an ETF, you are purchasing units of a trust that holds shares of the underlying stocks or bonds in a particular index. The ETF offers the same level of diversification that an indexed mutual fund offers.

ETFs can be tax efficient. When shareholders of a mutual fund redeem shares, the mutual fund is forced to sell underlying securities in order to pay them. These sales produce capital gains that are passed on to the remaining shareholders, creating a taxable event. ETFs do not have to sell underlying securities to meet redemptions. Shares are sold directly from one investor to another so the investor has more control over events that trigger capital gains. When an index modifies the underlying securities in it, the ETF is forced to sell securities and generate capital gains, but this will happen less frequently with an ETF than with an index fund. With ETFs, there is usually no end-of-year capital gains tax distribution as there is with mutual funds. The tax efficiency of ETFs makes them ideal for inclusion in taxable accounts.

There is no minimum purchase for ETFs. This is unlike most mutual funds that may require $1000–$3000 to open an account. Although this offers some flexibility, it may not be wise to purchase ETFs in small quantities. Purchased like stocks, you pay a brokerage commission every time you buy or sell an ETF. Larger quantity purchases are usually a more efficient way to buy through a brokerage. Once purchased, ETF fees can be lower than those for indexed mutual funds. ETFs should probably not be used when making regular small investments. The brokerage costs will be prohibitive.

ETF investments can be used to achieve an asset allocation that might not be possible through the selection of mutual funds available in one particular fund family. Investors who are happy with the service from their mutual fund company, except for the lack of a particular type of index fund, may be able to solve their asset allocation issues by purchasing ETF shares that track the same index. You can invest in ETFs today that track over 100 different indexes, including major U.S. stock indexes, bond indexes, industry sector indexes, international indexes, commodity indexes, and REIT indexes.

5.10. COMMODITIES

Commodities are an asset class that includes grain, metals, oil, electricity, beef, orange juice, pork bellies, natural gas, and other physical goods. They are most often used as inputs in the production of other goods or services. The characteristic that defines commodities is that here is little differentiation between a commodity coming from one producer and the same item from another producer. As an example, a bushel of wheat is basically the same product, regardless of the producer. This is in contrast to high-tech electronics, where the quality and features of a given product will be completely different depending on the producer.

The sale and purchase of commodities is carried out through futures contracts on specialized exchanges. Standards for quantity and quality of the commodity being traded are set by the exchange. Although participation in commodity trading has traditionally been more difficult and risky for individual investors, a number of commodity mutual funds now exist, making commodity investment much simpler.

Many financial planners and economic researchers believe adding a modest amount of commodities futures reduces the volatility of your portfolio. This belief is based on recent studies revealing a low-to-negative correlation of commodities to traditional asset classes like stocks and bonds. Commodities have offered superior returns in the past, but they also exhibit greater volatility than other asset classes. Funds dealing in commodities futures also carry high fees. This is not an asset for beginning investors.

REFERENCES AND FURTHER READING

1. Orman, S., *The Road to Wealth,* Riverhead Books, New York, 2003.
2. Mears, R. A., *Investing in Bonds,* Ohio State University FactSheet, Family and Consumer Sciences, January 2001, http://ohioline.osu.edu/mm-fact/0005.html.
3. Mears, R. A., *Investing in Stocks,* Ohio State University FactSheet, Family and Consumer Sciences, January 2001, http://ohioline.osu.edu/mm-fact/0006.html.
4. Bernstein, W., Why You Can't Afford a House in San Francisco, *Efficient Frontier,* 2005, http://www.efficientfrontier.com/ef/405/housing.htm.
5. Hevesi, D., Owning Is Hard, *New York Times,* September 11, 2005.

6. OFHEO, House Price Appreciation Continues at Robust Pace, Office of Federal Housing Enterprise Oversight, Washington, DC, March 1, 2006.

7. Burns, S., 7 Sins of Variable Annuities, *Dallas Morning News,* June 21, 2005.

8. Katt, P., Indexed Annuities: Too High a Price for Market "Protection," *AAII Journal,* volume XVIII, no. 10, November 1996, http://www.peterkatt.com/articles/aaii11.html.

9. Ameriks, J., R. Veres, and M. J. Warshawsky, Making Retirement Income Last a Lifetime, *Journal of Financial Planning,* TIAA-CREF Institute, December 2001.

10. Munnell, A., and M. Soto, How Do Pensions Affect Replacement Rates? An Issue in Brief, Center for Retirement Research, Boston College, November 2005.

11. Stevens, S., The Pros and Cons of ETFs, *Morningstar.com,* September 25, 2003, http://news.morningstar.com/article/article.asp?id=137219&_QSBPA=Y&hsection=Comm2.

12. Burns, S., ETFs Can Help Create Couch Potato Option, *The Dallas Morning News,* July 22, 2003.

ESTIMATION OF PORTFOLIO REQUIREMENTS INCLUDING SOCIAL SECURITY AND PENSION BENEFITS (EXAMPLE)

Social Security and pension benefits help to reduce the required portfolio needed to fund retirement. Consider the case of the 50-year-old engineer planning on retiring in 10 years at age 60.

1. Determine what you spend today. (See Table 3.1, downloadable Excel spreadsheets at www.golio.net , "Table of Contents and URLs," Section 3.3.) For this example, assume present average annual expenses amount to $68,000.

2. Evaluate your budget and estimate whether each category will increase, decrease, or remain constant. Revise your annual expense figure to represent your required annual budget in retirement. For this example, assume that your retirement budget requirements are reduced by $3,000 per year to $65,000. This is the amount your portfolio would need to support if you retired today. This figure needs to increase in order to match inflation each year in retirement.

3. Project your retirement budget requirements, S, forward to your retirement date. Use the formula

$$S = S_{today} \times (1 + i_{inflation})^n \tag{S5.1}$$

where S_{today} is your estimated budget requirement if you retired today (from step 2, this is $65,000), $i_{inflation}$ is the average inflation rate (use 3.5% for this example), and n is the number of years until retirement (10 for this example). Evaluation of Equation (S5.1) gives an estimated annual retirement expenses of $S = $91,689$ at retirement.

4. Modify your future retirement expense figure to account for Social Security benefits. Your modified expense figure, S', is simply the difference between your projected budget requirement, S, from step 3 and the Social Security annual

benefit, S_{ss}. Because Social Security benefits are inflation adjusted, the modification can be made directly as a cash flow requirement reduction in retirement:

$$S' = S - S_{ss} \qquad (S5.2)$$

For this example, assume projected annual Social Security benefits will start at $18,000 per year 10 years from now. Evaluation of Equation (S5.2) results in an estimated budget requirement after social security of $S' = \$73,689$. Estimated Social Security benefits can be obtained by request from The Social Security Administration or using the online calculators at http://www.ssa.gov/retire2/AnypiaApplet.html.

   5. Use the 4% rule to estimate the portfolio requirement to support the expenses calculated in Equation (S5.2):

$$P' = \frac{S'}{0.04} \qquad (S5.3)$$

For this example, $P' = \$1,842,223$. This amount would have provided inflation-adjusted income for a minimum of 30 years through the worst financial episodes in U.S. history.

   6. Compute a future lump-sum value, A', for a non-COLA pension benefit. If your pension can be taken as a lump sum, then use the estimated lump-sum value at your retirement date. If not, use your projected benefit amount in Equation (5.1) in this chapter, or one of the annuity calculators accessible at www.golio.net, Table of Contents and URLs, Section 5.4. Because the pension in this example is assumed not to have a cost-of-living adjustment, the portfolio amount, P', must be adjusted rather than the inflation-adjusted expense, S'. The 4% rule does not apply to an expense or benefit that is not inflation adjusted. For this example, assume a lump-sum pension benefit $A' = \$100,000$. You should be able to obtain an estimate of your future pension benefit from your company's Human Resources department.

   7. Modify the portfolio requirement at retirement to account for pension benefits.

$$P'' = P' - A' \qquad (S5.4)$$

Using the data of this example, the portfolio amount required at retirement would be $P'' = \$1,742,223$.

   The engineer of our example will need to amass a nest egg value comprised of 401(k) and other accounts equivalent to ~$1.74 million prior to retirement. This example does not include current or future mortgage payments, which are considered in Chapter 8.

6

YOUR INVESTMENT PLAN

Investment strategies vary significantly between individual investors. People will disagree on what to buy, when to buy, and how long to hold it. Some people follow and trade individual stocks while others prefer the stability of bonds. Mutual funds and real estate are additional asset choices considered by investors. Some investors focus on maintaining specific asset allocations (X percent stock, Y percent bond, Z percent real estate) regardless of market performance while others try to time the market (buy low, sell high). Holding times are also a distinguishing characteristic of investor strategies. Buy and hold investors tend to keep what they purchase for several decades before selling part of their holdings. Day traders may buy and sell the same stock several times in a single day.

Talking with investors about investment strategies is a lot like talking about politics or cars. A car enthusiast is likely to tell you what make of auto is best, the problems with all other makes, and that you are of inferior intelligence if you do not understand these simple facts. They may be able to speak at length in support of their world view of automobiles and automobile manufacturers. A different car enthusiast will hold another passionate view that contradicts everything you heard from the first. Conversations about investment strategies are often very similar to this.

With so many investing styles to choose from and plenty of passionate proponents and opponents of each style, how can you possibly choose the style that is best? The answer to this question depends on how "best" is defined. If you feel like the "best" strategy is the one that will guarantee maximum return in the future, you are almost certain to fail. You are more likely to succeed if you define the "best" investment style to be one that will get you to your retirement goals without causing undue stress and turmoil. Living below your means and investing regularly will likely bring financial independence and support your retirement lifestyle.

Adopting an investment style that you are not comfortable with is not likely to work for you. You may know a stock trader who does well, but if your temperament is different from the trader's, you will almost certainly buy too late, sell too early, and lose more money than you make. Similarly, many people earn significant wealth through real estate; but it is not likely to lead you to personal wealth if you do not understand the local real estate market, do not feel comfortable about putting your investment in the hands of unfamiliar renters, or feel like management and maintenance of property is unpleasant. Although many existing investment styles are extremely risky, there are examples of successful investors who employ every investment strategy. People earn money from many different investment styles, but the one that is most likely to make you a successful investor is the one you understand and feel at ease with.

If you learn to examine your investment performance honestly, over time you will learn more about investments and your own comfort level with investment risks. This knowledge will make you increasingly more effective. Honest assessment of investment mistakes, rather than rationalization, will turn them into a learning event and you into a better investor.

Evaluate investment performance in terms of decades, not months. Don't try to buy and sell based on breaking news events. Sound investment strategies do not change with the news. Markets are efficient and react or overreact instantaneously to news. An individual investor will not have time to dial a phone or boot up a computer before the market has responded. Markets, however, go up in the long run. That long-term trend is what will propel you to your goals. Forget about the erratic and unpredictable behavior that takes place over shorter periods of time.

Be skeptical of people who claim to always "beat the market." Most do not. At best, they are deluding themselves. At worst, they are lying. Most of your friends and neighbors spend too much, are loaded with debt, and do not understand their own portfolio or its performance. The advice they offer is not likely to help you achieve your goals. You have no control over the markets and your ability to predict optimum investment choices is not likely to be outstanding. Fortunately, you do not need to obtain market-beating returns in order to achieve financial independence. Controlled spending, regular investments, and time in the market are the requirements for that achievement. Steady, habitual savings and honest personal investment analysis will lead to financial independence.

6.1. ELIMINATE "BAD" DEBT

Carrying too much debt can eradicate all of the potential value of your investments. Paying interest on debt instead of investing in your future does not help accumulate a nest egg. Not all debt is "bad" debt, however. Debt might be characterized as "good" if what you are financing will (1) outlast your loan and (2) will provide additional financial value (positive leverage) to you. "Good" debt can help achieve long-term financial goals.

The most commonly misused debt is credit card debt. Carrying a credit card balance is almost always "bad" debt. Consider the case of credit card debt used to pay for an evening of fine dining. If a balance is carried beyond the initial billing, the debt clearly does not satisfy either of the conditions listed in the previous paragraph. The loan lasts longer than the meal, and no financial advantage is obtained from the debt. Many of the dangers of misused credit card debt were discussed in Chapter 3, Section 3.4.

An example of debt that is normally considered "good" debt is a house loan. A low-interest house loan satisfies both of the "good" debt requirements. The house will last longer than the mortgage, satisfying the first requirement. In fact, the value of the house is almost certain to increase. The loan also provides positive leverage, satisfying requirement two. Money not spent paying off the loan can be invested, with the potential to earn a higher rate of return than the mortgage rate. It is to your advantage to invest money at a higher rate than it costs to borrow it. At the end of the mortgage period, the investor will own the house, and will have earned enough from the invested house payoff amount to make all payments plus accumulate additional savings.

The house loan has other financial features that are also valuable to a patient investor. A fixed-rate mortgage provides significant protection against future inflation. No matter how much inflation increases, your payments remain fixed. You gain the advantage of paying for your house with less valuable, inflated dollars in the future rather than with full value dollars today. If inflation slows and interest rates drop, you can refinance to reduce your loan costs. Finally, the mortgage can be paid off at any time.

A car loan represents debt that can be "good" or "bad" depending on the specific situation. If you keep a car for longer than the terms of the loan, you can satisfy the first "good" debt condition. For example, if you tend to trade vehicles every 5 or 6 years, a 2 or 3 year loan satisfies condition 1. A 10 year loan would not. If you purchase a car to provide transportation to work, you are getting positive leverage from your financing since you will earn more than you have to pay. So a car loan can also satisfy condition 2. A car purchased for weekend recreation may not provide financial leverage.

A final example of "good" debt would be an education loan. The knowledge and credentials gained from the loan will outlast the loan period and provide positive leverage through increased salary and opportunity.

There are other interesting considerations related to the "good" debt examples just discussed. The leverage offered by a high-end sports car is no greater than that offered by an economy car. Both cars will get you to work. So the leverage applies only to the cost of basic, reliable transportation. Similarly, an expensive degree from a pedigree university may provide opportunities not available to the graduate of a less-known institution, but if those opportunities are not taken advantage of, the additional expense is not leveraged. If a home mortgage rate is higher than the expected investment returns over the life of the loan, the leverage may be lost. Even a home mortgage can be bad debt.

6.2. INVESTMENT ISSUES

Investing refers to the accumulation of some kind of asset in hope of getting future returns. Assets are anything owned that can produce future economic benefit. Securities in the form of stocks, bonds, or mutual funds are among the most common investments. Real estate and commodities are examples of other assets commonly invested in by individual investors. Each of these broad asset classes were discussed in Chapter 5. Although it is not necessary to understand every asset class, some understanding of the major asset classifications will be useful to investors.

Diversify

Most investors agree that it is wise to diversify. High diversification of an investment portfolio indicates that many dissimilar investments are included. Diversification can be quantified statistically as the intraportfolio correlation. The correlation measures the degree to which different assets in a portfolio can be expected to perform in a similar fashion. In other words, when different assets do not rise or fall at the same time, the correlation between them is low and the diversification is effective. When assets rise and fall together, the correlation is high and diversification is ineffective. The statistical formula to compute correlation is presented later in Equation (6.1) on page 126.

Diversification can be applied at many levels. Rather than own one million dollars worth of one stock, you can diversify by owning $100,000 worth of 10 different companies' stock. A $1 million investment in a stock mutual fund (which holds stock from hundreds of large companies) represents a diversification over a portfolio with 10 different stocks. Further diversification is achieved by investing $500,000 in a broad stock mutual fund and $500,000 in a broad bond fund. The stock and bond funds can be further diversified to include other classes of stocks and bonds. Each of these cases represents a $1 million portfolio. The same stock that was held in the first portfolio could be a part of all of the portfolios described, but with each diversification, the impact of that stock on the overall portfolio is diminished. The most diverse portfolio will not rise as rapidly if the company stock soars, but it also will not suffer as much if the company stock plummets.

Every financial market in America has experienced significant setbacks, and there is no shortage of examples in recent history. In 1994, bonds had their worst year in several decades. Commodity prices plummeted in 1997, 1998, and 2001. Stocks tumbled dramatically in 2000. Each of these markets have also performed better than expectations in recent history. Stock market returns in the late 1990s were record breaking. Bond holders celebrated outstanding returns from 2001 through 2004. Commodities surpassed all expectations in 2005. An investor who bought into these assets during poor performance years and sold during peak performance years would be doing very well today. Such a feat, however, requires that the investor predict which asset is about to change, the optimum time to buy, and the optimum time to sell. These three predictions must all be correct for an investor to achieve maximum profit. In addition, the predictions must be made prior to the market coming to the same conclusions. Once the market agrees with the predictions, prices will quickly adjust and eliminate the individual investor's advantage. Since most investors will get at least one of the three predictions wrong, or anticipate the performance too late, market timing tends to result in subaverage performance. The alternative to trying to place all of your money into the next hot market is to diversify your investments among several asset classes. By maintaining some money in several markets, you increase your odds of gaining some advantage when a market gets hot while reducing the risk when a market declines.

Stocks and bonds tend to move independently of each other. Sometimes, stock returns may be up while bond returns are down, and vice versa. When combined, these offsetting movements help to reduce overall portfolio risk. Figure 6.1 presents an example of how simple diversification into two asset classes (stocks and bonds) would have worked for a 1929 retiree. The 1929 starting date for retirement is chosen because it represents a time just prior to the catastrophic stock meltdown that started the Great Depression. The figure considers an all-stock portfolio comprised of the S&P500 index, an all-bond portfolio comprised of a corporate bond index, and a diversified portfolio consisting of 50% S&P500 and 50% corporate bonds. At the end of each year, the diversified portfolio is assumed to be rebalanced to adjust the portfolio to start each new year with a 50/50 split between stocks and bonds. A relatively diverse assortment of 500 stocks comprise the S&P500. The corporate bond index is a similar diverse selection of corporate bonds. Figure 6.1 presents the average annual rate of return for the retiree 10, 20, and 30 years into retirement. Although stocks have always performed better over the long term, the diversified portfolio provided much less volatility in the early years and performed as well as the

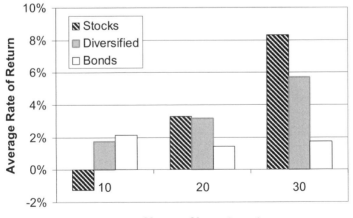

Figure 6.1. Illustration of how very simple diversification produced steadier returns for a 1929 retiree. The figure presents average annual return for three investment allocations: (1) Stocks (S&P500), (2) Bonds (commercial paper index), (3) Diversified (50% S&P500, 50% commercial paper). The results are given 10, 20, and 30 years after the initial investment.

all-stock portfolio for over 19 years. Although a January 1929 retiree and a September 1929 retiree would have slightly different experiences, the long-term story does not change significantly based on month of retirement. Diversification and rebalancing reduce volatility, even under extreme financial conditions.

Further diversification can provide even greater stability, but how you diversify is also important. The National Association of Personal Financial Advisors (NAPFA) presents a more complex diversification study. They considered 11 distinct asset classes and monitored the performance of each class for 15 years (1987–2002). The asset classes (and associated tracking indexes) included in their study are:

- Small-cap growth stocks (Russell 2000 Growth)
- Small-cap value stocks (Russell 2000 Value)
- Small-cap stocks (Russell 2000)
- Mid-cap growth stocks (Russell MidCap Growth)
- Mid-cap value stocks (Russell MidCap Value)
- Mid-cap stocks (Russell MidCap)
- Large-cap stocks (S&P500)
- International stocks (MSCI EAFE)
- Bonds (Lehman Brothers Aggregate Bond)
- Large-cap growth stocks (S&P/BARRA Growth)
- Large-cap value stocks (S&P/BARRA Value)

Three investment strategies were considered. The first strategy chased last year's hottest market sector. For this strategy, $10,000 was used each year to purchase the index that exhibited the highest performance in the previous year. The second strategy took the opposite approach. Each year $10,000 was invested in the index that exhibited the worst performance in the previous year. The third strategy allocated a $10,000 annual investment evenly across all eleven asset classes.

Table 6.1 presents the final portfolio values for the three investment cases. The investor who chased performance by investing in the previous year's top performing market segment would have finished the period with a portfolio worth a total of $310,064. The contrarian investor, who would have invested in the prior year's worst performing market, would have earned $292,390. The investor who diversi-

Table 6.1. Final portfolio value for three investment styles after 15 years. The study assumed that $10,000 was contributed to each portfolio each year.

	Prior year's best asset class	Prior year's worst asset class	Diversified portfolio
Final portfolio value after 15 years	$310,064	$292,390	$402,562

From the National Association of Personal Financial Advisors, http://www.napfa.org/consumer/index.asp.

fied evenly across the entire range of asset classes would have beaten them both, finishing the period with $402,562, approximately 30% and 40% greater than the other two investment strategists.

All three of the investment strategies used in this study are a form of diversification. Five of the 11 funds in the NAPFA study ranked as the worst annual performers during at least one of the 15 years of the study. Several ranked worst more than once. The bottom annual performers included Russell 2000 Growth, Lehman Brothers Aggregate Bond, MSCI EAFE, S&P500/BARA Growth, and Russell 2000 Value. The strategy that purchased last year's worst performer ended up with these five different securities in the portfolio at the end of the period. Six of the NAPFA study funds ranked at the top during at least one of the 15 years of the study. The top-ranked annual funds included all five of the funds listed as worst performers, plus the Russell MidCap Growth fund. The strategy that purchased last year's best performer ended up with six different securities in the portfolio at the end of the period, five of which were identical to those in the previous strategy. The diversified portfolio never exhibited annual returns that ranked higher than the fourth best fund return over the entire time of the study and never ranked lower than the eighth. Use of broad diversification resulted in both superior performance and greater stability when compared to market picking strategies.

Fees Matter

Investment fees can have considerable impact on your investment performance and your retirement lifestyle. They can be as critical to your financial success as inflation, risk, timing, or many other issues. Investors are often ignorant of the fee structure employed by their investment advisor or agent. It is a costly mistake to be ill-informed about expenses that accompany every potential investment decision. Fees and other investment costs diminish your income and erode your principal.

Whether you buy after-tax mutual funds, individual stocks, or tax-advantaged funds through your employer, you pay fees to someone.

When purchasing individual stocks, the *brokerage fee* or *commission cost* is specified when you make a purchase or sale. Brokerage fees may be a fixed amount per trade, or based on a percentage of the sale price. Besides the brokerage fee, there is a *bid/ask trading spread* that can be a significant cost. The bid/ask spread is the difference between the bid and offer price in a stock deal. The spread varies significantly among various stocks, from pennies to over a dollar per share. An individual investor buying a small-company stock can wind up with higher bid/ask costs than commissions. If you trade small amounts of stocks and bonds, or you trade often, trading fees can consume your returns.

Trading individual bonds involves similar costs to those involved in trading individual stocks. With bonds, however, the brokerage fees may be hidden in the price of the bond. Bonds are often sold out of an inventory that the brokerage holds. The sales spread is the difference between what you pay and what you can sell the bond for, and the commissions come from this difference. There are regulations that limit the sales spreads brokerage firms can apply to bond trades, but not all brokerages are the same. It pays to shop.

Costs for mutual funds and 401(k) plans are less visible to the investor investigating fund accounting statements. Mutual funds and 401(k) plans include administrative fees, investment management fees, and distribution and marketing fees. As an investor, the itemization of these fees may be less important to you than understanding the total fund costs. A metric used to calibrate total fund management expenses is the *expense ratio*. It is expressed as a percentage. The ratio is calculated by dividing a fund's annual operating expenses by its average annual assets. For example, a fund that holds $100 million in assets with $1 million in operating expenses would have an expense ratio of 1%. Typical fund expense ratios vary from as low as 0.1% to over 3.0%. That is more than a 30:1 variation in expense ratio. This number should matter to you because studies show that expense ratios are the best predictor of future performance available to investors. Fees are a better indicator of future long-term performance than turnover ratios, asset size, manager tenure, past performance, or any risk/volatility measurement. Over the long run, funds with high fees tend to underperform, whereas funds with low fees outperform. It really is that simple.

Figure 6.2 illustrates the effect fees have on portfolio value in retirement. The figure assumes that a retiree begins retirement with a portfolio worth $1 million. Annual return is assumed to be 5%. The retiree is assumed to withdraw 4% of the overall portfolio value each year for living expenses. Fees are expressed as an ex-

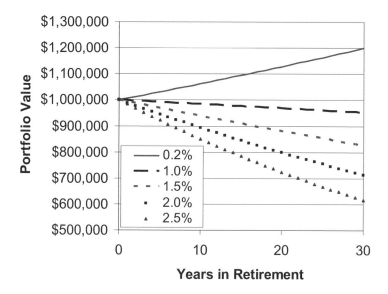

Figure 6.2. The impact fees have on portfolio value in retirement. The figure assumes an initial portfolio of $1 million, a 5% annual return, and a 4% annual withdrawal. Cases shown include expense ratios of 0.2%, 1.0%, 1.5%, 2.0%, and 2.5%.

pense ratio. The figure illustrates the fact that fees can be the difference between a retirement that rises with inflation and a retirement of diminishing lifestyle.

There are examples of mutual funds with above-average fees that have performed well over a period of time. But as the time period increases, the number of funds that are able to overcome high fees decreases dramatically.

When looking to optimize your portfolio performance, a good place to begin is to buy funds with the lowest fees. These are often broadly diversified index funds. If you choose to trade individual securities, searching for a low-cost brokerage house is a good starting point.

Timing Markets and Picking Stocks

People who speculate on the future direction of securities in order to achieve superior returns are engaging in *market timing*. In order to be successful at this strategy, market timers must identify market moves before they occur, and before the rest of the market also identifies them. Achieving this result requires superior information, rapid analysis, and fast action. With today's technology, it is very difficult for an individual to get information faster than everyone else.

Numerous studies have produced an overwhelming amount of evidence that most investors experience no advantage when they attempt to time markets or select individual equities. Stock picking and market timing is ineffective, expensive, tax inefficient, and unnecessary for the vast majority of investors. Most individual stock pickers also incur higher levels of risk than mutual fund buy-and-hold investors. There are times when people may get lucky and guess right, but over the long haul, the markets are efficient and the average investor does not beat them. There are no enchanted investments. Surges in popularity drive prices up, but panic often brings them down just as quickly. Unless your timing is impeccable repeatedly, you are more likely to lose than to gain.

Many studies reveal a second important result: although evaluation of their portfolios reveals that they have achieved poor performance, most individual investors believe they have achieved superior performance.

If you choose to invest in individual equities and time the market, you will need to understand your own emotions in order to avoid impulse buying or panic selling. It is also important to not hold equity positions for too long. Whatever technique is used to establish your buy-and-sell decisions, an honest evaluation of your performance is essential. That evaluation needs to include the fees and tax implications of your trading. Superior returns can be eroded by high trading costs and taxes on short-term gains.

Risk Versus Return

Your investments are at risk. Regardless of how you have chosen to save (stocks, bonds, commodities, annuities, houses, or buried in a jar in the backyard) there is a chance you could lose all or part of your investment. The underlying principle that drives investment results is that there is a direct relationship between risk and return. Greater investment risk brings greater potential returns. The underlying cause for this relationship is that investors expect to be compensated for taking on additional risk. A U.S. Treasury bond, for example, provides lower return than a corporate bond. The reason for the difference in returns is that the risk of a corporation going bankrupt is higher than the risk of the U.S. government going bankrupt. The corporation has to pay a higher rate than the government to entice investors to buy their bonds rather than U.S. government bonds.

Bankruptcy is only one kind of risk that investors experience. Other specific kinds of risk can be considered for an individual or portfolio of securities. *Price risk* or *market risk* is a risk that most investors are aware of. It is the risk that the value of the investment will decline in the future. *Event risk* is the risk that unforeseen events associated with the company will affect the price of its equities. Surprise announcements of a major reorganization or bond buybacks are examples of event risk. *Liquidity risk* comes from the lack of marketability of an investment when it cannot be bought or sold quickly. *Political risk* is the risk that a country or state will suddenly alter policies in a way that affects the companies. *Reinvestment risk* and *inflation risk* are normally associated with bonds. Inflation risk is the risk that inflation will outstrip your investment return, leaving you with less buying power than you started with. Reinvestment risk is the threat that when future proceeds are distributed, they will have to be reinvested at a lower interest rate.

All of the specific types of risk listed in the preceding paragraph can be broadly categorized either as *systematic risk* or *unsystematic risk,* depending, respectively, on whether the risk affects the entire market or only a portion of it. Diversification is useful to reduce unsystematic risk, but not systematic risk. An investor must learn to live with systematic risk.

Financial gurus have developed a number of simple numerical metrics designed to measure risk. *Beta* is the most commonly used risk measurement. Volatility of a particular security or portfolio can be quantified relative to the market using beta or the *beta coefficient.* It is calculated using regression analysis. By definition, the market has a beta of 1.0, and individual securities produce beta values according to their deviation from the market. A security that exhibits greater volatility than the market has a beta above 1.0. A security that moves less than the market has a beta less than 1.0. High-beta stocks are riskier but provide a potential for higher returns; low-beta stocks or bonds exhibit less volatility but also lower returns.

Other mathematically derived quantities used to estimate risk include *standard deviation, Sharpe ratio (CAPM), alpha,* and *variance.* All of these metrics quantify the past volatility of securities rather than estimate future risk; but the risk profile of companies can change significantly in a short period of time. Past volatility is not always a good indicator of future volatility. Risk also comes in more forms than volatility, and an investor must be concerned about all risk. The mathematical calculations have some value to financial and economic researchers when they develop theories on volatility and market performance. Coupled with additional knowledge, they can also help provide a qualitative appreciation for one kind of investor risk. The metrics have both technical and practical limitations, however, and these limitations seriously reduce their usefulness to individual investors interested in developing an appropriate investment strategy. Since risk and return are directly correlated, the question facing investors is, "What level of risk am I willing to live with in order to achieve higher returns?" Although a comparison of beta coefficients may indicate that one portfolio is in a different risk–return situation than a second one, the numerical value of beta does not indicate an investor's comfort level.

It is hard for investors to understand risk and its effect on comfort until they actually experience significant declines in their portfolios. Risk tolerance before a market decline is like courage before a battle. Until it is tested, it is difficult to distinguish someone who is brave from someone merely showing bravado. Establishing your appetite for risk involves gauging the potential impact of a major loss on both your portfolio and psyche. During the 1990s while stocks soared, many investors believed that they were comfortable holding portfolios with relatively high market risk and correspondingly high values of beta. When the S&P500 index plummeted more than 46% between August 2000 and September 2002, many investors were forced to recalibrate their personal risk comfort level. Knowing the value of the beta coefficient for their portfolio was not an indication of what they would feel like when they lost much of their net worth in a short period of time.

Although high beta portfolios may not be acceptable to some investors, minimizing numerical risk (as ranked by beta coefficient) is not an acceptable solution either. Make one kind of risk disappear and another kind will replace it. You can reduce the beta coefficient of your portfolio dramatically by placing all of your money in FDIC-insured Certificates of Deposit. You will eliminate market risk, but replace it with inflation risk. Unfortunately, market risk eradication is possible only if you are willing to accept deterioration of your purchasing power. This undesirable tradeoff is one more reason for investors to diversify.

Longevity Risk

A danger for retirees is that they outlive their portfolios. If you retire too soon, underestimate your longevity, or fail to adopt an appropriate spending model, you can run out of money before you run out of life. Economists refer to this as *longevity risk.*

According to the U.S. Internal Revenue Service, there is a 50% chance that a 65 year old in the United States will live for 22 more years, but there is also a 1% chance that the 65 year old will live for more than 40 years (see Chapter 1, Figure 1.6). This range in potential longevity corresponds to a significant difference in safe withdrawal rate. Historical simulators described in Chapter 2 (see Figure 2.13) indicate that survival of a portfolio for a 40 year retirement requires an annual budget reduction of more than 20% when compared to a safe budget for a 22 year retirement.

Social Security benefits and corporate pensions provide some insurance against longevity risk since these benefits are guaranteed for life, regardless of how long you live. For the worker with inadequate pension and Social Security benefits to meet their needs, additional strategies must be employed to guarantee portfolio survival for an indefinite period of time. One method to insure against longevity risk is simply to build a large enough nest egg to endure even if you live a very long life. Building the additional savings will require more time on the job and/or a higher savings rate, but it can provide adequate insurance against longevity risk. An alternative approach to accomplish longevity risk insurance is to convert part of your savings into an income stream by purchasing an annuity. Annuity benefits, like pensions and Social Security, are guaranteed for life. This provides further mitigation of longevity risk, but at a price. Annuities are expensive relative to other investments. Investors must pay for the security of an income stream guaranteed for life. When you buy an annuity, you are paying someone else to take on risk that you do not want to bear. If you have confidence in your investment strategies, it may be cheaper to simply increase your investments. You certainly do not want to pay for more risk insurance than you absolutely need. A second negative feature of annuities is that if you die early, the annuity company is the one that profits, not your heirs or favorite charities. For additional fees, annuity benefits can be guaranteed for the life of you or your spouse, whichever is longer. Although the annuity option can be expensive, it may provide anxiety reduction for some investors that make it worth the cost.

Investment Correlations

Effective diversification requires more than simply buying many different securities. In an ideally diversified portfolio, when one asset declines another advances. Buying multiple stocks or mutual funds that rise and fall at the same time does little to diminish volatility. The best selection of securities will increase returns while reducing risk.

The statistical measure of how two securities have moved in relation to each other is the *correlation coefficient.* The correlation coefficient between two sequences of n measurements can be calculated from the formula

$$r_{xy} = \frac{n\Sigma x_i y_i - \Sigma x_i \Sigma y_i}{\sqrt{n\Sigma x_i^2 - (\Sigma x_i)^2}\sqrt{n\Sigma y_i^2 - (y_i)^2}} \tag{6.1}$$

where x_i and y_i represent the data in the two sequences. Correlation coefficient calculations are also built-in functions for most spreadsheets and financial software. The value of r_{xy} as computed by Equation (6.1) ranges between -1 and $+1$. Perfect positive correlation ($+1$) implies that as one security moves, the other moves in an identical fashion. In contrast, perfect negative correlation (-1) means that if one security moves, the other moves in an equal but opposite direction. A correlation coefficient of zero implies that the movement of one security is random with respect to the other. In practice, securities tend to have some degree of correlation. Two securities with a correlation coefficient value of 0.95 are considered to have very high correlation, whereas values less than about 0.5 are typical of securities with weak correlation.

Although correlation coefficients can be computed between any two securities, this effort is of limited value. Correlations shift over time. The exact numerical value of the correlation coefficient that applied over the past several years may not be a good indicator of the correlations that will exist over the next several. It is more important to understand broad, long-term patterns in the returns of different asset classes. Between 1926 and the present, broad stock and bond indexes, for example, have exhibited correlation coefficients that ranged from about –0.4 to over 0.5. Despite the large swing in the value of the correlation coefficient, we can still conclude that stocks and bonds are weakly correlated. A mix of these two asset classes in a portfolio helps reduce volatility. Correlations between many other asset classes appear to be inherently unstable. Choosing which assets to include in your portfolio based solely on correlation coefficient is not advisable.

Asset Allocation

Choosing an appropriate mix of assets is far more important to your portfolio's performance than the specific securities you trade or when you trade them. *Asset allocation* is an investment strategy that establishes and maintains a target mix of investments in different asset classes. For example, a simple asset allocation target might be to hold 60% stock investments and 40% bond investments. A more detailed asset allocation plan might include 20% U.S. large-cap value stocks, 20% U.S. mid-cap value stocks, 20% international stocks, 20% short-term bonds, and 20% I bonds. Once targets are established, securities are purchased consistent with the asset allocation strategy. Periodic rebalancing of the portfolio is required in order to maintain the target asset mix. When practiced effectively, asset allocation dramatically reduces volatility as well as many underperformance issues related to market timing errors. Studies of the investment practices of large pension plans indicate that over a 10 year period, asset allocation accounts for over 94% of a plan's returns. Investment selection and timing account for less than 6% of a fund's results. These results can be applied to an individual investor's investment practices. It makes sense to devote time and energy to the development of an asset allocation strategy.

Asset allocation targets should vary slightly according to your age. As you age, your investment horizon changes to match your life expectancy and some modification of your asset allocation strategy is reasonable. For example, when you reach age 80, it probably makes sense to reduce your exposure to investments that exhibit short-term volatility. Many investment advisors offer a simple formula to compute a stock/bond asset allocation target appropriate to your age. The recommended stock allocation is given by

$$S_{\text{allocation}} = [T - A] \, (\%) \tag{6.2}$$

Where A is your age in years and T is a value determined by your own risk profile. For relatively aggressive investors, T might be 110, whereas for more conservative investors, T might be 90. Choosing the value of T is a decision based on an individual's personal level of comfort with risk. Bond allocation is then determined from

$$B_{\text{allocation}} = [100 - S_{\text{allocation}}] \, (\%) \tag{6.3}$$

Some shift in target allocation is appropriate as you age, but if you redefine your asset allocation targets each time you learn about a new asset class, you will lose many of the advantages offered by an asset allocation strategy.

A practical problem with developing an asset allocation strategy is that an investor needs to establish asset targets at the beginning of their investment career. Unfortunately, by definition new investors are less knowledgeable and lacking in investment experience than long-time investors. This is equivalent to asking the youngest engineer in the company to write the specification for a major system development program. As investors learn more about investments and as new investment vehicles become available, it seems foolish to maintain an allocation plan that was developed before many investment issues were understood. A new investor could adopt an asset allocation plan developed by a financial advisor or recommended in a book or article. The investor needs to be aware that when it comes to allocation plans, one size does not fit all. You should understand why each asset class is in the allocation plan, and make sure it is right for you. A more reasonable approach to the development of a new asset allocation plan is to begin with a simple strategy that considers only stock/bond/cash allocation. Then, as the investor learns more about stock asset classes (value–growth, cap size, etc.) the initial allocation can be further subdivided. Similarly, the bond allocation can be subdivided into bond asset classes (quality, maturity time frame, etc.). If asset classes such as real estate or commodities are to be added, the new asset class target investment levels can be increased gradually over a period of years.

Develop an Investment Plan

Before selecting your investments, it is advisable to develop a retirement savings strategy. Decide on more general goals for your final allocations. You must decide which markets to invest in, how much to invest in each, and whether to invest in individual stocks, bonds, and assets or mutual funds and REITs. A well-planned strategy also takes into account time horizon, tolerance for risk, amount of assets available for investment, and planned future contributions. Investors should have a clear sense of what they want to accomplish and the amount of volatility they are willing to bear. Once these general targets are established, you can begin to select specific investments.

If you have an investment plan that provides adequate performance and risk within your comfort range, then stick with it. If your plan is rudderless or leaves you uncomfortable, then develop a plan you understand and begin to shuffle your investments to match your plan. Guidelines for developing a basic asset allocation investment plan are presented in the rest of this section.

A rational investment plan with a time horizon of a decade or more will lead to some investment in the stock market. A plan without stock investments is likely to exhibit significant inflation risk. Developing a diversified portfolio of low-cost, indexed mutual funds is one of the best and easiest ways to achieve a fair return on stocks. Remember, it is time in the stock market, not stock picks or timing of your trades, that builds wealth. Standard & Poor's performs regular evaluation of S&P

indices versus active funds. These reports repeatedly show the same results: over periods as short as 1 to 5 years, indices outperform the majority of active funds. The number of active funds that outperform the indices diminishes with increasing periods of time. Buy a market-indexed mutual fund and spend your time more productively than combing through financial reports of companies looking for the next great pick. The returns of the market do a great job building wealth over a decade or two. As a well-paid technical professional, you do not have to beat the market. Let the market work for you. Accept the market return and you are likely to achieve your goals sooner and safer than any "beat the market" strategy.

Unless you are very young and have nerves of steel, you will also want to include fixed-income investments (bonds) as part of your investment plan. Diversification into bonds provides reduced volatility when compared to an all-stock portfolio. Many recent research studies indicate that the safest diversification choice for a bond component of a balanced portfolio is high-quality, short-term bonds or a short-term bond fund. Use of longer-term bonds has historically resulted in less return and greater volatility.

Using Equations (6.2) and (6.3) in conjunction with the stock and bond strategies outlined in the previous paragraphs will produce a simple portfolio that has performed outstandingly throughout U.S. financial history. Consider the case of a 40 year old who is comfortable with moderate risk. Using $T = 100$ in Equation (6.2), the 40 year old determines that a stock allocation of 60% is appropriate. A simple but effective investment plan is established by using 60% of investment funds to purchase a single, low-cost S&P500 index mutual fund and 40% to purchase a low-cost, short-term bond fund. This investment plan is also consistent with the portfolios that the historical simulators of Chapter 2 analyze. Thus, the safe withdrawal rates obtained from those simulators apply directly to this portfolio.

Since most technical professionals contribute some of their investment dollars through their employer's 401(k) or 403(b) plans, they often have limited choices for investment options. For someone without access to an S&P500 index fund, the asset allocation can be accomplished using one or more other funds to approximate the S&P500. Broader stock market index funds like Total Stock Market funds can also be substituted for the S&P500 index. The goal should be to achieve a set of investments that represents much of the stock market. Most employer tax-deferred investment plans will offer a choice of some broad stock funds and some bond funds.

One limitation of the S&P500 is that it underrepresents small-cap stocks. By splitting the stock allocation in half, a second-order allocation plan with three components is achieved. The new allocation includes 30% S&P500 index, 30% small-cap index, and 40% short-term bond. Introduction of small-cap stocks in the allocation provides greater long-term returns but also introduces greater volatility. The small-cap fund can be partially replaced by a REIT investment. REIT returns have been weakly correlated to S&P500 returns in recent years, but tend to exhibit less volatility than small-cap funds.

Further sophistication of the allocation plan can be added by differentiating between value and growth funds. Both the large-cap and small-cap portions of the stock investment can be further split to include large-cap value and small-cap value funds to complement the S&P500 fund and general small-cap fund. The additional weighting of value stocks in the stock portion of the portfolio has historically both decreased volatility and increased return. The resulting third-order allocation plan includes as many as six components: 15% S&P500 index, 15% large-cap value fund, 15% small-cap index, 15% small-cap value fund, 20% short-term bond, and 20% REIT.

The process of sudividing asset classes to refine an asset allocation plan can include international stocks and/or bonds, commodities, or any other asset class that an investor feels should be added. Before adding an asset class, you should understand what that asset is, the cost of owning it (fees), the risk it brings to your portfolio, and how it may correlate with the other assets in your plan. Adding asset classes without this basic understanding can hurt rather than help your investment portfolio. The number of assets in an investment plan is not an indication of sophistication. If you do not understand an investment, do not buy it. An investor who maintains the simple first-order stock/bond allocation has historically outperformed most other investors. This is often done with as few as two market-tracking index funds. Assuming that the future is like the past, you can outperform more than 80% of your fellow investors over the next several decades by investing in two index funds, and doing nothing else.[17] The simple stock/bond allocation plan, when coupled with a reasonable spending model and regular saving, will get you to a comfortable retirement.

Once you are within 5 to 7 years of retirement, you might also consider using a portion of your bond investment to develop a *bond ladder.* A bond ladder is a strategy for managing bond income by dividing a portion of your bond investment dollars evenly among bonds that mature at regular intervals (once every 6 months for 5 years, for example). The bond ladder provides consistent returns, low risk, and continuous liquidity. This can be very valuable to a retiree who wants to avoid having to sell other securities during a down market. Maturing bonds postpone the need to sell other investments for the length of the bond ladder while still guaranteeing an income stream.

Mechanics of Rebalancing

After initial design of an asset allocation plan, divergent performance of the asset classes will cause the asset mix to become out of balance. If stocks outperform bonds for several years in a row, the original 60/40 allocation can become a 70/30 allocation. Although there is nothing inherently wrong with the new mix, it does carry significantly more volatility risk than the original 60/40 mix. If the rationale for the original investment plan was to manage risk/return results, the new portfolio fails.

Periodic rebalancing offers a way to return the portfolio to an acceptable risk/return state. For example, if you have a target allocation of 60% in stocks but strong performance in the markets has left you with more than 70% in stocks, reduce your stock position by redirecting proceeds to portions of your portfolio that are below target. The *rebalance premium* is discussed in the financial literature. Mathematical derivations for the functional description of the premium have been published. Qualitatively, the argument is made that rebalancing is inherently a "buy low, sell high" strategy. You are a net buyer when an asset has underperformed and a net seller when a market outperforms. History tells a different story. Table 6.2 presents the results of historical simulation of the 30 year performance of a single investment split 50/50 between the S&P500 index and short-term treasuries. In one case, the investments were left alone to accrue in their separate accounts for 30 years. In the second case, the portfolio was rebalanced to achieve a 50/50 allocation at the end of each year. The two investment strategies were examined for 102 thirty year periods beginning in 1871. Starting dates of the thirty year sequences were spaced one year apart, the last sequence beginning in 1973. Historically, the unbalanced portfolio would have achieved greater returns than the balanced portfolio in 60% of the 30 year sequences. The average terminal value achieved by the unbalanced portfolio was more than 10% higher than that achieved using a rebalancing scheme. Although this example illustrates that rebalancing does not generally provide a return premium, it does reduce volatility and risk. The standard deviation in the terminal values of the 102 thirty year sequences is reduced by more than 25% by using rebalancing. It is also worth noting that at the end of the 30 year sequences, the average unbalanced portfolio is comprised of more than 78% stock, significantly more risky than the 50% stock allocation of the balanced portfolio.

Rebalancing can be done on a regular schedule or based on balances exceeding variation limits from their targets. When done on a schedule, studies indicate that rebalancing more often than once a year is not beneficial. Rebalance periodicity of between 1 and 3 years provides adequate risk reduction for most investors. Alternatively, rebalancing can be done when allocations deviate 5% to 10% from the ideal. During the accumulation phase of your investment career, it may not be necessary to rebalance at all. If you begin with a balanced portfolio and simply direct new investments to keep your portfolio in balance, redirecting funds may be unnecessary.

Financial Advisors Are Not Your Friends

Some people may feel that this statement is harsh or unfair, but it is a simple statement of fact. Friends are people who do you favors and help you in time of need. They do not take a portion of your money in exchange for following their advice. Do not confuse a financial advisor for your friend. You do not have any friends on

Table 6.2. Results of historical simulations of a 30 year investment. In one case, equal amounts are placed into an S&P500 fund and in a short-term treasury fund, and then left untouched for 30 years. In the second case, the identical initial investments are made, but the portfolio is rebalanced to achieve a 50/50 allocation at the end of each year. The average terminal value and standard deviation are given in multiples of the original investment. The simulation considers over 130 different starting years.

	Unbalanced portfolio	Annually rebalanced portfolio	Rebalance premium
Average terminal value after 30 years	9.57	8.45	−10.10%
Standard Deviation of terminal value	5.11	3.83	25.13%

Wall Street. Brokers and financial advisors work for themselves, not for you. You want to make money, but so do they. The more they make, the less is left for you. A broker gets a handsome commission when you trade and there is nothing like the prospect of a big bonus check to distort recommendations.

Your portfolio performance is driven primarily by your saving rate, your asset allocation, and time in the market. Personal values and frugal living drive your saving rate. Asset allocation is a matter of establishing your personal risk–return comfort level. Time marches onward for all of us. This leaves little or no reason to diminish your returns through commissions to an "investment expert."

Monthly Investing and Dollar Cost Averaging (DCA)

Developing disciplined investment habits is important if you want to develop a retirement portfolio. There is no investment advice that is a substitute for saving money. You should direct the first dollars from your paycheck to your investment portfolio. Budget the rest of your spending based on what remains after you have invested in your long-term goals.

Dollar cost averaging (DCA) is one way to implement regular investing habits. DCA means investing a fixed amount at fixed intervals of time. The typical interval is the length of your pay period. It is a sensible approach to regular investing. For the individual investor, the discipline demanded by DCA is its greatest benefit. DCA is also good for reducing the stress that comes from needing to make a decision every paycheck. Applying a DCA strategy makes you less tempted to make decisions based on short-term phenomena. Instead of trying to time the market in response to greed or fear, invest in an installment plan, knowing that the long-term trends in the market will cause your portfolio to grow.

Financial advisors often claim that DCA strategies also offer investment advantages because investing a fixed amount periodically tends to buy more shares when the price is low and less when the price is high. As appealing as that theory is, it is a myth. If you had a lump sum to invest, DCA investing would not improve your odds of achieving higher performance; it would reduce them. DCA investing of a lump sum will reduce risk, but the risk–reward continuum applies to investment timing the same way that it applies to investment returns. When you have money to invest (whether from a recent paycheck or from a windfall) your odds of achieving higher returns are increased if you invest the entire sum immediately. The reason DCA of a lump sum does not improve performance is because the market's upward bias is so strong that it is more likely that market prices will be favorable at some point in the future than it is that they will be unfavorable. Regardless of how you measure it, the market has more periods of increase than periods of decline, and the increases are likely to be of greater magnitude than the declines.

6.3. TAX-ADVANTAGED ACCOUNTS AND FREE MONEY

The government wants you to save money, and to encourage that behavior, they offer to defer taxes on certain kinds of accounts designed for retirement savings.

Tax-deferred accounts offer an economic bonus to investors who are willing to invest money when they are young and keep it invested until they reach retirement age.

By investing in special tax-advantaged accounts, an investor benefits in several ways. Tax-free growth is one important advantage. Instead of paying tax on the returns of an investment, tax is paid only at a later date. Without the tax-deferred status, the amount of money earning returns each year is reduced by taxation, and growth is impeded. Tax deferral means the money that would have been used to pay taxes is participating in investment growth. Mathematically, the one-year portfolio growth rate is given by

$$R_{\text{annual}} = r(1 - r_{\text{tax}}) \tag{6.4}$$

where r is the pretax rate of return and r_{tax} is the tax rate for the individual. As an example of the value of tax-deferred saving, Equation (6.4) indicates that a 7% pretax return becomes a 5% after-tax return for a person paying at a 28% tax rate.

A second advantage of these accounts is that investments are usually made when a person is in their peak earning years and, therefore, are taxed at a higher tax rate. Withdrawals are made from an investment account when a person is retired, earning limited income, and are taxed at a lower rate. Figure 6.3 illustrates

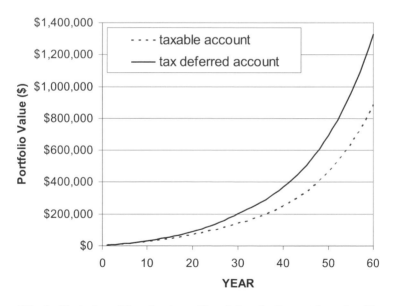

Figure 6.3. An illustration of the advantage of tax-deferred retirement investing. The example assumes a $2000-per-year investment for 30 years (preretirement) followed by a $2000-per-year withdrawal for 30 years (postretirement). For the taxable account, earnings during preretirement are taxed at 28%, earnings during postretirement are taxed at 18%, and withdrawals are untaxed. For the tax-deferred account, earnings are not taxed during preretirement, but withdrawals are taxed at 18% during postretirement.

the tax-deferral advantage of a hypothesized $2000 per year investment for 30 years, followed by a $2000 per year withdrawal for 30 years. The net investment after 60 years is $0, so the final portfolio values represent the earnings advantage of a tax-deferred retirement account. An annual rate of return on investments of 7% is assumed for both curves. The dashed curve represents a taxable account. Annual earnings are assumed to be taxed at 28% for the first 30 years (preretirement) then at 18% for the next 30 (postretirement). Withdrawals are not taxed for the dashed curve. The solid curve represents a tax-deferred account. Earnings are not taxed during the preretirement period. During the postretirement period, withdrawals are taxed at 18%. At the end of the 60 year period, the tax-deferred advantage has produced a portfolio that is more than 50% larger than one produced by the taxable-savings approach.

A final advantage of most tax-deferred retirement accounts is that they are accorded a protected property status. Under the Employee Retirement Income Security Act of 1974 (ERISA), tax-qualified retirement plans are exempt from creditors, except for some minor exceptions. Nearly all 401(k)s have complete protection from creditors under ERISA, no matter how much money is in the plan. Recent state laws as well as federal court decisions accord similar protection for most other retirement accounts.

401(k)s, 403(b)s, and 457 Plans

There are three common employer-sponsored, tax-deferred retirement plans: 401(k), 403(b), and 457 plans. Each plan is named after the section of the United States Internal Revenue Code that defines them. All of these plans are referred to as *defined contribution* plans to distinguish them from *defined benefit* plans such as pensions. Many technical professionals working in industry, education, or government are eligible to participate in one of these plans sponsored by their employer. A 401(k) allows a private-sector corporate worker to save for retirement while deferring income taxes on the saved money and earnings until the money is withdrawn. The employer acts as a plan fiduciary and is responsible for designing the plan, selecting the investment choices and monitoring the investments. This responsibility is usually outsourced to an investment or insurance company that actually runs the plan. A 403(b) plan is very similar to the 401(k) but is used to cover workers in educational institutions, churches, public hospitals, and nonprofit organizations. Similarly, a 457 plan is the tax-deferred equivalent to the 401(k) that covers employees of state and local governments.

Participants in a deferred plan elect to have a portion of their wages paid directly into the deferred account. This feature of defined contribution plans is very compatible with a DCA investment strategy. The investment options typically include an assortment of mutual funds that focus on stocks, bonds, money markets or a combination of these. Corporate 401(k) plans sometimes offer the option to purchase company stock. Employee pretax contributions are capped. The maximum annual contribution through salary deferral is $15,000 for the year 2006. For future years, the limit will be indexed for inflation, increasing in increments of $500. Special "catch-up" contributions of up to $5000 for employees over 50 are allowed and will also be inflation adjusted for future years.

Because the funds are meant to be retirement savings, there are restrictions to how withdrawals can be made. Unlimited withdrawals can be made after age 59½. With a 401(k), penalty free withdrawals can begin as early as age 55 *provided you do not terminate your employment earlier than the year in which you turn that age.* If you retire at age 53, for example, you could not begin penalty-free withdrawals until age 59½. There are allowable exceptions to the minimum-age, penalty-free distribution rules. One important exception that allows you to begin making early withdrawals from a retirement account is the 72(t) exception (named after another IRS paragraph). Withdrawals consistent with 72(t) rules can be exercised at any age by first executing a rollover of your tax-deferred account into an individual IRA, then following the guidelines for 72(t) withdrawals. These guidelines are presented in more detail in Section 8.3.

An employee who leaves a job can choose to maintain the 401(k) account for the rest of his or her life, but must begin to withdraw funds beginning at age 70½ or before. The departing employee can alternatively choose to roll the 401(k) account into a self-directed IRA at an independent financial institution or into another 401(k) account hosted by his or her new employer.

The 403(b) plans, also known as *tax-sheltered annuities,* are available to educational and nonprofit employees. These plans are very similar to 401(k) plans in terms of their tax treatment, but there are some significant differences related to withdrawal options prior to age 59½. A 10% penalty applies to early withdrawals unless the employee qualifies for an exception. Under many plans, termination of employment is an exception, so the employee can retire at any time and may have unlimited access to his or her 403(b) funds. Nonpenalized withdrawals are taxed as ordinary income.

Like the 401(k) and 403(b) accounts, 457 plans accrue tax-deferred interest. Unlike these other accounts, no 10% penalty applies for withdrawal prior to age 59½. Withdrawals are taxed as ordinary income.

Laws governing maximum contributions, withdrawal limitations, and tax treatment of deferred savings accounts have been changed in the past and will likely be changed in the future. There are also restrictions placed on these accounts specific to the plan sponsor. Organizations will all offer a different selection of investment options through their tax-deferred plan. For these reasons, employees need to research the options available to them and evaluate how these plans fit into their overall investment plan. Although each organization's plan is unique, tax-deferred plans are usually efficient ways to save for your future. In most cases, investors are best served by maximizing their employer-sponsored defined contribution plan before contributing to other accounts. This may not always be the case, but tax-deferral advantages should not be overlooked.

Company Matching (Free Money)

In order to encourage employees to save for their future, some companies match employee contributions to their defined contribution plan up to some level. The company pays extra money into the employee's 401(k) account as an incentive to save more money for retirement. Typically this money is paid as a match for employee dollars that are directed into the tax-deferred account up to some fixed percentage of the employee's salary. If the company match is a dollar-for-dollar match of up to 5% of the employee's salary, for example, this is equivalent to getting a 5% tax-deferred raise. An employee who fails to take advantage of such plans is truly passing up an opportunity for free money.

Some companies have restrictions to the "free money" 401(k) match that the employee needs to be aware of. Most plans vest over several years as an inducement for the employee to stay with the employer. Under such a vesting plan, the matching portion of the plan may not be available to the employee for the first year of employment. The portion of the match that is available increases each year until all of the matching funds are included. Some companies provide matching only in the form of company stock. As an investor, this may not be compatible with your ideal investment plan. Company stock may be more volatile and less valuable than the investments you would normally choose for your portfolio. Long-time employees may find that a very large portion of their portfolio is comprised of stock from a single company that they might otherwise never have purchased. However, the way to look at company matching is that it is free money. Regardless of how the stock rises or falls, it is still more valuable than no matching funds at all.

IRAs

Individual Retirement Accounts (IRAs) provide tax-advantaged investing for many taxpayers not covered by an employer-sponsored plan. IRAs can also be used to advantage by some taxpayers to augment their existing employer-defined contribution plans. There are a number of different types of IRAs. Table 6.3 presents a summary of IRA features for the various types of IRAs.

Traditional IRAs allow a taxpayer to contribute 100% of compensation up to a specified maximum dollar amount to their accounts. If you are 50 or older by the end of the tax year, you may also contribute an additional amount of catch-up contribution. Contributions may be tax-deductible depending on your adjusted gross income, tax-filing status, and coverage by an employer-sponsored plan. Withdrawals

Table 6.3. Features that distinguish various types of IRAs

Type of IRA	Contributor	Contributions	Transaction within account	Withdrawals
Roth	Taxpayer	After-tax dollars	Tax-free	Tax-free
Traditional	Taxpayer	Pretax dollars	Tax-free	Taxed as income
SEP	Employer	Pretax dollars	Tax-free	Taxed as income
Simple	Taxpayer and employer	Pretax dollars	Tax-free	Taxed as income

from a traditional IRA are treated as ordinary income. If your income is less in retirement, however, it may provide you the opportunity to be taxed at a lower rate.
With a traditional IRA, you must begin to take *Required Minimum Distributions*
(RMDs) from your account by April 1 of the year following the year you reach age
70½. This means you must reduce your IRA balance and add the distributed amount
to your income, even if you are not in need of the funds. Table 6.4 presents the IRA
contribution limits according to current law.

Contribution can also be made on behalf of a nonworking spouse. A spousal IRA
is subject to the same limitations as stated in Table 6.4 and must be held in a separate account. In order to contribute to spousal IRA, you and your spouse must file a
joint income tax return. All contributions to an IRA must be made prior to April 15.

If a household is covered by one or more employer-sponsored retirement plans,
the taxpayer's contributions to a traditional IRA may not be entirely deductible. In
2006, deductions are phased out for adjusted gross income (AGI) between $75,000
and $85,000 for taxpayers filing jointly. Taxpayers in that filing category earning less
than $75,000 can deduct all of their IRA contributions. Taxpayers earning more than
$85,000 cannot deduct IRA contributions. This phase-out limit will increase in 2007.

The phase-out range for a taxpayer filing single, head of household, or married
filing separately (and not living with spouse) is between $50,000 and $60,000. For
taxpayers in the married filing separately category (living with spouse), the phase-
out AGI range is between $0 and $10,000.

The Roth IRA works differently from the traditional IRA but has the same contribution limits as those presented in Table 6.4. Contributions are never tax-
deductible. They are made from earned income that has already been taxed. However, withdrawals are federal-income-tax-free. As in the case of traditional IRAs,
transactions inside the account incur no tax liability. You may contribute to a Roth
IRA at any age, even after you reach age 70½. Eligibility for a Roth IRA is limited
by AGI and tax filing status. For those filing jointly, Roth eligibility is restricted to
those with AGI less than $160,000. For single, head of household, married filing
separately (not living with spouse) filers, Roth eligibility is limited to those with
AGI less than $110,000. An AGI limitation of $100,000 applies to married filing
separate taxpayers living with their spouses. Roth IRA owners are never subjected
to RMD rules.

Table 6.4. IRA contribution limits

Tax year	Regular contribution limit	Over 50 catch-up contribution limit
2006	$4000	$1000
2007	$4000	$1000
2008	$5000	$1000
2009	$5000	$1000
>2009	$5000 indexed to inflation in $500 increments	$1000

If you qualify and your tax rate during retirement will not be lower than your current tax rate, the Roth IRA is probably a better choice than a traditional IRA. The Roth allows you to pay the taxes now, and receive tax-free distributions when your income tax rate is higher. If your AGI is too high to qualify for a Roth account or your tax rate will be lower during retirement, then the Traditional IRA may be a better choice. The traditional IRA is valuable if you are eligible to receive a tax deduction now when your tax rate is higher. If you are eligible to contribute to both types of IRAs, you might want to diversify by dividing your contributions between a Roth and Traditional IRA. This strategy is a hedge against unknown future tax rates, but could be costly since you will have to pay fees for two separate accounts.

When Roth IRAs were created, rules and regulations were established to allow traditional IRA owners to roll over funds into a Roth IRA account. The rules that determine rollover eligibility are the same as those for eligibility to make Roth IRA contributions. Since Roth IRA contributions must be made with after-tax dollars, an IRA conversion incurs ordinary income taxes for the rollover funds. The rollover decision depends on a number of factors including tax rates today, estimated tax rates in the future, taxes due from the converted dollars, and the size of your estate. Depending on your specific situation, rollovers can help reduce or eliminate tax on your Social Security benefits, reduce the estate tax burden on your heirs, or avoid required withdrawals at age 70½. The factors affecting a rollover decision can be complex. Specific details regarding IRAs and IRA conversions are found in IRS Publication 590.

IRA funds are protected by law. The United States Supreme Court ruled unanimously in 2005 that a debtor in bankruptcy can exempt his or her IRA from the bankruptcy estate, providing significant protection to money held in IRA accounts. Over half the states had already placed laws in effect to provide this protection for IRA funds, but the Supreme Court decision provides federal protection for IRAs.

Health Savings Accounts

Health Savings Accounts (HSAs) provide one investment alternative for those who have to pay for their own healthcare in retirement. The HSA is a special kind of bank account designed to help you build tax-free savings for healthcare throughout your lifetime. The account allows you or your employer to place money in an investment account through tax-free payroll deductions. The account earns money tax-free and can be used tax-free for expenses approved by the IRS. HSA accounts are portable. If you change jobs or locations, your account goes with you. After you retire, you can spend HSA money tax-free on eligible healthcare expenses such as prescription drugs, doctor's visits, and nursing home care. You do not have to spend the money each year. Unused dollars stay in your account. IRS-approved expenses include doctor and dentist visits, eye exams, hearing aids, prescription drugs, physical therapy, chiropractic expenses, and most other out-of-pocket medical expenses.

There are restrictions to who can use an HSA. Contributions to an HSA can only be made if you have a high deductible health plan consistent with specific IRS guidelines. If you are covered by other insurance that pays for medical services, you are not eligible to contribute to one of these plans. Those enrolled for Medicare benefits are not eligible to put money into an HSA (although you can collect previously contributed HSA funds). Finally, the amount you can contribute to an HSA is limited.

529 Plans (Saving for College)

The government will help you save for your family's education. See the discussion on Funding College in Chapter 4, Section 4.3.

6.4. TAXABLE INVESTMENTS

Saving inside of tax-deferred investment instruments like 401(k)s and IRAs has many advantages, but the amount you can invest in these accounts each year is limited by law. If you want to save more than the maximum limits allow, you will need to find other, taxable ways to invest. Depending on your investment plan and the options available through your employer's defined contribution plan, you may decide that your best options involve some taxable investments. The alternatives for this type of investing include mutual funds purchased directly through a mutual fund company, securities purchased through a broker, real estate purchased directly or through an agent, and treasuries bought directly from the U.S. Treasury.

A plethora of mutual funds and fund companies exist to address every need of the typical individual investor. There are actually more mutual funds than there are individual stocks in existence today. Mutual fund companies make it easy for an individual investor to establish an account of one or more funds that they manage. Typically, mutual fund houses allow investors to rebalance investment dollars between funds without charge.

Not all mutual funds are well managed and many are very expensive (high fees). When purchasing actively managed mutual funds, investors should evaluate and compare the fund's fees and tax efficiency. Mutual funds are evaluated and compared to benchmarks by Morningstar, an investment research firm that enjoys an excellent reputation for its fund information. Facts about fees, tax efficiency, past performance, and other useful information can be found there. Additional mutual fund issues are discussed in Chapter 5, Section 5.9.

If you choose to invest in individual stocks, you will need to establish a brokerage account employing a stockbroker or brokerage firm. Stockbrokers and brokerage firms charge a fee or commission for executing buy and sell orders submitted by an investor. A brokerage firm can also serve as your agent in the purchase of bonds, mutual funds, and preferred stock. In some cases, however, using a broker adds little value while adding to the cost through commissions and fees. Full-service brokerage firms charge significant fees for executing trades and providing investment advice. Investors should keep in mind that their full-service broker gets paid when they trade, regardless of the value of that trade to the investor. This makes a broker's advice highly suspicious. If you are curious about whether your broker is working to help you, try asking some simple questions: "What was the return on my brokerage account during the past year, past 5 years etc.?"; "How does that return compare to the S&P500 index?"; and "How much did I pay in commissions and fees as a percent of my account balance?" Good luck getting answers.

The internet has led to a proliferation of *discount brokers* who provide trading services for much smaller fees than full-service brokers. Discount brokers do not provide personalized advice. For investors intent on investing in individual stocks and who are comfortable doing their own research and making their own decisions, discount brokerage firms make sense.

Real estate represents another kind of investment that can be done outside of tax-deferred plans. The easiest way for individual investors to invest in real estate is through REITs. A REIT is a security that sells like a stock on the major stock market exchanges. They receive special tax considerations and often offer high yields. Unlike a stock, the REIT invests in real estate either by buying property or holding mortgages. Because REITs are traded like stocks, they can be purchased either through a mutual fund company or through a stockbroker. REIT investments are more liquid than actual property. These investments were discussed in more detail in Chapter 5.

Some investors prefer owning actual property to investment in other kinds of "paper" securities. Real estate investments that generate income (through rent) are considered investment properties. These kinds of properties include apartment buildings and rental houses. Rental properties also tend to appreciate in value and produce capital gains when the real estate investor eventually sells the property. In an escalating market, some real estate investors make money with a "fix 'n' flip" strategy. Homes or buildings that require some repairs or remodeling are purchased below market value, rapidly fixed up, and then sold at a much higher price.

Rental property requires management and maintenance. From mowing the lawn to unclogging plugged toilets, property maintenance requires effort. This is either done by the real estate investor or by a management company. Property purchase and sales usually require working with a licensed real estate agent. Successful real estate investors either develop a close relationship with an agent or become licensed and represent themselves. Use of property management organizations or real estate agents is a cost that must be accounted for in evaluating real estate deals. Property ownership can be lucrative, but it is not a passive investment like stock or bond ownership, and broad diversification is not possible for the small investor. This means property ownership carries significant risk.

Treasury Bills, Treasury Notes, Treasury Bonds, and Treasury Inflation-Protected Securities (TIPS) can be purchased directly from the U.S. Treasury Department. Investors can establish a TreasuryDirect online account and submit bids to purchase these securities. Account holders are able to purchase and hold savings bonds and marketable securities in a single online account with 24 hour access. There is no fee for this service. Purchase is made according to your account instructions. Bids to purchase securities are accepted automatically and funds are directly withdrawn from the financial institution established by the account. Interest and maturity payments are deposited automatically in your designated financial institution accounts.

If your investment plans include any U.S. Treasury investments, direct purchase through the department is the most efficient and convenient way to invest.

6.5. HOUSE—PURCHASE OR RENT?

Choosing to rent or buy affects your investment plan in several ways and should be considered as part of your investment strategy. If you choose to buy a home, you are likely to be taking on significant debt and regular monthly payments. Those payments are buying equity in property that is likely to appreciate in value and provide benefit in the future. You are also receiving preferential tax treatment for those payments. If you choose to rent, you are likely to reduce your monthly burden, but the money you spend is not buying any future value and you are not receiving any tax breaks on your payments.

The rent-versus-buy decision is almost always more about lifestyle choice than financial considerations. People often become passionate about their decision that one option is better than the other. Both from a financial and an emotional perspective, however, either decision can be better than the other. The best choice depends on the locality of the residence, timing of the purchase/rent decision, length of time the residence will be occupied, and priorities of the individual.

In some cities and regions of the country, purchase prices of houses are low and a shortage of rental properties places rental rates as high as or higher than mortgage payments. In addition, house prices may be climbing in these same areas. If you move to one of these areas, buying is likely to be the best financial decision. At the same time, soaring housing prices in many parts of the country have made renting a bargain. In these areas, renting can be financially advantageous. A few years from now, the housing/rental markets may be different in these areas.

Buying a house involves some fixed costs including real estate agent fees, inspection fees, document preparation fees, finance fees, and title fees. The number of people who have to be paid in order for you to complete a house purchase is staggering. In order to benefit from home ownership, you need to stay in the house long enough for the property value appreciation to exceed the fixed costs of buying and selling. In periods of rapid growth of a local real estate market, that time can be as short as a year. There are also cities that have experienced long-term declines in property value for more than a decade. From a financial perspective, rent/buy decisions, timing, and time of ownership are all locally determined.

Lifestyle preferences are as important as the financial aspect is to the rent/buy decision. Given enough time, home purchase is almost always financially advantageous. Having a mortgage ends up being preferable to paying rent, but if you move frequently and do not own a lot of things, renting often makes more sense and is cheaper than buying. If you would have trouble finding time to perform regular home and lawn maintenance, or to track down and hire appropriate services, you may not enjoy home ownership. Conversely, many people never feel settled and comfortable in someone else's property. For them, home ownership is a requirement to "feel at home" and caring for their property is a joy. Condominium ownership offers a hybrid of advantages and disadvantages that might also make sense for some people. It is important to consider what types of properties are available for rent and purchase in your area. If a one-room efficiency is plenty of home for you, it may be difficult to find equivalent property to consider for purchase. On the other hand, if you require a four-bedroom home with land, you may find the rental selection very limited. In the end, these lifestyle choices are often more important to the rent/buy decision than careful analysis of local housing markets and rental offerings.

6.6. MORTGAGE PAYOFF DECISION

The U.S. Census Bureau estimates that nearly 70% of American families own their own home. Eventually, most technical professionals will own a home. That home is likely to represent the largest purchase they will ever make, and the associated mortgage the largest debt they will ever incur. It is an important part of their overall investment strategy, but when it comes to mortgage payments, emotion often trumps reason. Many people do not feel comfortable with a mortgage debt. They feel less secure with a mortgage debt, and are determined to pay it off as soon as possible. At every opportunity they accelerate their payments to eliminate this debt.

If you just can't sleep at night because of mortgage worries, then paying it off is exactly the right thing to do. No analysis is likely to change your feelings about this decision. It is perfectly fine to pay off a mortgage early if doing so brings you satisfaction and comfort. If this is the case, skip the rest of this section and do what you know will make you most comfortable.

Keeping a low-interest, long-term mortgage can increase the value and reduce the risk of your retirement portfolio. Homeowners who see mortgage prepayment as a safety net could in fact be taking a risk by limiting their financial flexibility. A mortgage provides the opportunity for you to leverage a low-interest debt by placing the loan balance into long-term investments. If you can earn a better average return on your investments than the mortgage rate, you will increase the survivability of your portfolio by keeping your mortgage. You will also reduce your longevity risk. The results of a mortgage-versus-payoff analysis will depend on the years remaining on the loan, tax situation of the homeowner, investment allocations, and the mortgage rate of the loan.

You can use mortgage rate calculators to estimate the target earning rate you will need to beat a payoff option. Because loan interest is deductible, the effective loan payment, a_{eff}, is lower than the formal payment, a_{formal}, by an amount equivalent to the interest payment, i, multiplied by your income tax rate, r_{tax}:

$$a_{\text{eff}} = a_{\text{formal}} - i \times r_{\text{tax}} \tag{6.5}$$

For a conventional fixed-interest loan, the interest payment will change each year of the loan. In early years, nearly the entire loan payment is interest. For someone in a 28% tax bracket, in the early years of a 6.5% mortgage the effective mortgage rate is approximately 4.1%. This rate increases over the life of the loan to an annual rate of 6.4% in year 30. Over the entire loan period, the effective loan rate will be less than 5.3%. Over the duration of the mortgage, the odds of achieving greater investment return than 5.3% are very high. For example, in the past 130 years, only once has the stock market returned less than 5.3% per year on a 30 year investment.

The estimates of the preceding paragraph assume that the homeowner is able to benefit from itemizing their taxes throughout the loan period. This may not apply for people with low taxable retirement income. Also, mortgage payments increase the required portfolio withdrawal each year. If those withdrawals are taxable, keeping a mortgage can increase taxes. For most technical professionals, these issues are second-order effects, but each case is different.

Although none of us can predict the future or what our returns will be over the next three decades, we can use historical simulators to review the probability that various investment strategies in the past would have paid off. Historical simulation can provide much more detailed information about mortgage payoff decisions.

Figure 6.4 illustrates the historical probability of beating the mortgage payoff option using a $100,000 30 year loan invested in a 50% stock, 50% bond portfolio. The probability of benefiting financially from investing the loan amount rather than paying off the mortgage is plotted against the total annual payments, which include mortgage payments plus the tax implications of the loan. In the absence of income taxes, a $6000-per-year payment corresponds to a 4.4% loan and an $8000-per-year payment corresponds to a 7% loan. For mortgage payments in this range, there has

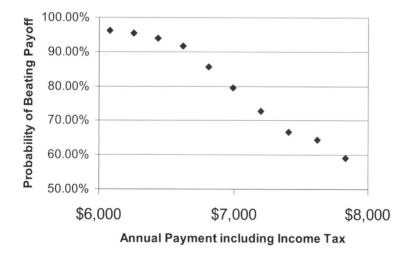

Figure 6.4. Historical probability of beating home payoff option using a $100,000 30 year loan with a 50% stock, 50% bond portfolio. The x-axis represents the total cost of the loan payments plus the income tax implication of making payments. In the absence of income taxes, $6000 per year payment on a $100,000 30 year fixed interest loan corresponds to a 4.4% loan and $8000 per year corresponds to a 7% loan.

historically been more risk to the homeowner choosing to pay off the mortgage than to the mortgage holder.

A common misconception about this analysis is that keeping a mortgage places you at risk of losing your home. A failure to outperform the payoff decision does not imply the loss of your house. When the mortgage decision does not lead to financial advantage, it simply means that the house will cost more than it would have cost had you paid it off at the beginning of the loan period. The converse statement is also true. Home payoff is more expensive than keeping a mortgage when the mortgage simulation predicts success. Nothing prevents the mortgage holder from paying off the mortgage at any time, thus locking in any gains or losses associated with the mortgage leverage strategy.

Another misconception about paying off a mortgage is that home ownership is without risk. When you pay down a mortgage, you are investing in your home and not diversifying into other alternatives. If your neighborhood declines, property values could dip or fail to keep up with inflation. You end up owning more of a declining asset and less of other assets. Also, if you need money after you have spent yours on your home, you might have to resort to taking out a home equity loan at higher interest rates.

Further use of historical simulation indicates that mortgage-leveraged portfolios can often survive bad economic times better than smaller portfolios of investors who have chosen to pay off their low-interest, long-term loans. The reason for this result is fairly easy to understand. Worst-case portfolio survival occurs when poor returns are realized in the early years of retirement. Any strategy that helps you to recover rapidly and solidly in the improved performance years that follow poor returns will increase the probability of survival. The mortgage option accomplishes this by maximizing the nest egg that is invested in the market when economic recovery occurs.

6.7. TAXES

A good investment plan considers the tax efficiency of your investments. Like it or not, the tax code affects your portfolio. If you overlook the tax consequences of your investment choices, the amount of money available to spend on yourself will be reduced. In the quest to establish a tax-efficient portfolio, some balance is required. An investor's first objective should be to make good investment decisions. It is not unusual for an investor to become so focused on avoiding taxes that they reduce their returns. Paying capital gains tax on an appreciated stock may not be attractive, but holding an overvalued stock too long may lead to a much less desirable collapse of the stock value. Tax advantages or disadvantages must be weighed against your investment objectives, tolerance for risk, and investment time horizon. Never let an obsession with avoiding taxes drive your investment strategy.

Investments trigger tax events of four important types: (1) payment of interest, (2) payment of dividends, (3) earning short-term capital gains, and (4) earning long-term capital gains. Interest is taxed as ordinary income. Under a law passed in 2003, dividends are taxed at a 15% rate for most individual taxpayers. Dividends received by low-income individuals are taxed at a 5% rate until December 31, 2007 and become fully untaxed in 2008. A long-term capital gain is the difference between the price that an asset sells for and what was paid for it, provided the asset was held for over one year. Long-term capital gains are taxed at a lower rate than ordinary income under current tax laws. When assets are held for a year or less, their sale produces short-term capital gains, which are taxed at a higher rate. Tax rates on the various types of income have been changed dramatically during the past decade and are likely to be changed again. This is one reason why investors should be cautious about over tax-engineering their portfolios. The rules may change at any time.

Some investments are better suited for tax-deferred accounts and some are better suited for taxable accounts. For example, bond and money market funds return virtually all their gains as interest. This type of earning is taxed at the relatively high ordinary income tax rate. As a result, bond and money market funds are inefficient investment vehicles for taxable accounts. They are better suited for tax-deferred accounts. Most individual bonds are also well-suited for tax-deferred holdings. Conversely, growth stocks and stock mutual funds tend to produce a very small amount of ordinary income. These holdings work well in a taxable account.

Mutual fund tax events are triggered when a fund manager sells holdings. A manager who trades often will incur more taxes than a buy-and-hold manager. On average, managed mutual funds buy and sell each holding more than once per year. This type of trading not only produces a large number of tax events, but many of these trades will produce short-term capital gains with the associated high tax rates. Since index funds rarely adjust their holdings, they tend to be very tax efficient. Morningstar has recently begun computing a "tax efficiency ratio" for mutual funds. The ratio represents the percentage of the fund's pretax return that an investor is able to keep after taxes. Fund ratings vary from 60% to 100%. This can significantly reduce the value of a mutual fund holding from that expected by looking only at pretax returns.

Municipal bonds (munis) and tax-managed mutual funds are two types of investments designed to limit taxable income. The income from municipal bonds is not subject to federal taxes and usually is not taxed by the state where they are issued. Although these investments can sometimes be used effectively by investors in high tax brackets seeking reduced portfolio volatility, there is no reason to own tax-managed funds or municipal bonds in a tax-deferred account. Even when municipal bonds are held in taxable accounts and produce no taxable events, the return may not justify the reduced tax for many investors. Paying a little tax on a large return may be preferable to paying no tax on a small return. The optimum decision will depend on the investor's tax bracket, risk tolerance, and time horizon.

As mentioned in Section 6.3, the benefits of tax-deferred accounts are substantial. Not only do these accounts defer tax payments, but they also provide an additional benefit of trading flexibility. An investor does not need to be concerned with the tax implications of a trade decision when the traded funds are inside a tax-deferred account. Short-term capital gains, for example, never apply to trades within a tax-deferred account.

Even greater tax advantage is realized from tax-free accounts such as education and health savings accounts. No tax is owed on the ordinary income from investments in these accounts. No capital gains tax is owed if you realize a profit when you trade investments in this account. No tax is owed on any accumulated investment earnings when you withdraw for the stated purpose of the account. The limitation of these accounts is that the money can only be spent on qualified expenses.

Investors can sometimes improve their tax situation by employing a liquidation strategy that uses investment losses as taxable account assets. If you are selling an investment that has appreciated significantly in value, you can offset gains by selling investments that have dropped in value. This can represent significant savings in taxes. You can claim only up to $3000 in capital losses in any given year, but you do not lose the value of the losses beyond that figure. The IRS allows losses to be carried forward on your tax returns indefinitely.

REFERENCES AND FURTHER READING

1. Fuerbringer, J., The Long-Term Lesson: It Pays to Diversify, *New York Times,* 28 August, 2005, http://www.nytimes.com/2005/08/28/business/yourmoney/28portfolios.html?th=&emc=th&pagewanted=print.

2. Farrell, P. B., Twelve Steps to Investment Peace, *Wall Street Journal,* 24 April, 2005, http://online.wsj.com/public/article/0,,SB111428448981715157,00.html?mod=sunday%5Fjournal%5Fprimary%5Fhs.

3. Guyton, J., Decision Rules and Portfolio Management for Retirees: Is the "Safe" Initial Withdrawal Rate Too Safe? *Journal of Financial Planning,* October 2004.

4. Whitehead, B., Good Debt vs. Bad Debt, Alliance of Cambridge Advisors, 2003, http://www.cambridgeadvisors.com/consumer/resources/articles/web/goodbaddebt/.

5. Burns, S., Account Managers Cost You, *The Dallas Morning News,* Monday June 6, 2005.

6. Bernstein, W., *The Four Pillars of Investing,* McGraw-Hill, New York, 2002.

7. Farrell, P. B., Are Fund Expenses Too High?, *MarketWatch,* July 31, 2005, http://www.marketwatch.com/news/story.asp?guid={b51087f0-4eb5-4d7d-b208-b38309e01620}&siteid=mktw&dist=SignInArchive&archive=true&param=archive&garden=&minisite=.

8. Wiles, R., Performance Chase, *Registered Representative Magazine,* October 1, 1997.

9. Erdoes, C., and J. H. Low, Investing as a Matter of Style, *Experience,* Summer, 1997.

10. Burns, S., Risk is Inevitable—Unless You're Rich, *The Dallas Morning News,* Thursday, February 17, 2005.

11. Merriman, P., The Ultimate Buy-and-Hold Strategy, *FundAdvice.com,* 2003, http://www.fundadvice.com/fehtml/bhstrategies/0108/0108a.html.

12. Benartzi, S., and R. Thaler, Naïve Diversification Strategies in Defined Contribution Saving Plans, *The American Economic Review,* pp. 79–98, March 2001.

13. DALBAR Financial Services, "DALBAR Issues 2001 Update to Quantitative Analysis of Investor Behavior" Report: More Proof that Market Timing Doesn't Work for the Majority of Investors, Boston, MA, June 21, 2001, http://www.dalbarinc.com/content/printerfriendly.asp?page=2001062100.

14. Barber, B. M., and T. Odean, Trading Is Hazardous to Your Wealth: The Common Stock

Investment Performance of Individual Investors, *The Journal of Finance,* Vol. LV, No. 2, April 2000.

15. Clements, J., Twenty Tips for No-Nonsense Investing, *Wall Street Journal Online,* February 19, 2006, http://online.wsj.com/public/article_print/SB114031062160177956.html.

16. Pane, R., and S. Dash, Standard & Poor's Indices Versus Active Funds Scorecard (SPIVA), www.standardandpoors.com.

17. Perry, A., Mortgage Payoff Attracts Heated Debate, *TheStreet.com,* August 23, 2004, http://biz.yahoo.com/ts/040823/10179250_2.html.

18. Hulbert, M., Buy and Hold? Sure, but Don't Forget the "Hold," *The New York Times,* July 2, 2006.

COMPUTING INDIVIDUAL INVESTOR RETURNS

Studies of individual investor's results indicate that most investors dramatically overestimate their portfolio returns. Investors tend to recall their best holdings but fail to account for underperforming investments. Individual investors also tend to make mistakes in calculating their personal performance results. The average investor obtains a far inferior performance compared to the performance of the funds. A common mistake investors make when evaluating performance is to assume that their personal performance is identical to the annual performance of their holdings. Although this may be true if no deposits or withdrawals have been added to their holdings during the performance period, an individual often experiences very different rates of return from the returns of their underlying holdings. A stock or mutual fund that rises 40% between January and June, and then loses 20% from July to December finishes the year with a 12% gain:

$$p \times (1 + 0.4) \times (1 - 0.2) = p \times 1.12 = p + 12\%$$

Based on the outstanding performance of the first 6 months, an investor may buy the security in July. This investor experiences a 20% loss. Even if the investor had $100 in the holding on January 1 and added another $100 on July 1, the personal holdings at the end of the year are only $192, a loss of $8:

$$\begin{array}{r} \$100 \times (1 + 0.40) \times (1 - 0.20) = \$112 \\ + \ \$100 \times (1 - 0.20) = \$080 \\ \hline \$192 \end{array}$$

Another mistake investors often make when calculating personal performance is to consider their deposits to be gains. The change in net worth an investor experiences over a year comes from a combination of gains and investment deposits. During the accumulation stage of your life, you should be making deposits into your investment accounts on a regular basis, but do not confuse those deposits with gains. The investor of the example in the preceding paragraph who held $100 on January 1 and $192 on December 31 did not earn a return of 92%. An annual rate of return for this investor is –24%. Twelve percent was earned for the year on the original $100 investment, and 20% was lost in only 6 months on the July investment for an annualized investment loss of 36%:

$$r_1 = (1 + 0.12) = +12\%$$
$$\underline{r_2 = (1 - 0.2) \times (1 - 0.20) = -36\%}$$
$$-24\%$$

The combined annual rate of return for both investments is –24%.

Further Reading

DALBAR Financial Services, "DALBAR Issues 2001 Update to Quantitative Analysis of Investor Behavior" Report: More Proof that Market Timing Doesn't Work for the Majority of Investors, Boston, MA, June 21, 2001, http://www.dalbarinc.com/content/printerfriendly.asp?page=2001062100.

7

WHAT WILL I DO WHEN I RETIRE?

Retirement offers choices. You can choose recreation, leisure, self-improvement, learning, or travel. You can choose to work part-time or start a new career. If you change your mind, retirement offers you the freedom to choose something else. Ideally, more choices bring excitement and anticipation to your life. New possibilities generate great potential.

Some retirees are not enthusiastic about retirement possibilities. They focus on what they are giving up rather than on their choices and opportunities. To some, a job provides not just money but lifestyle, self-image, purpose, and friendships. A job can also be a means of personal fulfillment and creative expression. On retirement, these people feel fear and upheaval rather than excitement and possibilities.

In order to achieve a successful transition into retirement, it is important to develop a personal plan for spending your time and energy. The personal plan is not a financial plan, but a plan based on personal goals and the time you will spend pursuing them. You should explore as many choices and possibilities as you can. Spending time developing a list of interests that you want to explore is time well spent. Your plan should consider any aspects of your work you believe you will miss. It will be important to find a replacement for these needs. Try to envision your retirement day schedule as you pursue your new possibilities. Expand that vision to your retirement week, month, and year. If there are gaps that need filling, reexamine your list of possibilities. If there is too little time, you may want to prioritize your list and focus initially on a smaller number.

Only after you have developed a reasonable personal plan for spending your time and energy should you consider the financial side of the plan. Is your retirement budget compatible with your retirement plan? This can be a problem if your vision of retirement includes expensive items. If you want to travel the world in

© 2007 Institute of Electrical and Electronics Engineers, Inc.

first-class accommodations or golf every day at exclusive country clubs, your retirement budget must include these expenses. Even if your first plan is a little bit too high-maintenance for your budget, a few substitutions and low-cost alternatives usually result in a realignment of the two.

Much of this chapter is devoted to the exploration of retirement possibilities and discussions on how to pursue them. Later sections examine retirement plans that involve part-time work, travel, volunteer work, and recreation. The lists and discussions of retirement possibilities is far from exhaustive, but provides a starting point for the development of your own personal plan. Reading this chapter is not going to magically compel you to "get a life," but it may remind you of interesting and rewarding activities you have not had time to pursue.

Even when people are dissatisfied with their job, they often find some form of fulfillment from it. That fulfillment can be difficult to replace in retirement. As you consider retirement options, it is important for you to understand what motivates you today. By identifying these motivators, it will be easier to find retirement activities that are even more rewarding than an objectionable job.

The most common motivators people gain from their jobs relate to self-worth or self-improvement. Many people enjoy feeling creative. They like feeling that they make a difference and feel good when they find solutions to problems. Intellectual stimulation contributes to their own feelings of accomplishment. In retirement, new activities need to replace work to provide this fulfillment. As you develop a retirement plan, consider how the activities you choose might satisfy your need to improve yourself and feel valuable. One possible replacement activity is to develop a hobby that cultivates your creativity. Such hobbies include everything from painting and cooking to metalworking and cabinet making. It is easy to transform almost any interest into a hobby with a significant creative component. Many volunteer activities also require you to learn and exercise new skills. If self-worth and self-improvement are important drivers for you, then approach each retirement activity with an eye toward creative expression and learning.

Friendship and interactions with other people is a second important motivator that many find in the workplace. Many people value friendship highly and gain satisfaction from feeling that they "belong." They enjoy camaraderie with colleagues even if the most common shared experience is complaining about work. If this is important to you, remember that retirement is not death. Nothing stops you from keeping in touch with old friends. Your newly gained freedom and their pressing need to meet deadlines, however, does place the responsibility of contact squarely on your shoulders. Stay in contact with your friends from work. Meet for lunch at a restaurant near their office and do not keep them too long. Try meeting former coworkers after work, but keep in mind that they have a shortage of time to spend with their family and other working friends. Chances are that after several months of retirement, you may find old coworkers less interesting. You might discover that the work issues that dominate their lives and used to dominate yours are no longer interesting to you. For that reason, it is a good idea to plan activities that involve joining organizations. If you have interest in a subject, look for clubs or take classes related to it. Take part in the activities and make new friends who share your new interests. These activities might replace several workplace fulfillment issues. Club or class participation provides social stimulation and meetings or classes satisfy your need to learn. After-class meetings might even provide you with a nightlife you never developed as a working professional.

Some people cite a need to wield power as an important driver that is fulfilled in the workplace. The need to be competitive, to be an authority figure, to mentor others, or to be a leader are closely related drivers. Such motivations can also be satisfied outside the workplace. Competition occurs in any sport or board game. Leadership opportunities exist in most clubs and organized volunteer activities. There are plenty of volunteer opportunities to serve as a mentor for teenagers and children. You can wield power as a tutor or as a little league umpire. You can structure your retirement activities, schedule goals you wish to achieve, and pursue them.

7.1. WORK PART-TIME

Traditional retirement is characterized by a lifestyle of leisure without work. Some people, however, have a different view of retirement. Although they may plan to escape their current wage-slave status through the achievement of financial security, they also plan on working part-time or cycling between work and leisure on an occasional basis. There are many different ways to remain in the workforce. You can continue in your present position, cut back to part-time, or take on a new job, often with less stress, fewer hours, and less money. Some surveys indicate that as many as 90% of baby boomers intend to keep working and earning for a period of time in retirement.

Although some who intend to continue working are trying to make up for inadequate financial planning, most say their goal is simply, "to keep busy." These people do not view retirement as an event, but as a process. One reason transitional retirement has become popular is that people are living longer. The life expectancy for people retiring today is approximately seven years longer than it was for the retiree five or six decades ago. Compared to their parents and grandparents, people retiring today expect to be active longer and need to fund a longer retirement. Work today also tends to be less physically demanding than work of several decades ago. The physical demands of work no longer play a significant role in a decision to retire.

Although a lifestyle that includes part-time work may not satisfy the strict definition of retirement, it has some of the same kinds of possibilities that typify traditional retirement. Work can be pursued primarily for fulfillment rather than money since transitional retirement begins after a worker has attained a significant level of financial security. Inadequate compensation, job volatility, office politics, and other issues that make a career job difficult are not as important for the transition-period retiree. Similarly, opportunities for leisure activities can be pursued freely since the transitional retiree decides when and how long to work. The addition of a transition period between full-time working status and full-time leisure also delays the need to tap retirement savings as the primary source of income. During the transition period, investments continue to earn and grow, thus reducing the amount of savings required.

Below is a short list of part-time work ideas for the transitional retiree to consider. As you review the list, you should keep in mind what kind of fulfillment you might want from your efforts and consider whether each job might satisfy those desires.

Work in community/government service

    Become a candidate in local elections (school board, zoning board, town council, coroner, etc.)

    Work at the polls as part of the Election Board

    Work concessions, security, or taking tickets at festivals, civic performance, or sports events

    Work for your local Irrigation Board

    Be a seasonal or part-time Park Service worker

Start a small business

    Start a community newsletter

    Do landscaping or yard work

    Start a used bookstore

    Buy a suitable property and build a hotel/apartment or store

    Collect and sell antiques

    Head a small nonprofit organization

    Run a laundromat

    Be a home inspector

    Be a finanical advisor

    Be a web page designer

    Start a computer repair business

Be an author

    Write a book

    Write freelance articles for newspapers and magazines

Be an artist

    Learn woodworking or metalworking and create sculpture

    Play an instrument in a band

Consult/technical

    Invent a device and obtain a patent

    Solve a company's current technical or manufacturing problem

    Serve as an interim executive

Teach

    Become a substitute teacher in nearby school districts

    Become a tutor, bus driver, or crossing guard

    Teach courses at local colleges or junior colleges

    Develop short courses in your field of expertise

Get trained for specialized temporary employment

    Be a tax preparer

    Be a temporary office worker

    Be a member of a campaign team

    Work for a special events security team

    Be a fitness advisor

    Become a tour leader (hiking, cycling, fishing, climbing, hunting)

    Work at a museum or gallery

Be a real estate agent

Be a landlord

Take a job in a local store

    Become a clothing store salesperson

    Sell power tools

    Sell sporting goods

    Work in a home improvement outlet

Take up a trade skill

    Build custom cabinets

    Become a handyman

    Make and sell jewelry

It is unlikely that all of the jobs listed above will appeal to any particular person, but it only takes one to complement a transitional retirement. Some of the jobs are temporary by nature. Tax preparation work, for example, is readily available only from January until April. Election board workers are needed during local, state, or national elections (typically two to four times per year). Event security, concession workers, and ushers are needed only during events (fairs, sporting events, performances, concerts, celebrations, etc.) The amount of income that can be derived by such jobs is limited and may not be enough for your retirement transition. Some of the listed jobs could easily become more than full-time and threaten to make your transition period more stressful than your original career. Finding the appropriate balance could take time and adjustments.

Training for certain kinds of specialized part-time jobs is often available at little or no cost. Many of the national tax-preparation firms, for example, go on a hiring spree every tax season and provide more than adequate training. A collateral benefit from this job is that you may learn how to improve your own tax situation. Similarly, health clubs are often willing to train and hire personal trainers. Security teams train and deploy people to monitor concerts, shows, and other special events. Temporary office worker agencies sometimes provide the instruction needed as part of the job assignment. National political campaigns hire some workers and the job includes significant on-the-job training. These part-time jobs can be very interesting and rewarding for someone who is motivated to learn new things.

One activity that can fulfill creativity needs and earn money is to become an author. This job offers significant flexibility in terms of work hours. Whether you are writing a novel or a technical book for Wiley-IEEE Press, you can work at your own pace and choose which days to write and which to take off. Other opportunities for a freelance writer might include writing articles for a magazine or writing copy for local businesses. It is important to research the publishing market you are interested in before you begin writing. Do not underestimate the task of getting your books or articles published. There are far more manuscripts and articles that never see the light of day than are ever published. You should also be realistic about the income that you might derive from writing. There are hundreds of starving writers for every best-selling author.

When your local housing market is hot, people who enjoy sales may enjoy being a real estate agent. This usually requires a state license, so an investment of time and money is required. Continuing education is also required if you continue to sell.

Many of the items on the part-time job list can be combined with other retirement activities in order to meet multiple fulfillment requirements. The transitional retiree can combine international travel with starting a business. This can be done, for example, by choosing to take trips to Europe, buy antiques there and ship them back to a gallery for profit. Take a job as an intern in a connoisseur restaurant and combine work with a desire to learn about gourmet cooking.

7.2. TRAVEL

Retirees with time on their hands are often excited about the opportunity to travel. They choose to go places they have never been or return to places they have enjoyed in the past. Retirees travel for a variety of reasons—to visit relatives, participate in volunteer projects, seek adventure, or for recreation and leisure. The list of destinations is endless. Travel anywhere—within your state, across the nation, or international. Spend a weekend or go on an extended trip. Many different travel styles are available and most budgets can be accommodated by choosing the appropriate style and number of trips.

If travel will be an important part of your retirement, it will need to be incorporated in your retirement budget. Where to go, how to get there, what to do, how long to stay and what class of accommodations you require all contribute to the cost of travel. Establish approximate trip budgets for your top-priority excursions. If you are inflexible about the details of your trip, budget limitations may establish how often you can travel once retired. Find ways to reduce your expenses while traveling and you may be able to travel more often.

Table 7.1 illustrates a basic travel-planning matrix. Destinations of interest are listed in the left column. Basic details for each destination are placed in the remaining columns. Each leg of the journey is associated with costs for transportation, dining, entertainment, shopping, and so on. Cost estimates can be determined for each trip by estimating the expenses listed in each row.

TABLE 7.1. Retirement travel budget planning

Destinations	How you will travel	Scheduled events and shopping	Length of trip	Accommodations/ dining
Paris	Fly to and from Paris. Use public transportation in city.	Visit Louvre, Eiffel Tower, Musée d'Orsay, Notre Dame, Musée Rodin. Shop for souveniers, perfume.	9 days	Hotel Lotti/ restaurants
Washington, DC	Fly to DC, shuttle to and from hotel, public transportation	National Spy Museum, National Zoo, National Art Galery, Jefferson Memorial, Washington Monument,	6 days	5-star hotel/ restaurants
Grand Canyon	Drive auto (one day, 1-way)	Hike Kaibab Trail to bottom, camp, return via Bright Angel trail	5 days	Phantom Ranch Campground/ campfire meals
Shawnee National Forest	Drive auto (two days one-way)	Explore Garden of the Gods, visit relatives	8 days	Highway motels and fast food on road. Stay and eat with relatives in Illinois
. . .	. . .	. . .	. . .	. . .

Creating a travel plan helps to set realistic expectations for the frequency of trips. If timing of your trip is not critical, the list of destinations can also be useful to locate bargains. For example, you can monitor flight costs and take your trip when airfares are low.

Indirect expenses can also affect travel budgets. All yard maintenance, house sitters, and/or pet care expenses should be considered in your travel plans. Be sure to adjust your thermostat accordingly. Savings in energy and water usage may offset some travel expenses.

Table 7.1 illustrates plans for several types of travel. Travel options, however, vary significantly. Other options include:

Tours and cruises
    Houseboat rentals
    Elderhostels
Adventure Travel
    Scuba or snorkel packages
    Trekking
    Around-the-world packages
Home exchanges

Some retirees intend travel to be the primary focus of their retirement. A multitude of books and internet sites are devoted to RV travel. Many retirees travel and live full time in RVs. Others travel and live full time on sailing vessels. This type of lifestyle can be costly or inexpensive depending on how it is approached. Budgeting for full-time travel requires specialized planning.

If you plan on extended or full-time travel, try to make sure your absence goes as smoothly as possible. Consider your financial assets, your health, and the consequences of a serious injury or death while traveling. Your finances, investment assets, power of attorney, and will should be in order before you leave home. Chapter 4 addresses these issues in more detail.

7.3. VOLUNTEER

Volunteer work can be as demanding as it is rewarding. Although part of the reason for volunteering may be altruism and selflessness, this is not the only motivation for volunteers. Volunteering is not generally one-sided; it is an exchange. Volunteers give time, skill, or knowledge in exchange for fulfillment of personal needs or in anticipation of a time when they may require help themselves. Some of the motivations for volunteering are the same personal fulfillment drivers discussed in Section 7.1. Volunteer jobs provide satisfaction from accomplishment, recognition for a job well done, challenge, and a feeling of self-worth. They can help people make new friends and feel like part of a team. Others see volunteering as a chance to gain experience, leadership skills, and knowledge that might be leveraged into a new career or job. In exchange for their efforts, the volunteers often receive valuable intangible rewards.

Your motivation for volunteering can be very personal and may change over time. A volunteer position should be rewarding to you. If it is not fulfilling, it is time to seek another form of volunteerism. Giving time and energy for a cause or organization should make you feel like you have accomplished something, that your talents were appreciated, and that you made a difference. Hopefully, you will also find something to respect in the people you work with. Volunteering should work for you as well as for the people and causes you choose to serve.

Professional Society Volunteer Activities

Many engineers and scientists choose to perform volunteer work for professional societies once they have retired. For some, this is simply a continuation or expansion of the volunteer work they were enjoying prior to retirement. There are some differences between volunteering for society work before and after retirement. Prior to retirement, such activities may be encouraged and supported by an engineer's employer. Although not all organizations are supportive of professional activities, many will sponsor active volunteers through travel reimbursement and time off work. Once in retirement, travel expenses required for certain types of volunteer activities are likely to come (at least partly) from the retiree's personal budget. In some cases, volunteer efforts may be subsidized by the society. Many retirees from technical careers find the cost of active volunteer participation to be easily worth the expense. Conference and meeting attendance can be coupled to retirement travel plans, and meeting with old friends in attractive locations is an enjoyable retirement activity. There are also many professional activities that do not require travel. Reviewing manuscripts, for example, is usually done whenever and wherever the volunteer can lug his or her laptop and find an internet link, even at the beach.

Professional societies depend on volunteers for a wide range of both technical and nontechnical tasks. These activities provide opportunities for retirees to remain in touch with friends and colleagues they worked with during the course of their careers. Technical tasks that professional organizations must address with volunteer help include review of research manuscripts, editing publications, selecting conference papers, and organizing conference sessions, workshops and tutorials. A further side benefit of this type of activity is that the retired engineer or scientist maintains a credible, up-to-date, technical resume while performing these volunteer tasks. If after a few years of retirement, retirees decide that performing some technical work for pay would be a welcome addition to their schedules, their technical involvement in professional activities would help bridge their resume gap, and their professional contacts would remain current.

In addition to the technical opportunities, professional societies also require volunteer assistance to organize and plan events, administer programs, manage the society, serve as reviewers for awards and recognition, and develop membership services. These types of efforts typically involve working on teams and committees with other professionals who share common concerns about professional issues in the field. A wide range of skills are needed to manage a large volunteer organization or to plan a large conference. Business negotiation expertise is useful when making conference center or hotel arrangements for society meetings. Publicity, food and beverage, registration, entertainment, and audio–visual capabilities all have to be arranged or managed by volunteers. Management experience is valuable to volunteers who become involved in society administration or large conference organization efforts. If you have skills in any of these areas (or wish to learn them) you may find a satisfying volunteer position available through your professional society.

Although professional societies are almost always in need of additional volunteer assistance, becoming involved may require some inquiry and effort if the retiree was not active in the organization prior to retirement. You should not expect to be appointed Editor-in-Chief of the organization's journal if you have not previously served even as a reviewer. You may quickly become a busy Editor's best friend, however, if you consistently deliver knowledgeable, constructive criticism and review of research papers on schedule. Expect to spend some time understanding the organization and its administrators before driving proposals for fundamental society change. If you take the time and develop thorough plans and proposals, however, you could have a significant and lasting impact on the profession.

Nonprofessional Volunteer Activities

If you are ready to branch out beyond your career field, there are many other types of opportunities for volunteers. Below is a short list of volunteer activities that are unrelated to technical careers. As you review the list, keep in mind the kind of fulfillment you might want from your efforts.

Be part of a community theater production or play

Coach a childrens sport team

Participate on nonprofit boards

Go to a developing country with an international aid organization

Join a volunteer band

Join a church choir

Start a charity to collect money or items for distribution to the needy

Visit a local nursing home

Maintain a website for a community group

Start an organization to plant trees in public spaces around your town

Deliver meals on wheels to elderly shut-ins in your community

Tutor children

Become a docent at a museum or historical site

Be a campground host

Become an aid at a pet center

Help out at a pound or humane center

Work with a wildlife rehabilitation group

Form a cancer support organization

Help an environmental group with a project

Organize your neighborhood and serve as liaison between it and your city

Become a hospital volunteer

Build a house with Habitat for Humanity

Help plan and run a local event

Help a Big Brother or Big Sister group

In addition to the ideas listed above, your local government may have a wide variety of volunteer opportunities. The city of Mesa, Arizona, for example, posts volunteer opportunities on its website. The opportunities listed below represent the volunteer positions that were recently advertised. Each position was hyperlinked to a description of the effort needed as well as suggested requirements. Although not every city will have a formal, online volunteer procedure, many welcome volunteer help.

Bilingual-Assistance Team Volunteer

Building Safety Division Office Intern

Center Against Family Violence Assistant

Communications Training Clerk

Community Response Team

Disabled-Parking Enforcement Volunteer

DUI Van Assistant

Gallery Shop Sales

Library Sales Desk Attendant

Mesa Fire Department Connector Program Office Assistant

Office Assistant (Fire Prevention)

Office Assistant Trainee

Performing Arts Dance Accompanist

Piano Accompanist, Voice Classes

Recruiting Specialist

Reference Services Librarian

Security/Office Assistant

Special Projects Volunteer

Transportation Division Office Intern

Transportation Marketing Assistant

Usher

Victim Assistance

Video Production Specialist

Voluntary Support Driver

The Internet can also be a valuable tool for identifying volunteer opportunities. Appendix A provides URLs for a number of sites that describe volunteer opportunities. An online version of Appendix A is accessible at www.golio.net, by selecting "Table of Contents and URLs." A quick search will turn up many other opportunities that are available in your area.

By definition, volunteers are not paid for their services. Volunteers, however, can receive tax deductions from the federal government on many costs associated with volunteering. Deductible expenses include mileage and other travel expenses, paper, copying, convention attendance fees, parking, required clothing (if the volunteer purchases his or her own uniform), and so on. These deductions only apply if you are not reimbursed for these expenses by the organization you are assisting, and you are itemizing deductions on your tax form. More details about tax deductions for volunteer efforts are provided in IRS Publication 526, Charitable Contribution, which can be downloaded from the IRS website.

7.4. RECREATION AND LEISURE

Your imagination is the only limit to the range and number of leisure opportunities you take advantage of. It is a sad individual who cannot imagine what he or she would do all day if they did not have to go to work. If you have been working too hard or too long to remember how to enjoy leisure time, the list below may remind you of a life you have not had time for. While reviewing the list, think about the opportunities in a lifestyle in which time is not limited by work.

Go on a trip or adventure

Restore an old car

Take a hot-air balloon ride

Go paragliding

Sit on the porch and enjoy the view

Build a deck and put a hot tub in it

Host a party for your friends

Visit with family

Get a dog or cat

Visit a museum

Visit the zoo

Visit an aquarium

Build a wooden boat

Become a wine expert

Tour Civil War sites

Go to battle re-creation events

Fish, golf, hunt

Go to a baseball game

Join an adult softball league team

Build a set of shelves and find things to put on them

Go trekking on a mountain trail

Ride a bike

Visit sculpture gardens

Go birding

Go camping

Go kayaking

Attend a theatre performance or concert

See a film

Transform your garden

Go sailing or boating

Learn to cook gourmet food

Take an island tour

Scuba dive

Go big-game fishing

Go on a whale-watching excursion

Take a ride in a helicopter

Enjoy live music at a local nightclub

Learn about and install a solar or wind-power system in your home

Eat out at a new restaurant

Read all the books by your favorite author

Go to the beach

Build a workshop and make things

Check out local parks

Travel in an RV

Tour a winery

7.5. HEALTH AND SELF-IMPROVEMENT

For many, retirement is a chance to devote time to their health and self-improvement. There is now time and no excuse for putting off important things like losing excess weight, getting back in shape, or learning to speak another language. The possibilities are endless. When asked what they are looking forward to in retirement, 60% of 3448 workers between the ages of 40 and 58 answered that they are looking forward to focusing on themselves. Nearly one-quarter indicated that they planned to take educational courses.[1]

There are good reasons to devote time to your own health in retirement. After many years as a wage slave, you have finally achieved financial independence. Your health, however, will have a direct impact on how long you will actually be able to enjoy your retirement freedom. A recent study by the University of Michigan Medical School and the VA Ann Arbor Healthcare System found that adults in their 50s and early 60s who were regularly active were about 35% less likely to die in the next eight years than those who were sedentary. Physical activity can help adults prolong their independence and improve their quality of life. Staying physically active on a regular, permanent basis can help prevent certain types of cancer, coronary heart deisease, high blood pressure, colon cancer, osteoporosis, and diabetes. Regular exercise can even improve management of some diseases and disabilities in people who already have them. Exercise contributes to the maintenance of bones, muscles, and joints. It reduces symptoms of anxiety and depression and fosters improvements in mood and feelings of well-being. Exercise, to put it simply, is one of the best things you can do for your health and retirement. Before embarking on any physical exercise program, it is essential that you obtain the advice of a doctor or qualified healthcare professional who is familiar with your health situation.

Americans are out of shape. One-third of U.S. adults are obese, and another one-third are overweight. Forty-year-old overweight males and females are likely to suffer a lifespan reduction of at least 3 years compared to those of normal weight. Obese male nonsmokers reduce their lifespan by nearly 6 years. According to studies, obesity reduces overall U.S. life expectancy by as much as 9 months. While this figure (averaged over the entire population) may seem trivial, it means that obesity currently lowers life expectancy more than homicide, suicide, and fatal accidents combined.

Although they are aware of their own lack of physical fitness and the importance of exercise, most Americans are too tired, too busy, or too lazy to exercise and maintain their health. Retirement offers the opportunity to alter this situation. Many retirees make their own fitness a priority in retirement. They lose extra pounds, eat better, and develop a regular workout routine. Exercise routines can be developed in a wide variety of ways. Although exercise and sport can be done at a club or gym, a pastime as simple and inexpensive as walking can keep people active. Generally, the more active you are, the healthier you will become.

Activities that engage your mind can also be important to achieving a satisfying and healthy retirement. Many find retirement an ideal time to take courses on topics that have always interested them. Others see retirement as an opportunity to develop a creative or artistic talent. According to the Department of Education, nearly 85,000 people over 50 are full-time students in undergraduate or graduate programs. Another 435,000 are part-time students. Millions of others choose to exercise their minds through activities that do not require a formal classroom structure. A healthy brain benefits from activity and may extend your life just as effectively as physical exercise.

Below is a short list of health and self-improvement activities to consider. As you review the list, keep in mind the kind of fulfillment you want from your efforts.

Exercise
  Learn yoga and practice it
  Join a sports team
  Take a long walk
  Run
  Ride a bike
  Play tennis
Develop a creative talent or skill
  Take a course in something that you have excelled at in the past
  Learn to play a musical instrument
  Learn to refinish furniture
  Learn to make sculpture
  Learn to make jewelry
  Learn woodworking
  Learn to paint
Pursue an educational goal
  Study genetic engineering/biotechnology
  Learn a new language
  Learn about astronomy

Research your ancestry/genealogy

Learn to build a website

Learn about photography

    Learn about digital cameras and the software used to manipulate images

    Build your own darkroom

Audit classes at a local university

Improve your health

  Study homeopathic medicine

  Get unhooked from coffee

  Learn to cook healthier meals

  Reduce sugar, salt, and fat in your diet

  Limit the amount of fast food you eat

  Reduce the amount of junk food you eat

REFERENCES AND FURTHER READING

1. The Merrill Lynch New Retirement Survey: A Perspective from the Baby Boomer Generation, Total Merrill, 2005.
2. Freedman, M., The Selling of Retirement, and How We Bought It, *Washingtonpost. Newsweek Interactive,* 2004.
3. Powell, R., Ten Hot Jobs for Today's Retirees, *CBS MarketWatch.com,* May 19, 2004, http://cbs.marketwatch.com/news/story.asp?guid={930AA498-9E59-40B2-8004-D3D88EEEFEE3}&siteid=mktw&dist=mktw&archive=true.
4. Americans Choosing Work after Retirement, *Associated Press,* March 9, 2005, http://www.msnbc.msn.com/id/7140314/.
5. Ruffenach, G., The Great American Retirement Quiz, *Wall Street Journal Online,* December 28, 2004, http://pf.channel.aol.com/moneytoday/wsj/investment/retirequiz.adp.
6. Preston, S., Deadweight?—The Influence of Obesity on Longevity, *The New England Journal of Medicine,* Vol. 352:1135–1137, March 17, 2005.
7. Report: Obesity will Reverse Life Expectancy Gains, *Associated Press,* March 16, 2005, http://www.cnn.com/2005/HEALTH/diet.fitness/03/16/obesity.longevity.ap/.
8. Mishra, R., Study Cites Obesity As Longevity Threat, *Boston Globe,* March 17, 2005, http://www.boston.com/yourlife/health/fitness/articles/2005/03/17/study_cites_obesity_as_longevity_threat/.

CONTINUING ADVENTURES OF BO CAMBERT & LEARY McFLY

Bo Cambert stepped into the elevator and pressed the button for the 15th floor. As he stepped against the back wall, a familiar face moved into the elevator with him. Bo inwardly cringed when he recognized Nick Tessle. Bo and Nick had gone to graduate school together, and Nick was widely considered to be the brightest and most well-liked student in the department. Bo, on the other hand, was considered by most to be a life form most closely resembling pond slime. That was 10 years ago, but Bo always felt threatened around people this bright and well adjusted.

There was no place to hide. After a second Nick looked up and recognized Bo. He smiled broadly as he reached out to shake Bo's hand. "Bo, how are you? It's good to see you."

Bo did his best to look pleased. "Good to see you too, Nick. What are you doing these days?" It was at this instant that Bo noticed that Nick was wearing some kind of a uniform and carrying a bag. His face registered his bewilderment at the clothing.

"Oh," Nick said in answer to the perplexed look on Bo's face. "I'm a mail carrier here." Nick noticed Bo's continued stare. "It's only part-time though."

Bo was dumbfounded. "Why are you working as a mailman, Nick? And what are you doing with the rest of your time?"

"Well . . . ," Nick answered, "I'm enjoying getting out, walking my route, talking to people, getting to know something about them, delivering mail a few days a week. And with the rest of my time, I play with Billy and Jenny. They're my kids. I get to spend a lot of time with them and my dear wife, Beth. We go camping and hiking and on family vacations a lot. On the weekends, I play bass in a band in a little bar at the edge of town—that kind of thing."

Nick smiled again. "But enough about me, Bo. What are you up to these days?" The elevator door opened on the tenth floor—Nick's stop—and Bo decided to step off with Nick. Before he got away, Bo needed to gloat about how important he was now. "I'm very successful, you know. I founded my own company and am currently President and CEO of the very successful company com.Wireless.com," Bo boasted. "I spend most of my time negotiating important business deals, seeking funding, planning corporate strategy, hiring, firing, and reprimanding employees—the sort of important things required to keep a company successful. It's very important work."

"That's great, Bo," Nick beamed. "It sounds like you are very successful and important. I'll bet you enjoy that."

This wasn't the response Bo had hoped for. He felt certain that Nick really was happy for him, but Bo didn't want him to be happy. He wanted Nick to realize how important Bo had become and how unimportant Nick was and to feel the same kind of insecurity that Bo used to feel around Nick in grad school. He wanted Nick to be jealous and envious. Clearly, Bo thought, Nick needed some advice and guidance.

"You should start your own RF/microwave company, Nick," Bo offered.

"Why is that?" Nick asked.

Bo was surprised at the question. "If you work hard at it, you can build the company into a significant force in the microwave community. You could have dozens, hundreds, or even thousands of people working for you. You could make a lot of money."

"Well, that would be something," Nick said. He looked at Bo as if he didn't really understand. Finally, Nick continued, "Then what, Bo?"

Bo couldn't believe the question. "Eventually, you could acquire and merge with other companies, Nick. You could dominate the world market for microwave systems, components or semiconductors. You could become a very powerful man"

"Imagine that," Nick said. He paused again and seemed to be thinking about Bo's answer. "What would I do then, Bo?"

Bo was exasperated. "Anything you want, Nick. You could do whatever it is you enjoy doing." Bo tried to think of how he could get this point across to Nick. Finally, Bo said, "Think about it, Nick. You could do whatever you wanted. What do you really want to do?"

Nick thought for only a second, smiled broadly and answered. "I really enjoy getting out, talking to people, getting to know something about them. I like playing with Billy and Jenny, spending time with Beth, camping, hiking, and going on family vacations. On the weekends, I like to play bass in a band in a little bar at the edge of town—that kind of thing."

From *IEEE Microwave Magazine,* September 2001, p. 128.

8

FINAL ISSUES

8.1. BEFORE YOU LEAVE THE BUILDING

It is never too late to start planning for your retirement, but once you have left the building, it may not be possible to go back in. Not all technical professionals are given the luxury of choosing the day they exit the workplace. Many are walked out of the building at short notice due to corporate layoffs or dark corporate politics. If you are fortunate enough to be able to pick the date of your exit, do not waste that opportunity. Think ahead and take advantage of your last days, weeks, and months to put things in order. Some of the office-related issues you should plan for are listed below:

- Take all of your personal possessions home before your last day. You will be busy and want to focus on the paperwork, exit interviews, goodbyes, and so on. Packing and juggling boxes is not the best way to spend that time.
- Review your computer files. If you have any personal files on your employer's computer, make personal copies and delete them from the computer.
- Take any vacation, personal holidays, or leave time that will be forfeited once you leave. This depends on the policy of your employer. Some organizations will pay you for unused leave days, others will not.
- Learn what your organization will allow you to do with your 401(k), 403(b), or 457 investments. You may be allowed to keep your money in the plan, roll it over, or be forced to take it out. Make sure you understand the options and the tax implications of those options. Be ready to execute your choice. You should also consider having extra deductions taken from your paycheck and

placed in these plans to ensure that you get your maximum allowable contributions for the year.

- Learn the details of any pension plan you are vested in. You may have a cash balance due to you. You may have annuity choices to make. Determine the options, the amounts, and tax implications.

- Learn your alternatives for any stock options you have. Are they exercisable? Are they under water? Can you take them with you? Do you understand the tax implications?

- Put a medical insurance plan in place. If you are not getting a medical benefit as part of your retirement package, this process should be started more than 6 months prior to your retirement (see Chapter 4, Section 4.1). If you are not prepared with your own plan on retirement day, check on COBRA transitional insurance. Federal COBRA law requires that you be allowed to keep your existing group insurance for up to 18 months. It may be expensive, but it will buy time for you to find your own solution.

- Surf your employer's internal websites for any information you may need after you have left. Make a hardcopy or a soft copy, but do not violate corporate policy.

- Compile the contact information (phone, address, email, URLs) for Human Resources representatives, benefits personnel, and other offices. Make sure you know who to contact with future questions about pensions, tax-deferred investments, medical benefits, stock options, and any other future benefit.

- Collect a list of e-mail addresses and phone numbers of any friends and colleagues you wish to keep in touch with.

- Draft a letter or memo of resignation. Keep it simple and keep it professional. See Table 8.1 for an example.

- Say farewell to friends and colleagues. Everyone and every situation is different. You may prefer to speak privately with a few people or slip out the back door unnoticed. Your office mates may want to have a party on your behalf. You might be asked to give a farewell speech. You might want to develop a farewell letter for distribution. However you choose to say it, you probably want to articulate four things:
  - Thank you. Thanks for being fun to work with, for helping me with some aspect of the job, . . .
  - I respect you. I have learned to respect and value your insights and opinions, your dedication, your genius, . . .
  - I'm sorry if I have failed to help you as much as I should have or if we have had misunderstandings in the past.
  - Good-bye and good luck.

In some companies, for some professionals, the employer asks the employee to leave immediately upon resignation. This does not normally occur for a retiring employee, but it can happen. Even if your supervisor is a life-long friend, the treatment

Table 8.1. Example of simple and professional memo of resignation

To:	*supervisor's name*
cc:	*HR representative's name*
From:	*your name*
Date:	*date of memo*
Subject:	*Resignation*

Dear supervisor's name,

I am submitting my written notice of resignation from *company's name* effective two weeks from today. My last day will be *date of last day.*

I am choosing to retire and pursue other interests at this time.

In my remaining time on the job, I will be happy to help train my replacement and do whatever is required to make a smooth transition.

I would like to thank you and *company's name* for a rewarding and productive experience. I wish only the best for you, and for the company.

---

you receive once you resign may shock you. Be prepared for this. Make sure all the other items on your list are completed before turning in your letter or memo of resignation. Being escorted from your own office can be a demeaning experience. Focus on getting through the exit process. Your retirement awaits you.

Many employers like to have all departing employees meet with a Human Resources person for an exit interview. Be careful. Keep your answers simple and keep them professional. There is nothing you can gain from this interview but your freedom.

There are some things outside the office that should be done before you leave the workforce. Have a plan for regular income flow to replace your regular paycheck. If your plan includes Social Security or pension benefits, start the process of initiating these payments several months prior to your scheduled needs. Become familiar with 72(t) rules prior to any anticipated early withdrawal from a tax-deferred account. Your taxable account holdings are likely to be easy to access, but you still need a withdrawal strategy. You may want to build a bond ladder. Section 8.3 discusses many of these income source issues. If you plan to refinance your home, it is important to do this before you leave the workforce. Without a job, you are not likely to be approved for a loan.

8.2. WHERE TO LIVE

Retirees have housing options open to them that could not be considered during their working careers. No longer are you tied to an office. You can move to a more suitable dwelling nearby, move to a far-away dream spot, or live a nomadic life in an RV or sailing vessel. While no place is likely to be perfect, methodical evaluations of possible locations can lead to a good match for your needs.

Start your search by developing a list of what you want and do not want in a community. Consider your preferences for each of the following:

- Size of town—small, medium, or large
- Climate—cold or hot, wet or dry, and so on.
- Cultural opportunities—museums, theater, live music, opera, zoo, pro sports
- Schools—public, Christian/parochial, progressive, university town
- Medical—major medical center
- Airports—major airport, driving distance to major airport, do not need it
- Leisure—golf, tennis, hiking, sailing, camping, fishing, water sports, gym, beach, spectator opportunities, gardening, National Forests, parks, snow sports
- Crime rate
- Public transportation
- Nightlife
- Social diversity
- Government
- Religious choices
- Family—same town, nearby, distant
- Housing—affordable, appropriate rentals
- Pollution levels
- State and local taxes

If you have an exotic location or a nomadic retirement in mind, the list above may not be applicable. Some people know they want to live in a foreign country, roam the highways in an RV, or sail the seas in retirement. If you are in one of those categories, you need to develop a custom list of preferences to guide location decisions. Conversely, if you have a single overriding preference (to be with family or current friends, for example) you may not need to consider more than one location.

Armed with a prioritized list of preferences, you can begin to develop a list of possible destinations. Use past vacation experiences, books, travel magazines, or the Internet to produce a list of potential retirement sites. Include your current hometown or others you are familiar with to serve as benchmarks for your comparison. Most retirees end up within 50 miles of where they worked. Consider what the possible locations will be like year round. Places with warm winters often have hot summers, and places with mild summers often have cold winters. Towns with tourist attractions can get both crowded and deserted. If you intend to live somewhere year round, it is important to understand what the location is like in all seasons.

Compare your target destination cities to your community preferences. Identify the cities that match up best. If you can manage, visit your top choices and stay a few weeks. Treat your visit like an interview with a city. See what you can learn about the location. If you are not ready to commit, visit at different times of the year, or rent a home for several months. If you are not unhappy where you are, and can afford it, there is no urgency to find a "better" location. Enjoy the search.

There is a good chance that your needs will change during a typical 30+ year retirement. The community preferences of an early retiree might not be identical to the same person's preferences at age 80. You might also find your first choice was not what you thought it would be. Moving can be expensive, so you should not take the decision of where to move lightly. If you are not in the right place, however, it is time to move. Avoid placing yourself in a situation in which you can't afford to move if you need to.

One hedge against getting "trapped" in the wrong retirement community is to rent, rather than buy, your retirement home. Buying a home is a commitment to more than the house price. Taxes, association fees, insurance, maintenance costs, and yardcare can easily cost 4% to 8% of the value of the home each year. A typical technical professional might have $350,000 tied up in their home and another $21,000 required for annual expenses. Using the 4% rule (equation 1.1), that $21,000 requires an additional $525,000 of nest egg to meet required house support payments through a 30 year retirement. If the home is larger than your actual needs, renting an appropriately sized house or condo may save you money. In addition, it provides insurance against becoming "trapped" in the wrong retirement community.

Even if you decide to stay in the same city, downsizing your home can be very cost-effective. Selling the family home and moving into a smaller "empty nest" home is likely to produce significant gains that can be added to your retirement portfolio. Home sale capital gains of up to $250,000 ($500,000 per married couple filing jointly) are not taxable if you have owned and occupied the house as a principal residence for at least two of the past five years. In addition to the tax-free windfall, the smaller home is likely to have lower associated tax, insurance, maintenance, and yardcare costs. The lower annual cost reduces the amount of your portfolio required to support your housing, freeing that amount for discretionary spending.

As an example, consider the couple that sells their $350,000 family home with associated $21,000 per year annual housing support costs. They move into a $250,000 "empty nest" home with $15,000 per year annual housing support costs. The couple gets $100,000 tax-free capital gains. They also reduce the portfolio amount required to pay annual housing costs from $525,000 to $375,000, a $150,000 reduction. The total portfolio amount that can now be used for spending other than housing is increased by $250,000. Using the 4% rule, this amounts to an inflation-adjusted increase in available spending of $833 per month throughout retirement.

8.3. SOURCES OF INCOME

In retirement, there is no paycheck. That steady stream of revenue needs to be replaced with other sources of income. Not only is it required for you to have saved plenty of money, but a plan is required to withdraw it on a regular basis. The way money is withdrawn has significant tax implications and contributes to your portfolio volatility.

In order to create a steady stream of cash, it is important for you identify all sources of income, the amount available from each source, when payments occur, and how to coordinate payments from different sources. The likely candidates for income sources include Social Security, pensions, annuities, tax-deferred accounts, taxable accounts, and, possibly, part-time or temporary work.

Social Security is a *cost-of-living-adjusted* (COLA'd) defined cash flow benefit. The amount of benefit depends on what has been contributed, when you begin taking the benefits, and whether you choose individual or joint survivor benefit options. Pensions and annuities also have defined cash flow benefits, but usually without COLA provisions. This means that the value of these benefits is eroded each year by inflation. All of these factors must be considered in planning your retirement income flow.

Tax-deferred retirement plans produce income in relation to the amounts you invested and the investment choices you made. Generally, the longer you can wait to tap into these sources, the greater their value. An exception to this is related to required minimum distributions (RMDs) at age 70½. For investors with large tax-deferred accounts, it can be advantageous to take funds as early as possible. This is discussed in Section 8.4. If income from tax-deferred plans is needed before age 59½, it must be taken in accordance with 72(t) provisions of the law (see 72(t) Withdrawals (SEPP) later in this section).

Income from taxable accounts is often the easiest to access. You should have complete access to broker, mutual fund, and treasury accounts that you established. Typically, these are the first accounts that should be withdrawn from since any income they produce is taxable. Depleting these funds reduces your taxes and places you in a lower tax rate for the eventual tax events triggered by withdrawal from tax-deferred plans. It is important to consider volatility of your taxable investments during the withdrawal stage of your life. If making withdrawals requires you to sell stocks or stock funds while the markets are down, you are not getting the maximum value from your investments. It is important to develop an appropriate rebalancing scheme for these accounts. This might include development of a fixed-income ladder (discussed later in this section).

As discussed in Chapter 1, many retirees choose to work part-time in retirement. This work produces an additional income flow that reduces the withdrawal requirements on other sources. If you participate in part-time work while you are collecting Social Security benefits, it may result in taxation of your benefits. This is discussed in Section 8.4.

If you own your home, you have an additional potential source of income—a reverse mortgage. This alternative is available to those age 62 and older. The reverse mortgage can supplement your retirement income but also reduces your heirs' inheritance. Reverse mortgages are discussed in more detail later in this section.

Retirement income arrives on different schedules. Social Security, annuity, and pension payments may come monthly. Stock dividends arrive quarterly. Interest on most bonds is paid semiannually. If you are used to a weekly or biweekly paycheck, you will have to adjust your habits and consider how to balance the various income sources to meet your expenses.

The best withdrawal strategy will be unique to each investor based on age, amount of funds in each income source category, and current tax situation. For many retirees, consideration of the following priorities will produce an efficient withdrawal strategy:

1. Take any required minimum distributions (RMDs). If you are age 70½ or older with a traditional tax-deferred account, you need to determine the distribution amounts required by law and take them by the required deadline in order to avoid paying significant penalties.
2. Consider selling loss positions in taxable accounts. You can use investments that are worth less than their tax basis to offset taxable gains.
3. Withdraw interest and dividends from taxable accounts.
4. Withdraw long-term capital gains from taxable accounts.
5. Withdraw remaining funds from taxable accounts.
6. Withdraw from traditional tax-deferred accounts.
7. Withdraw from Roth tax-deferred accounts.

Social Security Decisions

For most Americans, Social Security benefits represent a significant portion of their retirement income. Even the wealthiest families often receive a significant portion of their retirement income from Social Security. The amount you receive each month depends largely on when you choose to begin receiving benefits. Benefit flow can begin as early as age 62, but your benefits will be approximately 25% less than at full retirement age (65 to 67, depending on your birth year). If you postpone initial benefit payments to age 70, your benefits will be approximately 35% higher than your full benefit.

If your goal is to receive maximum payout and you know how long you are going to live, you can easily choose the optimum time to begin receiving Social Security benefits. Those living past 80 are likely to come out financially ahead by waiting for full benefits. If you live past 90, you are likely to profit by postponing initial benefits until age 70. Most of us do not know how long we are going to live, but if good health and long life runs in your family, delaying Social Security should be considered. There is risk in delaying initial benefits. If you live entirely off your portfolio and die prior to collecting benefits, less inheritance is left for your heirs.

Maximizing benefit payout is not the only consideration when choosing the date for your initial benefit payment. Some taxpayers worry that Congress will reduce or eliminate Social Security benefits in the future. Their proposed strategy is to get what they can as early as possible, before benefits are reduced. Others believe the benefit income is more likely to bring value to a 62 year old than it will to a 70 year old. Delaying the benefits could result in larger benefit payments, but less satisfaction and enjoyment. One strategy is to take the benefits early and invest part of them. The earnings from invested benefits can be used for expenses in old age or inherited by heirs in case of early death.

Married couples have an advantage in choosing a Social Security benefit strategy. The duration of Social Security benefits received by couples depends on their joint life expectancy, not individual life expectancy. Although an individual, at age 65, may expect to live about 20 more years, the joint life expectancy of a 65-year-old couple is over 28 years. One of the two of them is likely to survive long enough to profit by waiting for full benefits. When one spouse dies, the other is allowed to take either their own or their deceased spouse's benefits, whichever is greater. This suggests a strategy in which the spouse with the lowest earned benefits can begin taking payments as early as possible while their partner waits for higher benefits. No matter which spouse dies first, both will have received the advantage of some early payments, and the survivor will get higher benefits throughout retirement.

Pensions and Annuities

The considerations affecting when to begin taking pension or annuity payments are very similar to those that apply to Social Security. The payout details depend on the specific plan but, in general, postponing initial benefits increases monthly checks and reduces the period of time during which you will receive them. Choosing to take benefits based on joint survivor longevity will provide insurance for your spouse, but will reduce the monthly payments. As with Social Security, it is not possible to choose the optimum withdrawal strategy unless you know when both you and your spouse will die.

One significant difference between Social Security benefits and most pensions and annuities is that pensions and annuities are not typically adjusted for inflation. As years pass, the buying power of your benefits will get effectively smaller. One way to help offset this problem is to reinvest a portion of each payment. If 30% of each fixed annuity payment is invested in a diversified portfolio, the earnings are likely to offset inflation for approximately 30 years.

Fixed-Income Ladders

Stocks and stock mutual funds can decline steeply over time frames of several years. The possibility of a decline is a risk if you are depending on selling those funds for income. One method to ensure against this risk is to develop and maintain a *fixed-income ladder.*

The fixed-income ladder is a strategy to manage equity and fixed-income investments in your portfolio. The goal of the strategy is to reduce risk rather than increase returns. The strategy requires an investor to invest in short-term bonds, CDs, and/or Treasury bills with staggered maturity dates. If the amounts of the investment and maturity dates are tailored to match your expected cash flow needs, the bond ladder becomes a source of stable income. The ladder can be built with staggered maturity dates stretching out several years into the future. As fixed-income securities mature, the principal is swept into cash accounts and used for expenses. If the investment environment for stocks is healthy at the time of maturity, stocks or stock mutual funds can be sold to replenish the fixed-income ladder for future dates. If stocks are down, the investor can wait for market recovery to replenish the fixed-income ladder. Stable spending is guaranteed until the last investment in the ladder matures. With regular replenishing of the ladder, it can be continued indefinitely.

A typical duration for a fixed-income ladder used as retirement income is 5 to 7 years. To determine amounts and maturity dates required for the ladder, start with an estimate of next year's spending requirements (see Chapter 3, Section 3.3). Subtract from that amount any Social Security, pension, annuity, or other income you will receive. The remainder is the shortfall. It represents the amount of fixed-income investment required with a 1 year maturity date. For the second and later years, apply an assumed inflation rate to your spending requirements and repeat the process.

72(t) Withdrawals (SEPP)

Withdrawing IRA money without penalty prior to age 59½ is not difficult, but it does require that withdrawals be taken according to specific criteria. The loophole that allows these withdrawals is known as the *72(t) exception.* An investor with an IRA can avoid the 10% penalty if "substantially equal periodic payments" (SEPP) are withdrawn. The SEPP withdrawal amount is computed based on your age and the balance of your IRA. IRS regulations and rulings define the method for calculating acceptable SEPP withdrawals.

SEPP withdrawals must occur at least once per year and must continue for five years or until you reach age 59½, whichever is longer. If you started SEPP payments at age 58, you would have to continue taking SEPP withdrawals (beyond age 59½) until age 63. A 50 year old starting SEPP withdrawals would have to continue for 9½ years. Unlimited withdrawals from your IRA can begin as soon as 5 years plus 1 day has elapsed from your first SEPP withdrawal or you reach age 59½, whichever is longer.

Required Minimum Distributions (RMD)

Tax law requires that distributions be taken from traditional tax-deferred accounts once the taxpayer reaches age 70½. Technically, this means that withdrawals from the tax-deferred account must begin by April 1 following the year the taxpayer reaches this age. A minimum amount of distribution is also specified by law. The RMD amounts apply to traditional IRAs and 401(k)s, but not to Roth accounts.

The annual RMD amount can be calculated by dividing an account's year-end value by the distribution period determined by the IRS. The IRS offers three methods for calculating the distribution period. The most advantageous method for most taxpayers uses the Uniform Lifetime Table. Using this table, a 70 year old taxpayer must use a distribution value of 27.4. For an IRA account worth $1 million, this would result in a minimum withdrawal of $36,496 (= $1,000,000/27.4). A unique distribution value is determined each year. At age 80, the IRS distribution value has fallen to 18.7 and continues to diminish until age 115. If you are fortunate enough to live to that age, the distribution value remains at 1.9 for the remainder of your life.

For taxpayers with large tax-deferred accounts, RMD requirements can be larger than annual expenses. If this occurs, the taxpayer is forced not only to withdraw unneeded funds, but to treat these funds as ordinary income. This can have a significant effect on the taxpayer's taxes and tax rate. Those fortunate enough to have large tax-deferred accounts sometimes benefit from taking early withdrawals using 72(t) rules.

Reverse Mortgages

A reverse mortgage is a loan against your home that you do not have to pay back for as long as you live there. The equity in your home is turned into cash without the need to move or repay a loan each month. The cash received from a reverse mortgage can be paid as a lump sum, monthly income, line of credit, or combination of these.

To be eligible for a reverse mortgage, all of the coborrowers must be 62 years old or older. The home must have no mortgage balance and be owner-occupied. If you owe any money on your property, you generally must pay off the old debt before getting a reverse mortgage. If your current mortgage amount is small, you can use a lump-sum payment from the reverse mortgage to pay off the old debt. Single family homes as well as FHA-approved condominiums and two- to four-unit dwellings are also eligible. Since you do not have to make monthly payments, reverse mortgage qualification does not require you to have any income.

You can finance the loan costs using the loan. Loan costs are typical of a conventional mortgage and include an origination fee, appraisal fee, title fee, escrow fee, recording fee, and a monthly servicing fee.

The allowable equity available with a reverse mortgage is computed based on the youngest borrower's age, the appraised value of the home, and the FHA maximum loan limit for your county. The older you are when you take the loan, the more cash you can get. Similarly, the more your home is worth, the more you can get. The amount of money available also depends on the specific mortgage plan or program you select and the kind of cash advances you choose. You may be disappointed in the amount of money available with a reverse mortgage. Expect to get no more than 40% to 55% of the equity in your home. The bank is taking a risk if the house value plummets. They minimize their risk by accepting loans for only a portion of the current equity.

Reverse mortgages become due and payable when the last surviving borrower dies, sells the home, or permanently moves out of the home. Like most conventional loans, acceleration of the loan can take place if you fail to pay property tax, keep insurance, or maintain the property. Upon your death, your heirs can choose to repay the loan by selling your home or refinance the reverse mortgage and keep the home. Payment of only the outstanding loan balance is required. You or your heirs get to keep whatever equity has built up since you took out the mortgage. If the value of the house falls below the loan amount, the lender absorbs the difference.

Although your heirs may receive some appreciated value after settling the loan, a reverse mortgage means there will be less equity left for them than there would have been without the reverse mortgage. If you receive a lot of cash over many years from the loan, there may be little or nothing left for them. Many children will be pleased to know their parents are able to use their property equity to remain in their home. This is a personal and family matter that should be discussed and described in your will, trust, or other documents.

8.4. TAXES

In retirement, the various tax rates on different investments can become particularly confusing. Distributions taken from traditional 401(k) and IRA plans are taxed at ordinary income tax rates. Sales of mutual fund shares (if held for over a year) and some dividends are taxed at the capital gains rate. Distributions from Roth IRAs may be tax-free, depending on how long you have owned the account and when you begin taking distributions. The distribution priority list of Section 8.3 provides general guidance for retirees to avoid paying more tax than is necessary. Each family faces a unique tax situation, however, so it is more important for retirees to gain some appreciation for the tax rate issues than to follow a simple prescription.

There are some actions a recent retiree should consider in the year that they retire. If you donate to charity, you may want to consider setting up a charitable gift fund during your final year of work. The deduction will be better while you are in a higher tax bracket. During your retirement years, you will be able to direct money from this trust fund to your favorite charities. You do not get a deduction for trust fund distributions. Instead, you will have received the deduction when it paid the most.

If you have securities or property to sell that will generate capital gains, consider waiting until after the first of the year following your retirement. If timing is important, you should not let tax implications drive your decision, but you may benefit if waiting a few weeks or months places the event into the next tax year. Tax implications for those gains are likely to be lower during your first full year in retirement than they would be while you are working. Collect all the valuable treasures that have been lying untouched in your closets and take them to Goodwill before the end of the year. Again, a deduction will be worth more this year than next.

You may have to pay income taxes on your Social Security benefits. Taxes are incurred if you have other substantial income in addition to your benefits (for example, wages, self-employment, interest, dividends, and other taxable income that you have to report on your tax return). Based on IRS rules, you will never have to pay taxes on more than 85% of your Social Security benefits and some will pay on a smaller amount. The rules as posted on the IRS website are listed below:

- If you file a federal tax return as an "individual" and your combined income* is between $25,000 and $34,000, you may have to pay income tax on 50% of your Social Security benefits. If your combined income is above $34,000, up to 85% of your Social Security benefits is subject to income tax.

- If you file a joint return, you may have to pay taxes on 50% of your benefits if you and your spouse have a combined income* that is between $32,000 and $44,000. If your combined income is more than $44,000, up to 85% of your Social Security benefits are subject to income tax.
- If you are married and file a separate tax return, you probably will pay taxes on your benefits.

You can use your annual Social Security Benefit Statement when completing your federal income tax return to determine if your benefits are subject to tax. You can also choose to have federal taxes withheld from your Social Security benefits.

8.5. REBALANCING

Some investors undertake to dramatically alter their portfolios as soon as they retire. This is not necessary if your asset allocation has been developed appropriately. The decision as to whether or not you need to change your allocation when you retire should be dictated by changes in your risk tolerance, your time horizon, and your return needs, not by your retirement status.

It is a mistake to rebalance a portfolio too conservatively once retirement is achieved. An allocation that is shifted too heavily toward fixed-income investments is likely to suffer deterioration due to inflation and it will increase an investor's longevity risk significantly.

The requirement on your portfolio to fulfill your short-term needs changes when you retire. This may necessitate a modest adjustment of the fixed-income portion of your portfolio toward short-term securities. If you choose to produce income using a fixed-income ladder, rebalancing your fixed-income investments should begin several years prior to retirement.

As you spend your retirement savings from various income sources, your overall portfolio should be rebalanced to achieve your strategic asset allocation. If you are using a fixed-income ladder, you should consider replenishing it each year. Investors should attempt to rebalance inside tax-deferred or tax-free accounts so that taxes are not incurred. Tax implications should be considered when taxable accounts have to be used for rebalancing. Losses can be used to balance out gains. Securities that produce long-term capital gains are taxed at lower rates than those that produce ordinary income.

Rebalancing accounts once per year (associated with tax filing) is sufficient to maintain appropriate levels of risk for most investors. Even less frequent rebalancing (every other year) is often acceptable.

*On your 1040 tax return, your "combined income" is the sum of your adjusted gross income, plus nontaxable interest, plus one-half of your Social Security benefits.

8.6. HEIRS

If you hope to leave significant assets to beneficiaries, you need to engage in some estate planning. Estate planning involves deciding who your beneficiaries are and what they get. If you want to ensure that your heirs inherit what you want for them, you need to plan with more than income goals in mind. Estate planning requires that you also set wealth goals. To make sure the IRS does not turn out to be your major beneficiary and that your heirs receive the inheritance you have in mind, tax strategies may need to change.

There is a trade-off between income goals and wealth goals. The more income you spend, the less wealth you have, and vice versa. Leaving an inheritance to your heirs will require you to either build a larger portfolio or reduce your spending.

Using historical simulators, a 50/50 stock/bond allocation would have supported a 4% inflation-adjusted withdrawal through any 30 year retirement sequence in history. On average, those investments and that withdrawal rate would have resulted in an average portfolio balance of over 2.7 times the original portfolio amount (adjusted for inflation). In other words, a $1 million portfolio invested 50% in an S&P500 index fund and 50% in short-term treasuries would have risen to an average value of $2.7 million inflation adjusted dollars at the end of 30 years of inflation-adjusted withdrawals. This seems like a healthy inheritance for your heirs, but the average terminal value of over 130 historical sequences is not a guaranteed minimum value. In over one-third of those sequences, terminal portfolio value was less than the initial nest egg when adjusted for inflation. In order to ensure that an inflation-adjusted $1 million is preserved, an investor would need to either reduce the initial withdrawal rate to 2.75% ($27,500 in this case), or increase the initial portfolio value to almost $1.26 million. A side effect of beginning retirement with a portfolio 26% larger than needed to support income needs is that the average terminal value for the investor now rises to over 5.1 times the initial portfolio value. Table 8.2 presents a summary of the results of these historical simulations and illustrates the trade-offs between income and wealth goals.

Table 8.2. Historical simulations of 50/50 balanced portfolios assuming an inflation adjusted spending model using CPI as an inflation indicator. After 30 years, all three portfolios survived but each implies very different lifestyles for either you or your heirs

Initial portfolio allocation (stock/bond)	50/50	50/50	50/50
Initial portfolio value ($)	$1,000,000	$1,000,000	$1,260,000
Initial withdrawal rate (adjusted for inflation each year)	$40,000	$27,500	$40,000
Initial withdrawal rate as percentage of initial portfolio	4.00%	2.75%	3.10%
Average inflation-adjusted inheritance for your heirs (after 30 years)	$2,700,000	$4,200,000	$5,100,000
Worst-case inflation-adjusted inheritance for your heirs (after 30 years)	$570,000	$1,000,000	$1,000,000

Tax implications change if your primary concern is leaving assets to beneficiaries. Under current federal tax law, beneficiaries of securities held in taxable accounts receive an increased *cost basis* on assets that equals the assets' market value when you die. The increased cost basis effectively eliminates your capital gains and your beneficiary's capital gains tax burden. For this reason, you may want to avoid selling assets in taxable accounts that have risen significantly in value. If you liquidate the assets, you will expose yourself, your estate, and your heirs to capital gains taxes. Leave these assets to your heirs and they can avoid those taxes.

Beyond these simple guidelines, estate planning is unique to your family, the state you live in, and the size and type of investments you have. If your estate is significant and estate planning is a primary concern, you should consult an estate planning professional regarding taxes and other legal issues.

REFERENCES AND FURTHER READING

1. Burns, S., A Smaller Home Can Be a Big Help, *The Dallas Morning News,* August 25, 2004.
2. AARP, *Home Made Money: A Consumer's Guide to Reverse Mortgages,* AARP, 2004.
3. Burns, S., Assess Your Assets in Five Wealth Areas, *The Dallas Morning News,* January 3, 2006.
4. Ameriks, J., R. Veres, and M. J. Warshawsky, Making Retirement Income Last a Lifetime, *Journal of Financial Planning,* December 2001.
5. Burns, S., When to Take Social Security, *The Dallas Morning News,* January 29, 2006.
6. Franklin, M. B., Retire on the House, *Kiplinger's,* October 2005.

ESTIMATION OF PORTFOLIO REQUIREMENTS, INCLUDING MORTGAGE PAYMENTS DURING RETIREMENT

Both financial and emotional factors affecting a mortgage payoff decision were discussed in Chapter 6, Section 6.6. Regardless of whether a retiree chooses to pay off his or her mortgage prior to retirement or keep the mortgage for the full term, the mortgage payment requirements must be considered in determining retirement nest egg requirements.

Using the example from Chapter 5, a 50 year old engineer planning on retiring in 10 years needed a nest egg of approximately $1.74 million (neglecting any mortgage payoff or mortgage payments). Assume that this same engineer had a $150,000, 30 year, 5.25% fixed mortgage on his or her home and would be 15 years into the loan at retirement (i.e., the homeowner had held the loan for 5 years at the time of this calculation). By using a mortgage calculator (see www.golio.net , "Table of Contents and URLs," and Section 6.6 of this book) or by contacting the lender, the homeowner can determine that the amount required to pay off the loan at retirement will be slightly over \$98,000. The exact payoff amount depends on the amount and terms of the loan and the number of payments already made. The homeowner's nest egg requirement including payoff is the sum of the original computation plus the payoff requirement:

$$P = \$1,740,000 + \$98,000 \approx \$1,840,000$$

As discussed in Chapter 6, Section 6.6, a homeowner with a low-interest, fixed-rate loan is likely to benefit financially by keeping their mortgage and investing the amount that would otherwise be used to pay off the loan. Although this decision is likely to result in financial advantage, it is not guaranteed. Homeowners who keep their mortgages in retirement are still advised to increase their portfolio requirements by the mortgage payoff amount. The homeowner with a mortgage also needs to plan for annual cash flow requirements that are increased by the amount of the mortgage payments.

LIBRARY
THE NORTH HIGHLAND COLLEGE
ORMLIE ROAD
THURSO
CAITHNESS KW14 7EE

WEB SITE URLs: INFORMATION, ONLINE CALCULATORS AND SOFTWARE

A great deal of content that is of value to the retirement planner is available on-line. This content comes in the form of information documents (studies, surveys, articles, and summaries), online calculators, downloadable spreadsheets, and downloadable software. This appendix tabulates a number of useful content sources and organizes the URL according to the chapters of this book. Each URL is followed by an explanatory title indicating something about the content at that website. Although this information is potentially very useful, there are drawbacks to this kind of source material. Some of the sites are sponsored by commercial operations. Such sites have a vested interest in convincing the browser that they should buy their product. Although the author has seen something of potential value in the information available at these URLs, the browser should not assume that all of the advice available on the Internet is true. Another issue with online sources is that both the information and the URL address can change nearly instantaneously. The same address that provides an excellent mortgage payment calculator this morning may direct the browser to an advertisement for Viagra this afternoon. If the URL does not direct you to an appropriate website, you may find it useful to try searching for the explanatory title given immediately following each URL listed. One additional problem with URL source material is that many URL addresses are long, complex, and cryptic. The reader is instructed to be very careful and precise when entering the URL address information into your web browser. To avoid some of these pitfalls of URLs, the reader is directed to the author's website, www.golio.net. Click on *Useful URLs* next to the *Engineering Your Retirement* icon. This will direct you to a page listing the URLs that are provided in this index.

GENERAL INFORMATION SOURCES

Glossary of Financial Terms:

   http://www.infoplease.com/finance/tools/glossary.html

Retirement Discussion Boards:

   http://www.retireearlyhomepage.com/cgi-bin/yabb/YaBB.pl, Retire Early
      Home Page Discussion Board

   http://early-retirement.org/forums/index.php, Early Retirement Forum

INFORMATION BY CHAPTER

1. Retire On Your Schedule

1.1.   Retirement Options

   http://www.morningstar.com/Cover/Retirement.html?hsection=Centers7,
      Morningstar.com Retirement Center

   http://money.cnn.com/pf/101/lessons/1/, CNN Money, Lesson 1: Estab-
      lishing Goals

   http://money.cnn.com/pf/101/lessons/13/, CNN Money, Lesson 13: Re-
      tirement Planning

   http://www.mises.org/freemarket_detail.asp?control=147&sortorder=
      articledate, The Free Market

   http://www.careerjournal.com/myc/retirement/20031002-greene.html,
      Wall Street Journal Executive Career Site

   http://www.careerjournal.com/myc/retirement/20000821-epstein.html,
      Wall Street Journal Executive Career Site

   http://www.retirement.org.nz/graphs_statistics.html, Population, income,
      retirement statistics

   http://www.retireearlyhomepage.com/, Retire Early Home Page

   http://www.bls.gov/data/, U.S. Department of Labor Bureau of Labor Sta-
      tistics

   http://ceenews.com/mag/electric_record_engineering_unemployment/,
      EC&M

   http://www.retireearlyhomepage.com/mbti.html, Retire Early Home Page:
      ER Personality Type?

1.2.   Is There a Retirement Crisis?

   http://www.tiaa-crefinstitute.org/Publications/resdiags/77_9-2003.htm,
      TIAA CREF Institute

   http://www.globalaging.org/pension/us/private/losti.htm, US Pensions
      Lost $1 Trillion, Reuters

1.3 How Much Do I Need to Retire?

http://www.retireearlyhomepage.com/software.html, Generation X Retirement Calculator

http://www.bankrate.com/brm/calculators/manage-money.asp, Bankrate.com Retirement Calculator

http://www.bbc.co.uk/apps/ifl/health/gigaquiz?infile=health_calculator &path=calculator_living, Life Expectancy Calculator

http://flagship2.vanguard.com/VGApp/hnw/content/PlanEdu/Retirement/PEdRetPicLongRetireContent.jsp, Vanguard Joint Life Expectancy Calculator

http://www.nmfn.com/tn/learnctr—lifeevents—longevity, The Longevity Game

http://moneycentral.msn.com/investor/calcs/n_expect/main.asp, Life Expectancy Calculator

2. Analysis Tools and Calculations

http://www.gummy-stuff.org/gummy_stuff.htm, Gummy Stuff

http://www.soa.org/ccm/content/areas-of-practice/special-interest-sections/pension/retirement-planning-calculating-risk-of-retirement-woes/, Society of Actuaries Retirement Planning

http://www.soa.org/ccm/content/areas-of-practice/special-interest-sections/pension/retirement-probability-analyzer-software/, Society of Actuaries Retirement Probability Analyzer Software

2.1. Predictions Based on Average Returns and Inflation

http://www.troweprice.com/common/indexHtml3/0,0,htmlid=902,00.html?rfpgid=8278, T Rowe Price Retirement Planning Worksheet

http://www.analyzenow.com/, Analyze Now/Free Programs: Return Calculator

http://www.analyzenow.com/, Analyze Now/Free Programs: Pre-Retirement Savings Planner Calculator

2.2. Spending Models

http://www.gummy-stuff.org/sensible_withdrawals.htm, Gummy's Sensible Withdrawals

http://www.fireseeker.com/explain.htm, FIRECalc Explanations

http://www.fpanet.org/journal/articles/2005_Issues/jfp0605-art7.cfm?&, Reality Retirement Planning

2.3. Historical Data

http://www.econ.yale.edu/~shiller/data.htm, Shiller Data Online

http://www.bls.gov/cpi/, U.S. Department of Labor Bureau of Labor Statistics

2.4. Monte Carlo Simulation

http://www3.troweprice.com/ric/RIC/, T Rowe Price Retirement Income Calculator

http://www.quantext.com/SafeRetirementDraw.pdf, Quantext Safe Withdrawal Rates

http://www.gummy-stuff.org/TA.htm, Gummy Stuff Monte Carlo Simulator

2.5. Historical Simulation and the 4% Rule

http://www.fpanet.org/journal/articles/2004_Issues/jfp0304-art8.cfm, *Journal of Financial Planning*

http://www.retireearlyhomepage.com/re60.html, Safe Withdrawal Calculator

http://fireseeker.com/, FIRECALC

3. LBYM (Live Below Your Means)

3.1. Spending

http://www.choosetosave.org/, Choose to Save

http://about.com/, Practical Advice from About.com

http://savingadvice.com/, Savingadvice.com

3.2. Breaking the Relationship between Earning and Spending

http://moneycentral.msn.com/content/Savinganddebt/Savemoney/P90801.asp, MSN Money, Live Well on Less

http://www.simpleliving.net/, the Simple Living Network

http://www.strongnumbers.com/, Strong Numbers: Pricing Intelligence and Insight

http://www.stretcher.com/index.cfm, Dollar Stretcher

3.3. Establishing Budget Projections

http://office.microsoft.com/en-us/templates/CT011815531033.aspx?iStartAt=26, Microsoft Office Online Personal Financial Tools: Personal Budget Spreadsheet

http://office.microsoft.com/en-us/templates/CT011815531033.aspx?iStartAt=26, Microsoft Office Online Personal Financial Tools: Family Monthly Budget Spreadsheet

http://money.cnn.com/pf/101/lessons/2/, CNN Money, Lesson 2: Making a Budget

http://www.analyzenow.com/, Analyze Now/Free Programs: Post Retirement Budget Calculator

http://www.analyzenow.com/, Analyze Now/Free Programs: Replacement Budgeting Program

http://moneycentral.msn.com/investor/calcs/n_retireq/main.asp, Retirement Expense Calculator

http://office.microsoft.com/en-us/templates/CT011815531033.aspx?

iStartAt=26, Microsoft Office Online Personal Financial Tools: Retirement Budget Spreadsheet

3.4. Credit Cards

http://www.bankrate.com/brm/rate/cc_home.asp, Bankrate.com Credit Card Pages

http://www.transunion.com, Transunion Credit Reports

http://www.equifax.com, Equifax Credit Reports

http://www.experian.com, Experian Credit Reports

3.5. Increasing Earning

http://www.ieeeusa.org/careers/, IEEE-USA Career Navigator

https://salaryapp.ieeeusa.org/rt/salary_database/shop, IEEE-USA Salary Service

http://www.ieeeusa.org/careers/cpg/default.asp, IEEE-USA Career Planner (requires IEEE membership)

https://salaryapp.ieeeusa.org/rt/salary_database/shop, IEEE-USA Salary Service

http://www.ieeeusa.org/careers/salary/default.asp, IEEE-USA Salary Survey (requires IEEE membership)

4. Emergency Funds and Insurance (First Take Care of Stability)

4.1. Medical Insurance

http://www.healthinsuranceinfo.net/, Georgetown University Health Policy Institute

http://money.cnn.com/pf/101/lessons/16/, CNN Money, Lesson 16: Health Insurance

https://www.quickquote.com/cgibin/healthQuest.pl, Quickquotes Health Insurance Quote

http://www.retireearlyhomepage.com/ltcbuy.html, Retire Early Home Page: LTC Insurance

http://www.retireearlyhomepage.com/health.html, Retire Early Home Page: Health Insurance

http://www.medicare.gov/, Official U.S. Government Site for People with Medicare

http://www.cms.hhs.gov/hipaa/hipaa1/content/cons.asp, Centers for Medicare and Medicaid Services

http://www.medicare.gov/, The Official U.S. Government Site for People with Medicare

4.2. Emergency Funds

http://retireplan.about.com/od/caniretire/ht/emergency_fund.htm, About Retirement Planning http://www.bankrate.com/brm/news/financial-literacy/emergency-savings1.asp, Bankrate.com Building an Emergency Fund

4.3.   Personal Financial Concerns

http://www.divorcesupport.com/divorce/Cost-of-Divorce-112.html, Divorce support.com

http://divorcesupport.about.com/c/ht/00/07/How_Keep_Divorce_Costs0962932643.htm, How to Keep Divorce Costs Down

http://www.bankrate.com/brm/calculators/manage-money.asp, Bankrate.com Cost of Raising a Child Calculator

http://www.babycenter.com/popunder/pu71_halloweenA71.jhtml?_requestid=77114, Cost of Raising a Child Calculator

http://www.family.msn.com/tool/article.aspx?dept=raising&sdept=rks&name=index, MSN Family Resource Library

http://www.savingforcollege.com/, TIAA-CREF Guide to Funding College

http://office.microsoft.com/en-us/templates/CT011815531033.aspx?iStartAt=26, Microsoft Office Online Personal Financial Tools: College Costs Calculator Spreadsheet

http://money.cnn.com/pf/101/lessons/11/, CNN Money, Lesson 11: Saving for College

http://news.morningstar.com/doc/pfarticle/0,,529planscollegesavings~,00.html?pfsection=College&hsection=Centers3, Morningstar.com College Saving

http://www.bankrate.com/brm/calculators/college/investing/save.asp, Bankrate.com College Planning Calculator

http://www.irs.gov/individuals/students/index.html, Tax Information for Students

http://www.irs.gov/pub/irs-pdf/p970.pdf, Tax Benefits for Education

4.4.   Documents

http://money.cnn.com/pf/101/lessons/21/, CNN Money, Lesson 21: Estate Planning

http://news.morningstar.com/doc/article/0,,137725,00.html?rsection=Comm3, Morningstar.com Estate Planning

http://www.troweprice.com/common/index3/0,3011,lnp%3D10002%26cg%3D1270%26pgid%3D8282,00.html, T Rowe Price Estate Planning Tools

http://www.legacywriter.com/CreateYourWill_Process.html, Create Your Will Process

http://money.cnn.com/pf/101/lessons/3/, CNN Money, Lesson 3: Basics of Banking

5. Investment Instruments

5.1. Bonds

http://www.investopedia.com/university/bonds/, Investopedia Bond Basics Tutorial

http://news.morningstar.com/doc/pfarticle/0,,bonds~,00.html?pfsection =Bonds&hsection=Centers2, Morningstar.com Bonds and Bond Funds

http://www.investinginbonds.com/, Investing in bonds.com

http://money.cnn.com/pf/101/lessons/7/, CNN Money, Lesson 7: Investing in Bonds

http://www.publicdebt.treas.gov/, Bureau of the Pubic Debt U.S. Dept. of Treasury

http://www.treasurydirect.gov/, Treasury Direct

5.2. Stocks

http://www.investopedia.com/university/stocks/, Investopedia Stock Basics Tutorial

http://money.cnn.com/pf/101/lessons/5/, CNN Money Lesson 5: Investing in Stocks

http://www.morningstar.com/Cover/Stocks.html?topnav=stocks, Morningstar.com Stocks

5.3. Real Estate

http://www.realtor.org/, National Association of Realtors

http://realdata.com/viewlets/index.shtml, Real Data Software for Real Estate

http://www.mrlandlord.com/, MrLandlord.com

http://www.msfinancialsavvy.com/archive/real_estate_invest.html MsFinancialSavy 101

http://www.coldwellbanker.com/real_estate/home_search, Coldwell Banker Property Search

http://homebuying.about.com/od/realestateinvesting/, About.com home buying/selling

http://realtytimes.com/, *Realty Times*

http://www.nareit.com/portfoliomag/default.shtml, NAREIT Real Estate Portfolio

5.4. Annuities

http://office.microsoft.com/en-us/templates/CT011815531033.aspx? iStartAt=26, Microsoft Office Online Personal Financial Tools: Annuity Investment Calculator Spreadsheet

http://www.immediateannuities.com/, Immediate Annuities Instant Annuity Quote Calculator

http://www.analyzenow.com/, Analyze Now/Free Programs Tools: Annuity Calculator

5.5. Defined Benefit Plans (Pensions)

http://www.ebri.org/, Employee Benefit Research

5.6. Cash and Certificates of Deposit

http://www.bankrate.com/brm/calc/cdc/CertDeposit.asp, Bankrate.com CD Calculator

5.7. Social Security

http://www.ssa.gov/retire2/AnypiaApplet.html, Social Security Online Calculators

http://www.ssa.gov/planners/calculators.htm, Social Security Benefit Calculators

5.8. Mutual Funds

http://money.cnn.com/pf/101/lessons/6/, CNN Money, Lesson 6: Investing in Mutual Funds

http://www.investopedia.com/university/mutualfunds/, Investopedia Mutual Fund Tutorial

http://news.morningstar.com/doc/pfarticle/0,,bonds~,00.html?pfsection=Bonds&hsection=Centers2, Morningstar.com

https://flagship5.vanguard.com/VGApp/hnw/HomepageOverview, Vanguard Personal Investors

http://www.investopedia.com/university/indexes/, Investopedia Index Investing Tutorial

5.9. Exchange-Traded Funds (ETFs)

http://www.morningstar.com/Cover/ETF.html?topnav=etfs, Morningstar.com ETFs

http://www.ishares.com/splash.jhtml?_requestid=76808, Barclays iShares

http://mutualfunds.about.com/cs/etfs/a/exchangetraded.htm, About.com What are ETFs?

5.10. Commodities

http://www.commodities-now.com/, *Commodities Now Magazine*

http://cisdm.som.umass.edu/research/pdffiles/benefitsofcommodities.pdf, CISDM Research Report

6. Your Investment Plan

http://money.cnn.com/pf/101/lessons/4/, CNN Money, Lesson 4: Basics of Investing

http://www.efficientfrontier.com/ef/996.pdf, Efficient Frontier

http://www.hindsight2insight.com/mistake-holding.htm, Merrill Lynch Investment Managers Hindsight2Insight

6.1. Eliminate "Bad" Debt

http://money.cnn.com/pf/101/lessons/9/, CNN Money, Lesson 9: Controlling Debt http://www.equifax.com/, Equifax Credit Reports

http://www.bankrate.com/brm/calculators/credit-cards.asp, Bankrate.com Credit Card Payoff Calculator

6.2. Investment Issues

http://www.dol.gov/ebsa/publications/401k_employee.html, U.S. Dept. of Labor, 401(k) (fees)

http://flagship4.vanguard.com/VGApp/hnw/FundsInvQuestionnaire, Vanguard Investor Questionnaire (Risk)

http://flagship5.vanguard.com/VGApp/hnw/FundsInvQuestionnaire, Investor Questionnaire—Risk Assessment

http://omniweb.trustok.com/oweb/Newsletters/quiz1.htm, Trust Co. of OK, Asset Allocation Questionnaire

http://www.investopedia.com/terms/r/risk.asp, Investopedia—Risk

https://www.foliofn.com/content/education/edu_mut_costCalculator.jsp, Mutual Fund Cost Calculator

http://www.coffeehouseinvestor.com/default.htm, Coffeehouse Investor Asset Allocation

http://www.retireearlyhomepage.com/reallife05.html, Retire Early Home Page, Real Life Returns

http://money.cnn.com/pf/101/lessons/14/, CNN Money, Lesson 14: Asset Allocation

http://www.geocities.com/finplan825/ModelPortfolios-Data.html, Geocities Model Portfolio Data

http://easyallocator.com/, Easy Asset Allocator

http://www.gummy-stuff.org/rebalancing-bonus.htm, Gummy Stuff Rebalancing bonus I

http://www.gummy-stuff.org/rebalancing-bonus-2.htm, Gummy Stuff Rebalancing Bonus II

http://www.moneychimp.com/features/dollar_cost.htm, Dollar Cost Averaging Calculator

6.3. Tax-Advantaged Accounts and Free Money

http://office.microsoft.com/en-us/templates/CT011815531033.aspx?iStartAt=26, Microsoft Office Online Personal Financial Tools: 401(k) Planner Spreadsheet

http://money.cnn.com/pf/101/lessons/23/, CNN Money, Lesson 23: 401(k)s

http://news.morningstar.com/doc/pfarticle/0,,4307,00.html?hsection=Centers1, Morningstar.com 401k Guide

http://www.403bwise.com/, bWise Guys 403b Page

http://www.troweprice.com/common/index3/0,3011,lnp%3D10002%26cg%3D1270%26pgid%3D8278,00.html, T Rowe Price 403b Contribution Calculator http://www.retireearlyhomepage.com/roth2.html, IRA Withdrawal Calculator and Roth Analyzer

http://www.rothira.com/, Roth IRA Website

http://moneycentral.msn.com/investor/calcs/n_roth/main.asp, Roth IRA Calculator

http://partners.financenter.com/hrblock/calculate/us-eng/rothira02.fcs, H&R Block IRA Conversion Calculator

http://www.retireearlyhomepage.com/wdraw59.html, Retire Early Home Page 72(t) Withdrawals

http://www.irs.gov/pub/irs-pdf/p590.pdf, IRS Publication 590 on IRAs and IRA Rollovers

http://www.healthsavingsaccount-hsa.com/, Health Savings Account

http://www.savingforcollege.com/, TIAA-CREF Guide to Funding College

http://www.troweprice.com/tools/cic/cicNational?scn=Can_I_afford_to_send&rfpgid=8281, T Rowe Price College Investment Calculator

http://money.cnn.com/pf/101/lessons/11/, CNN Money Lesson 11: Saving for College

http://news.morningstar.com/doc/pfarticle/0,,529planscollegesavings~,00.html?pfsection=College&hsection=Centers3, Morningstar.com College Saving

6.4. Taxable Investments

http://www.creonline.com/, Creative Real Estate Online

http://www.dfin.com/ldisc_brokers.htm, Discount Stockbrokers

http://stocks.about.com/od/findingabroker/, About Finding a Stockbroker

http://www.vanguard.com/VGApp/hnw/CorporatePortal, Vanguard Investing

https://www.fidelity.com/, Fidelity Investing

http://www.morningstar.com/Cover/Funds.html?pgid=hetabfunds, Morningstar Mutual Fund Page

http://www.treasurydirect.gov/, Treasury Direct

http://www.publicdebt.treas.gov/, Bureau of the Public Debt

http://wwws.publicdebt.treas.gov/BC/SBCPrice, Savings Bond Calculator

6.5. House—Purchase or Rent?

http://partners.leadfusion.com/tools/motleyfool/home10/tool.fcs, Motley Fool, Am I Better off renting?

http://www.bankrate.com/brm/rate/calc_home.asp, Bankrate.com Mortgage Calculators

http://office.microsoft.com/en-us/templates/CT011815531033.aspx?iStartAt=26, Microsoft Office Online Personal Financial Tools: Buy vs. Rent Home Calculator Spreadsheet

http://office.microsoft.com/en-us/templates/CT011815531033.aspx?
iStartAt=26, Microsoft Office Online Personal Financial Tools: Closing
Cost Calculator Spreadsheet

http://www.fdic.gov/bank/analytical/fyi/2005/021005fyi.html, FDIC U.S.
Home Prices

http://www.pmigroup.com/lenders/media_lenders/pmi_eret05v1s.pdf,
PMI Economic and Real Estate Trends

http://office.microsoft.com/en-us/templates/CT011815531033.aspx?
iStartAt=26, Microsoft Office Online Personal Financial Tools: ARM
vs. Fixed Mortgage Comparison Spreadsheet

http://office.microsoft.com/en-us/templates/CT011815531033.aspx?iStar-
tAt=26, Microsoft Office Online Personal Financial Tools: Balloon
Loan Calculator Spreadsheet

http://mortgage-calculators.org/calculators/template2.php3?calc_type=28,
Mortgage Calculators

http://money.cnn.com/pf/101/lessons/8/, CNN Money, Lesson 8: Buying a
Home

6.6. Mortgage Payoff Decision

http://biz.yahoo.com/ts/040823/10179250_2.html, Yahoo Finance Financial News

http://www.dinkytown.net/java/MortgagePayoff.html, Mortgage Payoff
Calculator

6.7. Taxes

http://www.irs.gov/, Internal Revenue Service Website

http://news.morningstar.com/doc/pfarticle/0,,taxplanning~,00.html?
pfsection=TaxPlan&hsection=Centers8, Morningstar.com Tax Planning

http://www.brookwoodtax.com/personal_tax_guide/deduct_noncash_
charitable_donations.htm, Brookwood Tax Service: Donating Non-Cash
Items to Charity

http://www.salvationarmysouth.org/valueguide.htm, Salvation Army Valuation Guide

http://money.cnn.com/pf/101/lessons/18/, CNN Money, Lesson 18: Taxes

7. What Will I Do When I Retire?

7.1 Work Part-time

http://www.megajobsites.com/MKT/Content/JS/Channels/AccountingFi-
nance.asp, Mega Job Sites

http://askmerrill.ml.com/html/mlrr_illustrate_flash/, Merrill Lynch New
Retirement Illustrator

http://www.ieee.org/portal/site/mainsite/menuitem.818c0c39e85ef176fb-
2275875bac26c8/index.jsp?&pName=corp_level1&path=pubs/press&
file=kit.xml&xsl=generic.xsl, IEEE Press Author Information

http://www.ieee.org/portal/site/mainsite/menuitem.818c0c39e85ef176fb-2275875bac26c8/index.jsp?&pName=corp_level1&path=pubs/press&file=prpgd.xml&xsl=generic.xsl, IEEE Press Book Proposal Form

http://www.sfwa.org/, Science Fiction & Fantasy Writers of America

http://www.thrillerwriters.org/, International Thriller Writers, Inc.

http://www.idealist.org/en/ip/idealist/AdvancedSearch/Job/default?SID=0cd7def748bdfbea072db49166ae0f42

http://www.ieeeusa.org/business/consultants/cgi-bin/con-sultant.cgi?task=display_page/page=home.html, IEEE Consultants Database

http://www.educationplanet.com/search/Education/Teacher_Resources/Substitute_Teaching, Education Planet

http://www.bls.gov/oco/ocos120.htm, U.S. Department of Labor, Bureau of Labor Statistics

7.2. Travel

http://www.priceline.com/, Priceline

http://local.msn.com/special/results/2003_budget.asp, MSN Travel Center Best of Budget Hotels

http://www.weather.com/?from=globalnav, The Weather Channel

http://www.garybeene.com/retire/ret-trav.htm#b, Gary Beene's Retirement Information Center

http://seniortravel.about.com/od/extendedtravel/, Senior Travel About.com

http://www.cruiseamerica.com/hot_rental_deals/default.asp, RV Rental Deals

http://www.fulltiming-america.com/, Full Timing America

http://www.campingworld.com/cforum/index.cfm/fuseaction/thread/tid/264829.cfm, Camping World

http://www.catamaran-yacht-charter.com/sailing-vacations/long-term-yacht-charter.html, Yacht charter Neverland

http://cruisenews.net/index.php, Guide to Sailing and Cruising Stories

http://usparks.about.com/cs/usparklocator/l/blmaptemplate2.htm, National Parks by State

http://camping.about.com/od/campgroundreviews/l/blpcgndx.htm, Campground Reviews by State

7.3. Volunteer

http://www.pointsoflight.org/centers/find_center.cfm, Points of Light Foundation

http://www.serviceleader.org/new/virtual/2003/04/000026.php, Service-Leader.org: Virtual Volunteering

http://www.idealist.org/, Idealist.org

http://charityguide.org/charity/homecg.htm, Charity Guide.org

http://www.aarp.org/about_aarp/community_service/, AARP Community Service

http://www.amigoslink.org/, Amigos de las Americas

http://amizade.org/, Amizade

http://ofcn.org/networks/By_State.txt.html, Organization for Community Networks

7.4. Recreation and Leisure

http://www.1fghp.com/, The Fishing Guide

http://www.passportintime.com/, USDA Forest Service Passport in Time

http://www.learnspanishtoday.com/, Free Online Spanish Lessons Center

http://www.france-pub.com/french/, Free French Lessons

http://www.bikeforums.net/index.php, Bike forums

http://www.rudyprojectusa.com/links/index.htm, Golf, Cycling, Tennis Links

http://www.sierraclub.org/outings/, Sierra Club Outings

http://directory.google.com/Top/Sports/Golf/Courses/North_America/United_States/North_Carolina/, Google Golf Directory

7.5. Health and Self-improvement

http://www.ahrq.gov/ppip/50plus/index.html, U.S. Agency for Health Research and Quality

http://www.cnn.com/2005/HEALTH/diet.fitness/03/16/obesity.longevity.ap/, Report: Obesity Will Reverse Life Expectancy Gains

http://www.webmd.com/, Web MD

8. Issues in Retirement

8.1. Before Leaving the Building

http://www.writeexpress.com/resignation-letters.html, Write Express Retirement Letter

8.2. Where to Live

http://www.homefair.com/homefair/cmr/salcalc.html?NETSCAPE_LIVEWIRE.src=, Realtor.com Cost of Living Calculator

http://www.homefair.com/homefair/calc/crime.html?NETSCAPE_LIVEWIRE.src=, Realtor.com Crime Statistics by Location

http://www.realestatejournal.com/toolkit_res/bestplaces.html, Real Estate Journal Choose Your Best Place to Live

http://www.findyourspot.com/, Find Your Spot Quiz

http://money.cnn.com/best/bplive/, CNN Money Best Places to Live

http://www.fortune.com/fortune/investorguide/articles/0,15114,1076994,00.html, Fortune Retirement Guide: Where to Retire Abroad

http://www.americanchronicle.com/articles/viewArticle.asp?
articleID=1336, American Chronicle: New Places to Live and Retire
Around the World

http://belizeretirement.org/, Welcome to Belize

8.3.   Sources of Income

http://www.i-orp.com/model.html, ORP Distribution Planner

http://www.troweprice.com/common/index3/0,3011,lnp%3D10002%
26cg%3D1270%26pgid%3D8278,00.html, T Rowe Price Retirement
Income Calculator

http://moneycentral.msn.com/investor/calcs/n_retire/main.asp, MSN Money Retirement Income Calculator

http://www.seniorjobbank.org/rm/index.html, Reverse Mortgages

http://www.analyzenow.com/, Analyze Now/Free Programs: Social Security at 62, 66, or 70 Software

http://www.ssa.gov/retire2/AnypiaApplet.html, Social Security Online
Calculators

http://ssa-custhelp.ssa.gov/cgi-bin/ssa.cfg/php/enduser/
std_adp.php?p_faqid=236&p_created=957878244&p_sid=krSQ-
c2i&p_lva=&p_sp=cF9zcmNoPSZwX3NvcnRfYnk9JnBfZ3JpZHNvc
nQ9JnBfcm93X2NudD02MTcmcF9wcm9kcz0mcF9jYXRzPSZwX3B2
PSZwX2N2PSZwX3NlYXJjaF90eXBlPWFuc3dlcnMuc2Vhcm
NoX25sJnBfcGFnZT0x&p_li=&p_topview=1, Social Security Benefits
and Earning in Retirement

http://www.aarp.org/money/social_security/, AARP Social Security Information

http://www.ebri.org/, Employee Benefit Research

http://www.retireearlyhomepage.com/wdraw59.html, Retire Early Home
Page: SEPP

http://www.72t.net/, 72t on the Net

http://www.calctools.com/newrmd.htm, New Required Minimum Distribution Calculator

http://www.aarp.org/money/revmort/revmort_basics/Articles/a2003-03-
21-revmortfactsheet.html, AARP Fact Sheet on Reverse Mortgages

http://www.reversemortgage.org/, Reverse Mortgage.org

http://nrmla.edthosting.com/, Reverse Mortgage Calculator

8.4.   Taxes

http://news.morningstar.com/doc/pfarticle/0,,taxplanning~,00.html?
pfsection=TaxPlan&hsection=Centers8, Morningstar.com Tax Planning

http://www.brookwoodtax.com/personal_tax_guide/deduct_noncash_
charitable_donations.htm, Brookwood Tax Service: Donating Non-Cash
Items to Charity

http://www.salvationarmysouth.org/valueguide.htm, Salvation Army Valuation Guide

http://money.cnn.com/pf/101/lessons/18/, CNN Money Lesson 18: Taxes

http://www.vanguardcharitable.org/, Vanguard Charitable Endowment Program

http://www.charitablegift.org/index.shtml, Fidelity Charitable Gift Fund

8.5. Rebalancing

http://www.gummy-stuff.org/sensible_withdrawals.htm, Gummy Stuff: Rebalancing Discussion

8.6. Heirs

http://www.estatplanninglinks.com/, Estate Planning Links

FUNDAMENTAL FINANCIAL EQUATIONS

To apply the following equations, the interest rate is expressed as a fraction (use 0.05 for a 5% interest rate). If the rate is an annual rate, monthly rates can be computed by dividing the annual rate by 12.

HOME LOAN REPAYMENTS

The repayment amount for a set principal over a set number of payments is given by

$$a = \frac{p \times r \times (1 + r)^n}{[(1 + r)^n - 1]} \tag{B1}$$

where
p is the principal
a is the payment per month
r is the interest rate per month
n is the number of months

The number of payments for a set principal and set repayment amount can be computed from

$$n = \frac{\ln\left(\dfrac{a}{a - p \times r}\right)}{\ln(1 + r)} \tag{B2}$$

Engineering Your Retirement. By Mike Golio
© 2007 Institute of Electrical and Electronics Engineers, Inc.

FUTURE VALUE OF AN INVESTMENT

The future value of a an amount invested for a fixed rate and time when recurring investments are not made ($a = 0$) is given by

$$f_p = p \times (1 + r)^n \tag{B3}$$

For the case when an investment is recurring, ($a \neq 0$) the future value is given by

$$f_a = a \times \sum_{j=0}^{n-1} r^j = a \times \frac{r^n - 1}{r - 1} = \frac{a \times [(1 + r)^n - 1]}{r} \tag{B4}$$

where
f is the future value of the investment
p is the principal invested (initial investment)
a is the amount added each month or year (if investment is recurring)
r is the interest rate per month or year
n is the number of months or years

For the case when you begin with an initial principal and add an amount each month, calculate the future value of the principal and the future value of the added amounts and add the two totals:

$$f_{total} = f_p + f_a \tag{B5}$$

When both the initial and final amount of an investment are known, the annualized return can be computed as follows:

$$r = \left(\frac{f}{p}\right)^{(1/n)} - 1 \tag{B6}$$

LONGEVITY TABLE

Current age	Average years to live	50 Percentile	75 Percentile	90 Percentile	95 Percentile	99 Percentile
15	67.4	70.3	77	82.2	85.1	89.9
16	66.5	69.3	76	81.2	84.1	88.9
17	65.5	68.4	75	80.2	83.1	87.9
18	64.5	67.4	74	79.2	82.1	86.9
19	63.5	66.4	73	78.2	81.1	85.9
20	62.6	65.4	72	77.2	80.1	84.9
21	61.6	64.4	71	76.2	79.1	83.9
22	60.6	63.4	70.1	75.2	78.1	82.9
23	59.6	62.4	69.1	74.2	77.1	81.9
24	58.7	61.4	68.1	73.2	76.1	80.9
25	57.7	60.4	67.1	72.2	75.1	79.9
26	56.7	59.4	66.1	71.2	74.1	78.9
27	55.8	58.4	65.1	70.2	73.1	77.9
28	54.8	57.4	64.1	69.2	72.1	76.9
29	53.8	56.4	63.1	68.2	71.1	75.9
30	52.9	55.4	62.1	67.2	70.1	74.9
31	51.9	54.4	61.1	66.2	69.1	73.9
32	50.9	53.5	60.1	65.2	68.1	72.9
33	50	52.5	59.1	64.2	67.1	71.9
34	49	51.5	58.1	63.2	66.1	71
35	48	50.5	57.1	62.2	65.1	70
36	47.1	49.5	56.1	61.3	64.1	69
37	46.1	48.5	55.1	60.3	63.1	68
38	45.1	47.5	54.1	59.3	62.1	67

(*continued*)

Current age	Average years to live	50 Percentile	75 Percentile	90 Percentile	95 Percentile	99 Percentile
39	44.1	46.5	53.1	58.3	61.1	66
40	43.2	45.5	52.1	57.3	60.1	65
41	42.2	44.5	51.1	56.3	59.2	64
42	41.2	43.6	50.1	55.3	58.2	63
43	40.3	42.6	49.1	54.3	57.2	62
44	39.3	41.6	48.2	53.3	56.2	61
45	38.4	40.6	47.2	52.3	55.2	60
46	37.4	39.6	46.2	51.3	54.2	59
47	36.5	38.6	45.2	50.3	53.2	58
48	35.6	37.7	44.2	49.3	52.2	57
49	34.6	36.7	43.2	48.3	51.2	56
50	33.7	35.7	42.2	47.3	50.2	55
51	32.8	34.8	41.2	46.3	49.2	54
52	31.9	33.8	40.3	45.4	48.2	53
53	31	32.8	39.3	44.4	47.2	52
54	30.1	31.9	38.3	43.4	46.2	51
55	29.2	30.9	37.3	42.4	45.3	50
56	28.3	30	36.4	41.4	44.3	49
57	27.4	29	35.4	40.4	43.3	48
58	26.5	28.1	34.4	39.5	42.3	47.1
59	25.6	27.1	33.4	38.5	41.3	46.1
60	24.8	26.2	32.5	37.5	40.3	45.1
61	23.9	25.3	31.5	36.5	39.4	44.1
62	23.1	24.3	30.6	35.6	38.4	43.1
63	22.2	23.4	29.6	34.6	37.4	42.1
64	21.4	22.5	28.6	33.6	36.4	41.2
65	20.5	21.6	27.7	32.7	35.5	40.2
66	19.7	20.7	26.8	31.7	34.5	39.2
67	18.9	19.8	25.8	30.7	33.5	38.2
68	18.1	19	24.9	29.8	32.6	37.2
69	17.3	18.1	24	28.8	31.6	36.3
70	16.6	17.2	23	27.9	30.7	35.3
71	15.8	16.4	22.1	26.9	29.7	34.3
72	15.1	15.6	21.3	26	28.8	33.4
73	14.3	14.8	20.4	25.1	27.8	32.4
74	13.6	14	19.5	24.2	26.9	31.5
75	12.9	13.2	18.6	23.3	26	30.5
76	12.3	12.5	17.8	22.4	25.1	29.6
77	11.6	11.8	16.9	21.5	24.2	28.6
78	11	11.1	16.1	20.7	23.3	27.7
79	10.4	10.4	15.3	19.8	22.4	26.8
80	9.8	9.7	14.6	18.9	21.5	25.9
81	9.2	9.1	13.8	18.1	20.7	24.9
82	8.7	8.5	13.1	17.3	19.8	24
83	8.1	7.9	12.3	16.5	19	23.2
84	7.6	7.4	11.7	15.8	18.2	22.3

Current age	Average years to live	50 Percentile	75 Percentile	90 Percentile	95 Percentile	99 Percentile
85	7.1	6.9	11	15	17.4	21.4
86	6.7	6.4	10.4	14.3	16.6	20.6
87	6.2	5.9	9.8	13.6	15.8	19.7
88	5.8	5.5	9.2	12.9	15.1	18.9
89	5.4	5.1	8.6	12.3	14.4	18.1
90	5.1	4.7	8.1	11.6	13.7	17.3
91	4.7	4.4	7.7	11	13	16.5
92	4.4	4.1	7.2	10.5	12.4	15.8
93	4.1	3.8	6.8	9.9	11.8	15
94	3.9	3.6	6.4	9.4	11.1	14.3
95	3.6	3.4	6	8.8	10.6	13.6
96	3.4	3.1	5.7	8.3	9.9	12.8
97	3.1	2.9	5.3	7.8	9.4	12.1
98	2.9	2.8	5	7.4	8.8	11.5
99	2.7	2.6	4.7	6.9	8.3	10.8
100	2.5	2.4	4.3	6.4	7.7	10
101	2.3	2.2	4	5.9	7.2	9.4
102	2	2	3.7	5.5	6.7	8.7
103	1.8	1.9	3.4	5	6.1	8
104	1.6	1.7	3.1	4.7	5.6	7.5
105	1.4	1.6	2.8	4.2	5.1	6.8
106	1.3	1.4	2.6	3.8	4.7	6.2
107	1.1	1.2	2.3	3.5	4.2	5.7
108	0.9	1.1	2	3	3.8	5
109	0.7	0.9	1.8	2.7	3.3	4.5
110	0.6	0.8	1.6	2.4	2.9	3.9
111	0.5	0.8	1.4	2	2.6	3.5
112	0.3	0.7	1.1	1.8	2	2.9
113	0.2	0.6	0.9	1.5	1.8	2.5
114	0.1	0.6	0.8	1	1.5	1.9
115	0	0.5	0.8	0.9	1	1

Note: Life expectancies are based on the mortality table in IRS Revenue Ruling 2002-62 Appendix B. See link: http://www.irs.gov/pub/irs-drop/rr-02-62.pdf.

INDEX

ABOUT THE AUTHOR

As a teenager, Mike Golio worked in the coal mines, on road crews, clearing brush, and in a wide variety of other manual labor positions. Management of the earnings from this work served as his first lessons in saving, budgeting, and balancing long- and short-term personal/financial goals. With some help from his parents, an Old Ben Coal Corporation scholarship, and part time work in a dormitory dish room, he was able to fund his undergraduate studies and receive his BSEE degree in 1975. Mike spent two years as a microwave design engineer before earning enough to return to school and complete his MSEE and PhD studies in 1980 and 1983.

During his career as a technical contributor, Dr. Golio published hundreds of technical papers and served as editor for six books. He has held a variety of volunteer positions in both IEEE Microwave Theory and Techniques Society and IEEE Electron Device Society. These organizations have presented him with several awards for his service and contributions. Working over 31 years in the electrical engineering field, Dr. Golio designed and built electronics hardware, developed models for microwave transistors, managed both small and large engineering organizations, and directed corporate research and development strategies. Each advance on the corporate ladder was associated with increased responsibility for planning and budgeting. Dr. Golio recognized a similarity between balancing R&D priorities and budgets and planning retirement investments. Thus began his extensive and thorough research to develop a personal retirement plan.

Mike and his wife, JJ, have published articles in archaeology volumes about their investigations of prehistoric cultures of the Southwest, and have cowritten two children's books. In 2003, at the age of 49, he and his wife achieved their goal of financial independence and disengaged themselves from full-time engineering work. They remain very active, volunteering at community functions, working for their county election board, and serving as liaison to the city for their neighborhood. Financial independence has also provided them the opportunity to travel, visit family, and pursue interests outside of electrical engineering. The Golio's enjoy the outdoors and hike over 40 miles each week. Although mostly retired, Dr. Golio still enjoys spending time on technical efforts and participating in professional activities. He currently chooses to work approximately quarter-time for a start-up company in Phoenix, Arizona, serves as volunteer Editor-in-Chief of *IEEE Microwave Magazine,* and is a reviewer for several professional journals, IEEE conferences, and book publishers.